A Long Road Home

A LONG ROAD HOME

In the Footsteps of the WPA Writers

GEOFFREY O'GARA

HOUGHTON MIFFLIN COMPANY · BOSTON

For information about permission to reproduce selections
from this book, write to Permissions, Houghton Mifflin
Company, 2 Park Street, Boston, Massachusetts 02108.

Library of Congress Cataloging-in-Publication Data

O'Gara, Geoffrey.
A long road home : in the footsteps of the WPA writers / Geoffrey
O'Gara.
p. cm.
ISBN 0-395-53758-4 (pbk.)
1. United States—Description and travel—1920–1940. 2. United
States—Social life and customs—1918–1945. 3. Federal Writers'
Project. 4. United States—Description and travel—1981–
5. O'Gara, Geoffrey—Journeys—United States. I. Title.
[E169.034 1990] 90-30032
973—dc20 CIP

Printed in the United States of America

VB 10 9 8 7 6 5 4 3 2 1

Book design by Margaret M. Wagner
Map by Hannah Hinchman

Photos by permission of the Farm Security Administration.
Lyrics from "Little Sister" by Doc Pomus and Mort Shuman,
copyright Elvis Presley Music, administered by Rightsong, Inc.
All rights reserved. Used by permission.

Houghton Mifflin Company paperback 1990

For Agnes Wright Spring and the many other writers who contributed to the Federal Writers' Project American Guide series. May the brooks go on forever.

Emergency mule power. *Arthur Rothstein.*

Contents

Illustrations

Author's Note

MY grandfather, when he was dying, would put on a brown tweed sport coat, a scarf, and a straw boater, pull a walking stick from the collection in the coatroom, and amble down a brick path in the gardens behind his house. He was a jaunty figure, even when his neck had grown noticeably thin in his collar. The type of man whom lifelong acquaintances still addressed as "Colonel Griffin" but whom I would see laughing at ribald jokes with his gardener; the type who until the last would insist on dressing formally for dinner in the dining room, and then after brandy liked to step outside with the men and piss on the boxwood. I followed a step behind, jumpy as a crown bearer, wondering with his every wobbly stride if he would topple over sideways into his beloved roses.

We had never been close, but he had offered me a chance, very late in the game, to record his recollections of an interesting life. This was difficult, because I lived in Wyoming, while he lived on the Monterey Peninsula in California, and time was short. But it was a chance for me to hear him describe the world in which he'd grown up and to revisit the setting of my own childhood in California.

We did our best. When I could get away from work, I would fly out for a few days with a list of questions. When he was too fragile to rise and walk with me, I would interrogate him as he lay propped up with pillows, like a doll on a child's bed.

Cancer seems to ebb and flow, even in its last stages, and I could not always count on productive sessions—remembering is an exhausting effort. Our interviews often trailed off, as he would arrive at an eddy of memory and sink into a pause, which could stretch into hours. But he tried and tried.

He was disdainful of the pain that weakened him, and scornful, too, of imprecise questions. He rejected those questions as he would a cold dinner plate, and I found myself reduced from the Intimate Confessor I imagined myself to the Feckless Grandson of old. I had hoped that fellow, the F.G., was gone for good, bound and gagged perhaps in a closet in a distant wing of the enormous house, one of those remote rooms where the F.G. used to flee his grandfather's formal dinners. But no. My grandfather could resurrect the red-faced F.G. in an instant with a curt "That's irrelevant" or "No one's interested."

When his pauses sometimes became slumber, I had frustrating gaps of time to fill. On one visit I picked up from a used book dealer a 1930s guide to the Monterey Peninsula, to read while I sat amidst the boxwood on the veranda facing Point Lobos, waiting for his strength to return. The book was the work of the Federal Writers' Project, part of the Works Progress Administration, a New Deal program of the 1930s, written during the early years of my grandfather's career as publisher of a Monterey newspaper. One evening, when my questions were eliciting only monosyllabic answers, I pulled the book out and read aloud from it.

His eyelids flickered up. Being a certain kind of man, he was quick to take issue with some statement in the book. He was stirred by his lifelong, and somewhat hopeless, desire to correct the world, to get it right, whether it was a troop movement or a grandson's manners, and so after a tonic admonishment of the guide's authors he was off telling his own story again. That story is not for telling here, at least not in full, but in the most general terms it is the story of a man constructing himself, brick by brick, into pretty much exactly what he thought he ought to be. Mobility was a liberating force in his life, as it is to an extraordinary degree for many Americans. He was the son of a plumbing contractor, who came from England by way of Canada, and an immigrant Polish woman; he finished life as a successful newspaper publisher and decorated Army officer, living in a baronial mansion, with membership in the sort of country club that excluded Jews such as his mother. His was a very different story, I suspect, from the ones we will tell our grandchildren fifty years hence. In our story there may be fortunes made and lost, wars, and much moving about, as there always have been, but the routes traveled will be less direct, the goals more equivocal. My grandfather lived in a very different world.

I began studying the Federal Writers' Project American Guides for clues to just how different a world it was for members of his generation. The American Guide Series was an extensive undertaking. There were guides to all the states and most of our big cities. Reading them, one can get a distinct flavor of the places and people of America in the 1930s, that adolescent America transforming itself in depression and war.

I thought at one time the guides were my exclusive discovery, since most of them were out of print, but they had long been favorites of writers such as John Steinbeck and Lewis Mumford. There has been a revival of interest in the years since I first came across them, bringing many back into print, wrapped in nostalgic Art Deco covers.

They remain surprisingly useful half a century after publication, describing or prefiguring much of what the landscape still holds. Back in 1979, a couple of years before my grandfather's final illness, my wife and I decided to move from Washington, D.C., to the Rocky Mountain region, and I went to the Library of Congress in Washington, searching

for information about Wyoming. We had decided that
Washington lacked whatever it was we wanted in a home,
not actually knowing what that *was*—like-minded friends?
Risk? Natural beauty? We were taking a blind, hopeful leap
into the remoteness of the West. The library's Wyoming
pickings were surprisingly slim, but I found a worn copy of
Wyoming: A Guide to Its History, Highways, and People, published in 1941 by the Federal Writers' Project. The guide
had no dust jacket, and the green cover had darkened with
age. The pages, as I rapidly thumbed them, smelled of musty
neglect. An earlier reader had underlined favorite passages on
paper so yellowed and brittle that the pencil had sometimes
broken through. In the guide I found history, economics,
landscapes described, and a wide range of essays. On a shelf
in one of the alcoves were similar guides to all the states,
credited to state and federal writers' projects, all dating from
the 1930s and early '40s.

We journeyed west to Wyoming, where I had a job. In
the years that followed, I corresponded with rare book dealers
who specialized in Americana, filling a shelf in the old shep-
herd's cabin where we first lived, and then more shelves when
we moved our growing family to a larger house. I collected
dozens of the guides, rummaging beyond the state series into
the volumes on particular highways and counties and pockets
of ethnic culture. By the time I sat on my grandfather's veranda reading about the Monterey of fifty years ago, I was well
versed in writers' project lore.

On one of my last visits to my grandfather, I walked again
behind him down the brick path toward the rose garden; he
moved rather more slowly, taking shorter steps than before.
When we reached the roses, he examined one peach-colored
bloom that was beginning to brown. He pulled a pair of
clippers from his side pocket, snapped the rose off, and threw
it on the path, scattering petals. The motion almost toppled

him. He gave me a "That's how it's done" nod and walked on.

He told me about a trip he'd taken, in his middle age, to the little town of Eyegreen, in Lincolnshire, England, where his father's family, the Griffins, had lived until the late nineteenth century. My grandfather, who was born in Kansas City, had never been there before. Nevertheless, a man in a cloth hat stopped him in front of a cottage by an abandoned brewery, and said, "Be you a Griffin?"

How did he sense that? I asked. Was *he* a Griffin?

Oh, no, said my grandfather. The Griffins had been gone for over two generations, to Canada and the United States, and the property had fallen into others' hands. He said, "But what had been passed on was the myth of prosperity, the Griffins and the good old days, when the brewery made beer, and the brickyard made bricks, and all those little houses were occupied by men who worked on the Griffin place, farmed there, and so forth. They forget the bad times. They remember certain things. The way men walk, the shape of their heads, that sort of thing. The things that farmers remember. It was odd. Mysterious." He paused and examined another rose. I wondered if one irresolute little brown petal spelled doom for the whole brilliant flower. But he turned away, saying, in a rolling cadence, "And the brooks go on forever."

I could only look at his back, his straight, narrow back, and wonder what face he had on. I hear the untypical words now whenever I think of him, like a last bright rose among the hips.

One winter not long after he died I took out my collection of Federal Writers' Project guides and set them out on the kitchen table, thumbing them and ordering them for an imaginary trip. I searched them for eccentric places, odd conjunctions of history and landscape, wonders that had never made it into tourism brochures, pockets of old culture pre-

served. It is difficult now to say just what I was after. Certainly I had a curiosity that bordered on hunger for places
where the inhabitants felt an indelible kinship with a particular piece of ground, places where an old soul by the road
would remember the shape of heads in a particular family.

The row of books on the table gradually took on an order.
The biggest, fattest book of all came first: Washington, D.C.,
where I could return to the Library of Congress and delve
deeper into the collections of old material assembled by the
Federal Writers' Project. Already the guides had offered up a
few scents to follow—the original ramshackle cabin of "Home
on the Range," the colonies of oystermen sequestered out in
the Gulf of Mexico—and I knew I would find more among
the yellowing notes sent back to Washington by writers' project
"fieldworkers" around the country. Out there somewhere, I
hoped, was the contemporary equivalent of the little towns
where the brickyards make bricks and the breweries beer.
The guides would be my ancestral voices, and I would follow
them to unlikely places and beyond, in search of those brooks
that go on forever.

THE accounts of the journeys that follow convey the landscapes and voices as faithfully as I am able, with only minor
editorial manipulations for sense and concision. My travels
with the American Guides are a few years behind me now,
and there have already been changes in lives and landscapes I
observed—last year I was notified that the luminous Agnes
Wright Spring, author of the Wyoming volume of the
American Guide Series, had passed away, and word comes,
too, that the U.S. Army Corps of Engineers has bulwarked
the Mississippi River flood control structures around Baton
Rouge—mentioned in my Louisiana travels—to its own satisfaction. Perhaps a book about how places change over half

Ready to roll in Montana. *John Vachon.*

a century *should* be mildly confounded by events over the much shorter period of time between execution and publication. My account, though, is of things as they were when I was there, and my aim is to render the people and places vividly alive in those moments, without hedging against the sudden twists life will inevitably take the minute we turn our backs.

With chronology, I have taken some liberties, condensing elements from a series of trips between 1984 and 1987 into a single narrative. Thus, a punctilious Louisiana reader will note that the New Orleans World's Fair took place in 1984, while Hurricane Elena—a much less costly event, as it turned out—arrived in 1985, whereas my version would have them occur in the same year. My intent here is to spare the reader the details of numerous arrivals and departures, as well as the interludes of wage work I found necessary.

Finding a structure for this book was much more difficult than locating its subjects. I originally conceived it as a book of continuous, headlong travel, only to find once I began that particular places waylaid and captivated me, demanding a more lingering examination. I wanted to describe, though, through the fresh senses of the road traveler and try to capture the extemporaneous beguilement of what one sees and hears when arriving unexpected in a new place. So it is patched together this way: a series of "Points of Departure" and "Destinations." Departure Points were really way stations for me, well-traveled places that will be familiar to many readers, where I caught my breath, took a quick look around, and readied myself for another segment of my journey, putting myself in a critical and questioning frame of mind. Destinations were the more obscure places where I lingered longer and sought answers.

Readers already familiar with the American Guide Series may know that in 1939 the work of the Federal Writers' Project was divvied up among the states, and titles published thereafter would list, for example, the Louisiana Writers' Program as author. Work on the guides was still funded primarily by the federal Works Progress Administration—participating states after 1939 made a 25 percent contribution—and Washington had final approval of all publications. For the limited purposes of this book, I saw no reason to confuse readers by distinguishing between Writers' Program and Federal Writers' Project publications, but anyone interested can consult Jerre Mangione's excellent history of the Federal Writers' Project, *The Dream and the Deal* (Little, Brown &

Co., 1972) and a list of publications assembled therein by Pittsburgh bookseller Arthur Scharf.

It should be remembered throughout that this is a book of travels, with a travel book's sins, the most common of which is the subjective and sometimes cursory nature of its observations. I have no intention of competing with the credibility of witnesses who have known these places for a lifetime; rather, I offer a new and idiosyncratic perspective, like the aerial photographer who flies over at a considerable remove and gives us a useful new view of a landscape we know, but still might know differently.

Acknowledgments

THOUGH this book is largely made up of firsthand experiences, it began in a library, the Library of Congress, where I first picked up the Federal Writers' Project's *Wyoming: A Guide to Its History, Highways, and People.* I returned there again and again to pore over writers' project books and research materials stored in the Madison Annex. For a time I looked over the shoulder of Joe Sullivan, who in the early 1980s sorted and cataloged reams of material written for the writers' project. In various state and university libraries there were helpful archivists like Sullivan, and many a small-town librarian helped me find local history written in local voices. When I needed to have a copy of a particular writers' project guide at my side on the road, it could usually be found in the basement of Arthur Scharf, a Pittsburgh rare book collector who specializes in the American Guide Series.

The idea of revisiting and writing about places described in the writers' project Wyoming guide got its first tryout in the *Denver Post*'s *Empire Magazine,* with encouragement and unlimited space provided by editor Bob Wallace. My agent, Amanda Urban of ICM, somehow got book publishers interested in letting an unknown writer from Wyoming try this project on a broader scale.

A number of people who helped me during my travels—with ideas, interviews, encouragement, and meals—are mentioned in the book. Among the many who are not, dozens of friends, new acquaintances, and relatives have my gratitude. I will single out a few whose solicitude came at crucial times: Jean Griffin Ward; J. B. Jackson; Tom Bell; Bill Webb; Deborah Grant. I got a push when I needed it most from writer Dick Prouty, who may not have realized at the time how galvanizing were his words.

The computer has made manuscript preparation less of a chore, but early on Laurie Allen and Ginger Tillemans helped with transcription, typing, and research.

A number of people read parts of the manuscript and gave constructive criticism, but only my wife, Berthenia Crocker, and my editors at Norton have traveled the full length of this manuscript. Editors Linda Healy and Carol Houck Smith never complained about the deadlines I missed; they kept shaping the book, from its overall concept to the minutiae of its sentences. Berthenia and our children—Genya, Rosaleen, and Nicholas—tolerated my absences and preoccupation and made home a happy place to work. Berthenia read and made suggestions, told me what worked and what didn't, and kept me at work when my spirits flagged.

The past presses so closely on the present. . . .
—*Wyoming: A Guide to Its History,*
Highways, and People

Lander, WY

Southern
Wyoming

Smith
Center, KS

Monterey

Eastern
Colorado

Los
Angeles

BARRY CARPENTERS

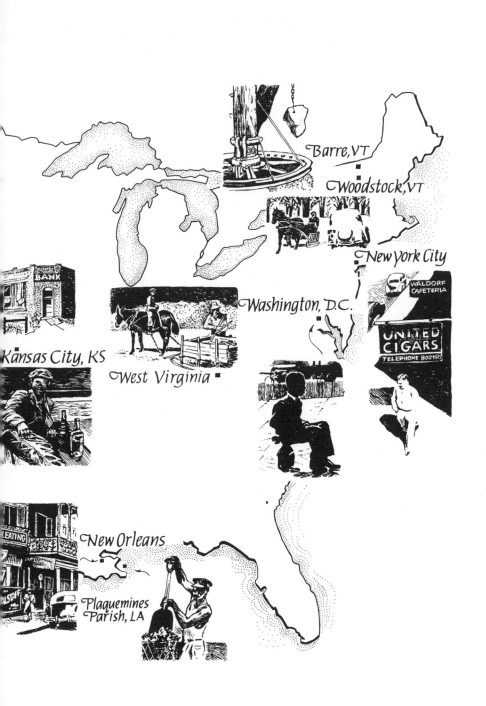

Barre, VT

Woodstock, VT

New York City

Washington, D.C.

WALDORF CAFETERIA

UNITED CIGARS
TELEPHONE BOOTHS

BANK

Kansas City, KS

West Virginia

New Orleans

EATING

ALSTAFF

Plaquemines
Parish, LA

Prologue

Leaving Wyoming

*Tall shade trees and trim flower gardens surround pressed-brick,
stucco, and frame buildings. . . . Willow-fringed Popo Agie
River meanders through the town, and behind it are blue-black
timbered foothills, rising to snow-capped peaks on the west. . . .
'Where the rails end, and the trails begin' is the local slogan.*
—Wyoming: A Guide to Its History, Highways, and People

I LEFT in the middle of a May night, when in the town of
Lander, Wyoming, in 1985, only one all-night market-cum-
gas station stayed open, and the countergirl killed her time
riding the mop up and down the aisles. The streetlights blinked
orange. Main Street, where yesterday cattle window-shopped
on their way to higher pasture, lay glistening and bare. The
brimming, soily scent of the river carried across the street.
Cottonwood branches lay tangled in the gutters.

My wife and I had agreed it was best to leave this way. She
and our children were sleeping when I closed the door behind

me. No labored good-byes with two sleepy, uncomprehend-
ing young girls and a baby boy. My wife exacted only a promise
that I would orbit back regularly while I scratched this traveling itch.

She knew as well as I that these were uncertain and hum-
bling times for our adopted town, with many despairs and
departures caused by a depressed economy; that, and perhaps
some better understanding than my own of wanderlust, were
the reasons she encouraged me to do a little searching for
both of us. Lander had been our home for six years. We had
arrived from Washington, D.C., in 1979 with our first baby
a month old; adventurers, we thought, with a yen for a change
of climate, and an interest in the people who live away from
the civilized centers. We slept on the floor of a cabin belong-
ing to new friends for the first few weeks, and discovered that
at least in this town and for us, the doctrine that rural communities share individual burdens was no myth. The small
cabin we first rented was reroofed in a day by a jolly crew of
new acquaintances; they even brought the beer. My wife opened
a law office; I worked as a journalist. We moved to this larger
house in town as our family grew: a second daughter in 1981;
a son in 1984.

The planks that edge our house were wet from a thunder-
shower earlier in the night. Shielded by the dark from the
inquiring faces of neighbors, I stumbled along, feeling the
give of the boards as if it were my own spongy resolve. A
towering cottonwood, a century old like the house, rustled
above me, and an engine turned over down the block.

I stopped just beyond the tree to look at the sky. At this
altitude, five thousand feet, you stare into a dense pocketful
of stars, spare change to rattle if the world is yours to wander
in. I found the rainmaking Hyades, and Arcturus, orange
and intense in the north.

Then the planks creaked behind me; the dog had arisen from one of the cool garden spots he favored, and followed. He had faithfully trod my path for fourteen years, through thin mountain air and thick southern humidity, into leaky cabins and slum houses, always anxious at another departure, always ready to shake out his leonine mane and come along. He'd put up with a lot. A foxtail in his eye driving home from a dog pound in the Sierras began things for us. A black teenager in Oakland had once waved a gun and threatened to shoot him. But misadventures never diluted his resolve to accompany me. He was now precariously old.

This was his best time of day, when the night wind cooled his heavy fur and he could stumble around in the dark, unembarrassed by his arthritic gait. Watching the way his hips wandered sideways, I was reminded of my grandfather's stiff-legged movements of a few years before, wobbling down the brick paths.

We sat shoulder to shoulder for a moment on the wooden walkway, the old house behind our backs. He was not as happy in town as he had been in that first cabin. There he had had a broad hill of high grasses, cut by an irrigation ditch where he chased an elusive fox. He used to march the hillcrest importantly, watching the world, and we did, too. Off to the west were the white nubs of the Wind River Mountains; to the east, the grazing horses and then the cottonwoods along the North Fork of the Popo Agie River; and to the south, below us, the bright lights of the town. It was a wondrous first winter. We trucked our water from town, using a precarious old International on icy or muddy roads, and filled a cistern beneath the cabin; some evenings a snowy owl would whoosh up out of the darkness onto the utility pole by the south window.

Life in town was a little less arduous, a little more settled, though the house was old and needed plenty of work. It was a noisy, genial place, pathed by young children and their pet retainers, busy in the warm and inconsequential way of families, with a nook or two for writing and reverie. Cattle were less likely to eat your front yard, so my wife planted like crazy, both for eating and for looking. The harsh weather of the high plains and mountains snugged the house and the town, and neighbors helped and gossiped about each other, in the way of communities where paid jobs are only part of the work you do. But times got hard in Wyoming in the 1980s, and little by little the town began to change. A tiny plot of zinnias next to a trailer was left to dandelions and weeds one spring; the weekly newspaper grew lighter and thinner; less dust was raised at the softball diamonds. If I had placed on a map of the United States, one by one, the faces of those people who sweated on our cabin roof back in 1979, they would have been spread all over the country in 1985.

Since my grandfather's death I had been reading extensively in the old Federal Writers' Project guides, forming mental pictures of American places as they were fifty years ago, from the Gulf Coast to the Northwest. Partly I read to distract myself from the decline of my own community and the departure of friends, partly simply for the vividness of the descriptions and history.

The guides became a window out of the present, to a time when my grandfather had been my age. I had always been well aware of the differences between him and me, and I had wondered how much of it was generational shift. If many of my contemporaries seemed to lack his certainty and confidence when it came to shaping a home, and a self, out of the raw materials immediately at hand, it might be because the materials, as much as the shapers, had changed.

The dog and I lingered for a moment on the porch. There

was a faint smell of rain; clouds were bunching around the rising moon. My stomach tightened a little, anticipating. When I put my arm around the dog, he turned his embarrassed gaze toward our neighbor's toolshed; then he pulled free of my arm and ambled away, putting his bones back in order. He headed for a little mud wallow he'd excavated beneath the rhubarb.

I threw my bag among a pile of American Guides in the back seat of an old, ramshackle Mustang. I slid in, turned the key, and was off. The mild, musty smell of the carpets, the faint pattern of dust on top of the dashboard, the elfish glow of the radio—surely almost any American born in the twentieth century knows that excitement when you climb into a car in the dead of night.

It was the first departure on a journey that would include many departures, many returns, a regular traveling forth to find places and coming back to contemplate what it was I'd found; then a little planning, and off on the next leg. I would start in Washington, D.C., home of the Federal Writers' Project archives. Then, I imagined, I would disappear onto the back roads of the guides' back pages. I had no particular agenda, just a good set of maps and the guides.

———

Wyoming is a land of great open spaces with plenty of elbow room;
in 1940 the population density was only 2.1 persons to the square
mile. There are sections of the State where it is said you can look
farther and see less than any other place in the world.
— *Wyoming: A Guide to Its History, Highways, and People*

MIDNIGHT sped by on the blacktop south of Lander, just beyond the Rawlins cutoff, where U.S. 287 crosses the Little Popo Agie River and you look back at the sleek foothills that

rise westward toward the Wind River Mountains. I put on a
cassette tape, and the Mustang thundered like a freed pony
across the High Lonesome of Wyoming.

> Little sister don't you kiss me once or twice,
> say it's very nice,
> and then you run—
> Woo-woo-woo-woo,
> Little sister don't you do what your big sister done.

I was alone on one of the loneliest stretches of road in
America. No more than half a dozen vehicles would pass this
way before dawn, and I could zip across this empty plain at
eighty miles per hour in my ragged, revved-up car without
fearing the highway patrol or any other authority. The population of Wyoming is now about 430,000, or a density of
4.4 per square mile. Compare that to Rhode Island, which
people inhabit like coats in a closet, more than 900 per square
mile. In Wyoming people mass in isolated towns, and the
long stretches in between are as empty as they were fifty years
ago, or five hundred.

The body of the Mustang was a dark, dented green, touched
up with squirts of candy-flake green spray paint; the spray
paint had dripped down the damaged metal and frozen in
icicle shapes. The grille and bumper were askew, like the face
of a palsy victim who smiles on one side and frowns on the
other. And the convertible top was so tattered and torn that
for all the good it was doing I just slung it back, despite the
chill. It was an old-shoe sort of car, and it would be my
companion on many of my trips, though not all of them. We
were good companions from the moment I pressed the accelerator, free with each other and uninhibited. So there sat I,
beneath the stars, singing at the top of my lungs.

Well I dated your big sister,
And I took her to the show.
I went out to get some candy,
Along came some dandy
And they snuck right out the door—

Eighty miles per hour is a dawdling pace on these masking-tape highways. The landscape is all distance, with shadowy sentinel outcrops here and there in the starlight, and the convex band of the eastern horizon. There is nothing to intrude on radio dreams. There is nothing to inhibit the adrenaline surges that seem to put the big 289 engine right in your chest, pistons sliding and valves going tappety-tap. I scribbled in a notebook with my free hand: "coyotes whisper," "7th grade band," "Conestogas," "Zydeco beat," "UFO?" Begin a trip at night by yourself, and in the first few minutes you've traveled in time, and been almost anywhere.

———

Although there are many . . . old-time residents and their families, 58 per cent of the present population of Wyoming has come from somewhere else. Many of these people were headed for other horizons and intended merely to pass through Wyoming. Because of various accidents, such as a horse dying, a guide breaking his leg, a car being wrecked, or a blizzard blocking the road, they were delayed in the State.
— *Wyoming:* A Guide to Its History, Highways, and People

LANDER, the town I departed, is tucked into a sun-blessed valley at the southeastern end of the Wind River Mountains. Its first non-Indian settlers were emigrants who dropped out of the caravans on the Oregon Trail and began growing vegetables to sell to the travelers that followed. On one side rise steep, granite peaks; on the other side, in the direction I was driving, extend miles and miles of high desert plains, the kind of sagebrush country which dejects all but the antelope hunter and a few sheepherders.

According to the 1941 guide to Wyoming, more than half the 250,000 residents of the state at that time were born somewhere else. It was a land of opportunity for the resourceful and self-reliant, and if you showed you were made of that sort of stuff, you assimilated quickly; there was no problem getting yourself elected to state office after a few years' residency. Oil and mining were the quickest route to riches.

Many of the people who live in Wyoming now arrived during the boom years of the 1970s, when workers poured in to work on oil and gas rigs and in coal strip mines and pushed the population up by over 30 percent. Even as developers cashed in on the boom, they and the politicians clucked about the need to diversify the economy before the inevitable crash, and vowed never again to let the state's natural resources be taken away for mere cash. But the developers, egged on by office-bound demographers, dreamt that this joyride had a long way to go, so they let diversification wait.

They waited too long. The bust came, and now businesses are shutting down and property prices are dropping, and just about everybody in Wyoming wishes someone would come rushing in to take more coal or oil for mere cash. A few community leaders have even begged the rest of the country to use Wyoming as a disposal site for nuclear wastes. While the rest of the United States enjoyed a kind of hysterical prosperity during the first half of the 1980s, Wyoming limped along. Costly efforts were made to nurse indigenous Wyoming industries during these years, but one wonders what will happen to them as the rest of the country sobers up and stops bingeing on consumption. I had read and written about the unhappy economic cycles in mining regions like Appalachia, as an outsider, often hiding a nagging skepticism about the inability of the locals to pull out of their bad circumstances; now I was getting a more convincing education.

In the 1930s, though, the Wind River Valley stood a little apart from Wyoming's history of plunder. It was an agricultural center. The best fruit in the state came from the orchards around Lander, said the guide, as well as "excellent honey." The valley was called "Pushroot" by the Shoshone Indians because of the way grasses and other plants shot up in the spring. It had then, and I suppose it must have still, the lowest wind velocity of any town in the United States, which must be a shock to those who know Woming only by the biting blows of its southern plains.

U.S. 287 going south climbs out of the Popo Agie River drainage, where Lander lies, and up onto high sagebrush plains; it climbs up Beaver Rim to another alkaline, desert plateau, once an inland sea, and follows the meandering Sweetwater River for a while. Then the road turns south at Muddy Gap and makes haste across one of the world's most empty landscapes to the town of Rawlins.

About seventy miles from Lander I drove through ghostly Jeffrey City, a town where there would be no more than a fuel pump, if that, were it not for that mineral hunger that brings so many people to this barren country. Jeffrey City is a latter-day company town, updated by its sharp-cornered, Kleenex-box trailers. In my 1941 Wyoming guide it doesn't exist. A year or two from now it may not again: The two uranium mines that were its lifeblood have been nearly completely shut down, and few are likely to stay on here without a fifteen-dollar-per-hour wage to convince them it's livable. The population of Jeffrey City, a huddle of trailers and prefab housing in a lunar landscape, has dropped from forty-five hundred in 1980 to a few hundred today. In a desperate attempt to meet payments on bonds that funded school construction during the boom, the Jeffrey City district has offered free housing to families that'll move there and put children in the schools. Bureaucracy always lags, and so highway improvements, a necessity during the boom years and improvident now, are presently under way.

———

In 1916 Wyoming adopted a constitutional amendment that made it possible for the State to participate in the Federal aid for post roads. A State highway commission was created the next year, which has since carried on an extensive building program. The production of oil on State-owned lands has been responsible in large measure for the network of . . . roads spreading over the state.
—Wyoming: A Guide to Its History, Highways, and People

OFTEN this is what compels transportation improvements in Wyoming, where there is still so much open space for asphalt to conquer: Highways follow the hunt for the raw mineral and energy resources, which in turn provide tax revenues to build roads. Beyond that, much time and money are devoted to upkeep. Shoulders are forever being widened to ease a flow of traffic that would hardly disrupt a single on-ramp to the Pasadena Freeway.

With the uranium mines shut down, Jeffrey City's two-lane highway has less traffic, but it still serves as one of a few routes ferrying tourists from Interstate 80, the busy zipper that crosses southern Wyoming, to the beauties of Wyoming's northwestern corner, where Yellowstone and Grand Teton national parks lie. This little highway also crosses the route of the Oregon Trail, which was pioneered in the early 1840s and runs just south of Lander.

There are many things along a roadside worth seeing that aren't plainly marked. I pulled over on 287's shoulder a few miles beyond Jeffrey City within view of Split Rock, a cleft chunk of weathered granite that thrusts skyward out of the plain to the east. Near the highway the Sweetwater River meandered in the starlight, and along its banks followed the Oregon Trail wagon ruts. The rock served as a landmark for travelers on the trail, and from the right vantage point you can watch the sun rise behind it.

Probably, too, at a much earlier time it helped nomadic Indians find their way. A year earlier I stopped here in the high dust of road construction to look at an array of tiny red flags that marked a prehistoric pit house. While huge graders and front loaders and dump trucks lumbered a few feet away, a small group of volunteers led by a ponytailed archeologist named Dan Aiken scraped away with toothbrushes and small tools at the clay below the road's shoulder, searching for flint and bowl fragments left sometime after the last Ice Age. While the heavy equipment moved a ton of dirt at a scoop, these folks lifted it by the teaspoonful.

State archeologists, who are allowed to poke around—in fact, must, whenever federally funded road construction lifts some topsoil—preceded the road-widening project here and found the usual fire rings and arrowheads and flake tools. This was a natural route for nomadic Indians to travel two thousand or more years ago; like the immigrants to California in the nineteenth century, they liked being a stone's throw from fresh water and the wildlife it attracted.

But the red flags marked an extraordinary find: a pit house, evidence that Indians here excavated rooms, stored food, and made it their home. "Home" may have been a concept outside the vocabulary of these prehistoric people, who had to be primarily concerned about natural cycles of drought and game and temperature—matters of less concern in today's homes. But it was the idea of "home"—a stable abode, a community, a culture—that I thought about as I sat on the soft gravel shoulder where the red flags had been.

The archeologists pecking at the site last year were wide-eyed and energized. Relics from nomadic Indians—fire rings, arrowheads, and the like—were common around here, and experts had assumed that in the northwest plains the early Indians had been strictly wandering hunter-gatherers. Even as they dug, completely new images of this prehistoric way of life were forming in their heads. In the entire northern Great Plains, only two sites of permanent prehistoric habitation like this have been found.

The dig had to be completed within weeks of the discovery, coming as it did under the dominion of road building; archeologists seemed grateful that the engineers worked around them that long. Dan Aiken, whose clothes, skin, and wispy beard were all merging into the same desert color, refused to criticize the tyranny of highway construction, admitting only that his crew would have been slower and more methodical if time had been available. A little half-smile creased his young face, and he said he guessed there were a few other prehistoric houses out there they would never get a chance to find, unless a million dollars dropped in their laps.

The archeologists with toothbrushes had speculated an ancient world, a world that contradicted accepted notions of prehistory. They had imagined a people seeking safety in rush-covered huts as the world around them dried up; they conjured trees along a river that is now bare-banked; they tasted native grass seeds stored dozens of centuries ago in these bowl-shaped hollows.

After a few short months the excavation was over, and the road builders moved in. The state spent $3.8 million to add a few feet of shoulder to this old highway so the big Winnebagos could make their way more comfortably to the national parks in the summer. No one even suggested the construction crews hold off for a year or two, or change their route by fifty feet, so history hunters could scratch the ground for answers about how people lived. Scratch a little deeper, and the question becomes: How do *we* live?

A breeze reversed itself; it blew downriver from my home to the west and then came back the other way, up the sinuous Sweetwater. The moon was dropping behind the Wind River Mountains. As I sat myself back in the Mustang's vinyl bucket seat, I thought about the muscle and money we have put into motion. We have built so many highways like this one, erasing petroglyphic messages without a thought. All to make it easier for someone like me to run away when I get an itch.

———

Barren country stretches southward . . . bordering the Great Divide Basin, an eastward continuation of the Red Desert. Patches of alkali alternate here with clumps of sage and greasewood; occasional jutting red rocks disturb the monotony of gray salt soil and greenish-gray shrubs. Winter winds sweep the snow into deep arroyos and gulches, leaving the sparse plants uncovered for sheep feed.

—*Wyoming: A Guide to Its History, Highways, and People*

I HIT Interstate 80 in Rawlins, Wyoming, and immediately felt sleepy. That's the way I react to interstates, and I'd been driving most of the night as well. There was a glimmer of light in the east, and the only thing open by the freeway was a familiar fast-food operation. As an orange yolk sagged on the eastern horizon, I drank some coffee and ate a fanciful fist-size "breakfast," an egg and bun with a piece of unidentifiable meat tucked in it. It hardly gave the traveler a sense of locality to be fed his first meal on the road by a chain food vendor, and I vowed then and there that I would sin no more, or as little as possible. Beware the narcosis of an interstate: It is in league with the corruption of franchise food.

A long, uneventful drive lay ahead of me, rolling east and
then south into a landscape thickening with the urban overflow of Denver. My last Wyoming memory would be Elk
Mountain, a peak near Interstate 80 west of Laramie that
stands on the brown plains, wearing a green shawl of evergreens. It is all alone here, too far from anything to be useful
to real estate developers, or the recreationists who abound in
the Medicine Bow Mountains farther east. It is an island, one
that a sleepy eye can surround with imaginary water and place
somewhere in those vast gaps of the South Pacific, rising up
into its own solitary environs, rare and magnificent. I found
a pullout near its base and slept beneath it for a short while
before I drove on into Colorado.

"Elk Mountain has always looked the same," Agnes Wright
Spring was telling me a few hours later. Ms. Spring was ninety-
one and living in a tall, quiet apartment building in Fort
Collins, Colorado, that catered to older folks. A published
historian and author, she was dictating another book. But
her most popular work, even though it hasn't got her name
on it, is the FWP guide to Wyoming.

She had occasion to drive by Elk Mountain frequently in
the thirties. She occupied the passenger seat and scribbled
notes while her husband, Archer, an oil geologist, drove her
fifty thousand miles around the state, interviewing, observ-
ing, and gathering material for the guide.

When I visited her, she was about to move to another
apartment, forced out by condominium conversion, but she
faced the change with brio and pawky reproach for the absen-
tee landlord. Blindness made writing and moving difficult,
but she seemed to have plenty of energy for both. She must
have devised a system that allowed her to dress herself well
for strangers, for she greeted me wearing a blue ascot and
Hopi jewelry on her long forearms. Spunk had kept her
memories neat, too.

U.S. 30 across southern Wyoming. *Arthur Rothstein.*

"The highways were just dirt, not concrete. I don't think we ever drove over fifty—probably more like thirty-five miles per hour. At night we did our own cooking, because we were in small hotels. They were mostly crude. When we got a place without bedbugs, we figured we were all right.

"I couldn't get anywhere telling people I was with the WPA. When I started out, I got nothing but frozen faces; we were boondoggling, they thought. Then I started saying I was the women's editor of the *Wyoming Stockman-Farmer.* . . . And from then on all the doors opened, and I got anything I wanted all around the state.

"In Wyoming people ate a great deal and said nothing. I noticed the food when we went around the state, it varied so. Up in the northeast part of the state, around Gillette, they had so much starch—they would have potatoes and beans and all sorts of starchy food at one time. In Lander they had nice gardens and a variety of food. And, of course, down along the Union Pacific they had"—she paused—*"substantial* food."

My breakfast, eaten down along what is still the UP line, sat in my stomach like a rock.

"There were lots of tourists, and then there were what we called 'jalopy gypsies,' drifting around. Okies and people like that, looking for work."

She said she hadn't been back to Wyoming in some time, because of her blindness, but she imagined it had changed less than most of the country. She was dismayed, though, by the new people drawn there by the energy industry. "I heard a television broadcast recently interviewing people in Gillette and Douglas and Evanston [Wyoming], and I couldn't believe it. These people were living in trailers, hating Wyoming, only staying to get some money. How bitter they were! Mostly women, complaining.

"I loved Wyoming. I think more of Wyoming as home because that's where I grew up [Spring was born in Colorado]. My father had a stage line which went from Laramie up to the mines in the Medicine Bow Range. We had sort of a stage stop where people would stop for meals. Fishing was my hobby, and I'd go out and catch lovely trout. We had a stream with no limit. The air was so clean, and the stars!"

The blind woman beside me actually could see it, and I would like to believe that I will someday sit at night by the rushing water near the town of Centennial, Wyoming, and find the feelings of that young, spirited woman inscribed in that landscape. The traffic intensified as I drove down the freeway toward Denver, but I don't think I woke up again to the present until I was up in the air somewhere over Illinois on my flight to Washington, D.C.

Point of Departure

Washington, D.C.

WITHIN a long trip there are many beginnings and endings. Generally, the trips I took with the Federal Writers' Project guides began at metropolitan centers, where I could find libraries to haunt, authority figures to quiz, and usually bright, ambitious people struggling with questions about the importance of where you live and where you came from. The cities were preludes to my destinations, which were generally out beyond the reach of commuters or experts.

Washington was the first city to serve me as a point of departure, a most sensible place to begin, because here were stored many of the materials produced under the Federal Writers' Project, some of them never published. In addition, there were certain books in the American Guide Series that were virtually unattainable through rare book dealers—South Dakota's guide, for instance—which were available for perusal in the Library of Congress collections. And it was from

Shoeshine boys at Union Station in Washington, D.C.
Esther Bubley.

Washington that my wife and I, six years before, had set out for the West, pulling a U-Haul trailer after reading the Federal Writers' Project guide to Wyoming.

I spent my days in Washington rushing between the library and the U.S. Bureau of Census, where I groped like a blind man among the statistics, looking uncertainly for numbers that would illuminate half a century of change. Usually I lugged the 1,140-page Federal Writers' Project guide to the city under my arm. It described a more leisurely, less populated place, laid out on, but not yet fulfilling, the grand design of Pierre Charles L'Enfant. This was, in 1937, "the best-shaded city in America," and it still is. But even fifty years ago, according to the guide, Washington was suffering "the curse of the motorcar . . . more congested and perilous than . . . even London or Paris or New York." The nation's great adventure in city planning failed to anticipate Henry Ford.

So I rode the subway, whooshing under the hopeless jam on Pennsylvania Avenue, beneath the milling humanity on the Capitol Mall, and up to Capitol Hill, where it was a short jaunt to the rotund old Library of Congress. South across Pennsylvania from the main library is the new Madison Annex, a sharp-cornered marble Dumpster that catches the overflow of over twenty million books and pamphlets, thirty-five million manuscripts, and over six million pieces of music. The Library of Congress collections grow by ten new "items" every minute.

Inside the Madison Annex, the walls were high and smooth and tidy as ice. A marble Madison sat larger than life to the left, at the end of a hall flanked by twelve pillars. Cold, sterile efficiency, his stern visage insisted. Daily the guards by the manuscript room made me surrender every tablet and paper scrap on my person; I filled out forms and punched codes and waited at my assigned table to handle old writers' project files. Computers whirred and microfilm hissed behind the walls.

In these surroundings I discovered what an ambitious, scruffy enterprise the Federal Writers' Project had been. It was a minor program in the broad sweep of the New Deal, but it left behind so much material that even today it is still being laboriously sorted by sleepy-eyed researchers wearing aprons and plastic gloves. The more famous guides—to states like Massachusetts and cities like New York and New Orleans and, yes, Washington, D.C.—have been rediscovered and are back in print now, but most of the others never will be. Is there an audience for guides to 1930s Chillicothe County, Ohio, and the Smoke Hole, a tiny hollow in West Virginia?

Between 1935 and 1939 the writers' project produced 320 books; before it was finished, over 1,000 publications were issued. All you had to do was call yourself a writer and qualify as "indigent"—not hard to do in those times—to get a low-paying job with the project. Richard Wright, Nelson Algren, Jack Conroy, and Saul Bellow all served. Algren later gave wry thanks to the project for the afternoons he "took work home"; a number of successful novels got their start this way.

On withered yellow newsprint I read the longhand reports that "fieldworkers," some of them virtually illiterate, submitted to the editors of the American Guide Series. There were folklore collections, and guides to loggers' ax brands, and other books that never got into print. When the project fell on hard times, underfunded by a Congress that suspected the writers' project was up to its quill in Communists, books were delayed, and then, with America's entry into World War II, abandoned. But the scraps are still here—a massive history of grazing, notes for a book of "industrial folklore," a collection of regional recipes called "America Eats," and other unfinished stuff. I found a recipe for beaver tail in a memo from the Montana office.

I wandered through the materials day after day, less and less aware of time passing. The bloodless machinery of information awed and arrogated me; I felt obligated to turn over every slip of paper in the collections. But one day, when I entered at my usual time, 8:30 A.M., there wandered behind Madison's marble chair a couple of steers. They were pointed in the direction of an "American cowboy" exhibit tucked in the rear of the building. The stony gaze of the President seemed to waver. The nonchalant gait of the plywood steers disrupted the normal order of business in Madison's annex; a sneering clerk warned me to watch out for plywood cow pies. That same day a clerk told me that many of the oral life histories collected by the FWP folklore division would be hard to find because they were "in a box in the attic somewhere." Things were not so efficient and orderly in President Madison's house as they'd seemed, and I came out of my stupor. I'd found alluring descriptions of West Virginia hollows, interviews with Vermont stonecutters from the 1930s, opinionated fragments like the Washington guide's description of the Lincoln Memorial: "[T]he immense pedestal of the statue serves to raise the heroic head of Lincoln above the midpoint between floor and ceiling—an effect that belittles the chamber without heightening the figure of Lincoln." I read that as I walked around the outer circle of the library's main reading room, guide in hand, around the gently curved tables encircling the main desk, the bowed heads of spike-haired students in loud sweat shirts, blue-suited Africans, a grizzled bum sleeping on Hegel. I opened the guides at my desk to the back pages, where you could ride vivid description and historical detail down the remotest highways, out to the tip of the Mississippi Delta or into my own small corner of the Rocky Mountains. It was time to get out of the stacks and on the road and let the senses take over.

It was twilight when I walked from the Madison Annex across the Capitol's east side parking lot. Three soft-edged men in dark lobbyists' suits came down the steps on the House of Representatives side; some Marine joggers crossed my path; the usual pink-cheeked congressional interns did their optimistic hop down the avenue; a couple of black kids passed dribbling a basketball, heading for the game at the Eastern Market courts.

Congress was in recess, and this was a peaceful hour at the Capitol, so I walked around the building to the other side. The sun was dropping into the folds of low cloud to the west, and the rug of grass stretching from the Capitol steps went slightly gray, as color evaporated from the lawn and the sky and the buildings and the clothes of the people walking the mall. A small assemblage gathered on the west steps for a concert by the U.S. Navy Band. Unhurriedly, people began to bunch on the steps as the band wet its reeds and shuffled its music. An overweight lady in a purple print dress settled regally into her lawn chair at the top and center of the stairs. A family of five, uniformed in tourist fatigues—tank tops and running shoes—positioned itself near her; the kids, two boys and a girl, made faces and acted spastic, while the parents looked dully past them toward the band. In the crowd there were bald heads, alligator shirts, backpacks, gold watches, and some long cotton dresses of the kind sensible southern women wear when it warms up. A black man with a visor sun hat, a paunch, and muttonchop sideburns moved his legs to a calypso version of "Charade."

The brass was muted by the hum of evening traffic and the open vista to the west. The crowd on the esplanade looked down on the band, the manicured grandeur of landscape and monuments, and the setting sun. From that vantage the sun was like a large-headed adjutant, bowing as it retreated, eyes lowered, until it was out of presence of the fat lady in purple and on off across the empire to pursue its duties.

I was enjoying this scene, just sitting there, when I felt a tap on my shoulder. It was an old friend, a press aide to a senator, whom I'd befriended six years ago. A smart fellow with the deceptively soft and youthful look of many southern men, he expressed his surprise at seeing me, then told me his news: He was moving back to a small town in his home state. He remembered the conversations we'd once had about the benefits and costs of life in Washington. His decision was a hard one; after a decade on the Hill he had a parking space right there between the Supreme Court and the Capitol, and he had a ground-floor office in the Dirksen Building, with a window looking out at the trees between the Capitol and Union Station.

When a congressional staffer gets a ground-floor window, he has indeed arrived. My friend was not immune to the infection that everybody here catches: "About this time, I come out of my office, and the sunset reflects off the Capitol dome, and there's not many people still around. I know that one hundred of the most powerful people in the world work here, and *me*."

We walked to my car. He bounced side to side when he walked, as he always had, and every now and then he looked over his shoulder at the Capitol. Now the band was playing "Moon River," and I was thinking how even the most bathetic song gains a certain force in the presence of difficult choices. Shaking hands, he asked me if I thought he was doing the right thing. A small-leafed maple shrugged in the breeze, and with my senses awakened I could smell the grass and the mix of fabric and sweat from the people on the steps, and I knew fleetingly how he would miss that. I said good-bye and shook hands, then drove down Independence Avenue, playing chicken with the taxi drivers and limousines in the thickening murk, heading for the Lincoln Memorial, where I could wait for the last clots of commuter traffic to dissolve.

Navigating these streets and freeways, I had been thinking ugly thoughts about the coral growth of this and other cities, with their dying centers and the suburban whorls that grow out from them.

Practically, Washington could never have remained a small southern city or an uncrowded landscape of monuments. But I could sense in the tired faces I saw on my drives around the capital's outskirts that few of these new people had found a home here on the perimeter—only a place from which they could commute to work. The narrow, twisting roads on which we jousted in the Maryland suburbs had clearly been designed for less hurried folk, in smaller numbers, farm folk whose fields were now built over with innumerable caterpillarlike town house rows, designed to resemble the estate houses of an imagined gentrified past. My grandfather did a stint here, in his early twenties, and so had I. I liked the city then, when I lived near the Eastern Market, on the edges of the poorer black neighborhoods. The atmosphere on the basketball courts was charged, and so, too, in the press gallery, where there were plenty of young journalists like me, racing after opportunity and challenge. You could walk off the tension, enjoying the low skyline and the greenery everywhere. Why, then, did my friend at the Capitol dream of being somewhere else? Only a visitor now, I wasn't sure I knew.

The last stop on my way out of Washington was at the Lincoln Memorial, where the Emancipator broods on matters other than the height of his pedestal, or what the Washington guide called the "somewhat dubious skylight arrangement." Two boys of seven or so in T-shirts that said, "Maryland is for crabs," raced up and down the steps; a white-haired man, scarily similar to the patriotic immigrant in a Frank

Capra movie, stood reading the Second Inaugural Address, lips moving silently; a pair of teenagers in matching rugby shirts embraced down by the pool; there were brief outbreaks of laughter from little clots of strolling families. It was dark now, and down at the other end of the mall the Capitol was lit. I cannot imagine a finer monument than one in which the honored figure sits instead of stands, sits in craggy preoccupation and asks nothing of the children playing about him, though they were the very object of his thought. But our puckish monument critic, brimming with vinegar, went on to describe the "unfortunate sense of crowding" at the Lincoln Memorial, an assertion that would have been vigorously disputed by me and the varied folk who sat peacefully and informally on the steps below Lincoln looking back toward the reflecting pool. It was growing too dark to read, so I put the Washington guide down on a step, along with the West Virginia guide I had also brought, and sat next to them. It may be that every other opinion, maybe even every other fact, in these guides is wrong, as my grandfather seemed to think about the Monterey guide, and as I would have agreed here. It didn't, just then, seem too important; an infallible companion would only get on my nerves. I preferred books like these—cheeky and charming, primed like me with prodigal opinions and enthusiasm for what lay down the road.

Destination

The Smoke Hole

*John Brown's Fort. . . , the engine house in which John Brown
made his stand against the marines, occupies the cliff top
overlooking the Shenandoah River. . . . When the armory was
burned during the War between the States this was the only
building left standing. . . . In 1892 it was dismantled and
shipped to the World's Columbian Exposition at Chicago. After
the exposition it was sold and would have been used for a stable if
the Negroes of the country . . . had not raised funds to buy it and
have it shipped back to Harpers Ferry. . . . Although "bricks
from John Brown's Fort" have been sold to tourists ever since the
War between the States, the structure is believed to contain the
greater part of its original brickwork.*
—West Virginia: A Guide to the Mountain State

YOU are still within the gravitational field of Washington,
D.C., when you drive into Harpers Ferry, West Virginia;
the capital extends several long, six-lane fingers through the

green hills, and one of them, Interstate 270, crooks an asphalt knuckle, Highway 340, at Frederick, Maryland, and tugs at the steep-cliffed confluence of the Shenandoah and Potomac rivers.

Big freeways continue south, to haul agricultural produce up and down the fertile Shenandoah Valley, and north into the industrial landscape of Pennsylvania. But I would drive west, onto the dinky, winding two-lane roads of an earlier time, climbing up and down the sandstone ridges and limestone valleys along the eastern front of the Appalachian Plateau.

The eastern side of the plateau is difficult country. It lacks the coal deposits that lured energy companies to rip open the soil farther west, and for this its residents might be grateful. But it also lacks the broader, flatter bottomlands that farmers to the east enjoy. When West Virginia seceded during the Civil War, Virginia got rid of its most inhospitable and tragic lands.

John Brown's small, bloody skirmish with U.S. Marines here presaged bigger, bloodier battles between the North and South. Today's residents, many of them retired, struggle only with time—shoring up the old buildings, taking care of their own aging bodies. Those who still work make the long commute to the capital or provide services for the tourists.

South of town, Paul Becker sat in a lawn chair on the porch behind his garage, enjoying a Rolling Rock and his own raspy version of retirement. In 1935, at twenty-three, Becker earned $110 a month pulling together the Federal Writers' Project West Virginia guide. Then he spent a lifetime working at various congressional jobs on Capitol Hill; he still drove down there every week to sit scowling in the congressional cafeteria "just to make 'em nervous." It kept his mind fresh, he claimed, and from Washington contacts he picked up his own diacritical vision of the future: "You will see, within five years, young man, the absolute end of the threat of nuclear war. It'll be as useless as a fuckin' broomstick." He offered no details, but since we talked, Star Wars has emerged.

Becker wore stained khaki pants, black leather shoes, white socks, and no shirt. Behind thick glasses, his eyes glared pugnaciously, one of them fully and permanently dilated. But the real fury was in his mouth; pinched like an owl's, it crunched down on words and spat out the bones.

In Washington nothing was done right. "The government cannot make a job," he said flatly, as if he'd forgotten the 1930s, when he went on the government payroll and wrote a graceful, loyal guide to his home state.

It was while working on the West Virginia guide that Becker discovered the Smoke Hole, a remote hollow in the Potomac Highlands south and west of his present home. Harpers Ferry is east of the Blue Ridge, lapped by the cosmopolitan tides emanating from D.C.; the Smoke Hole is high in the mountains, beyond any such influence. Becker was smitten, and produced a small writers' project publication about this hollow. His writing then had much of the hurling rhetoric, but none of the vituperation, of his present orations from the lawn chair: "Almost untouched beauty, a haven of escape, a Shangri-la where topography still grants seclusion, and the virgin perfection of all things—trees, flowers, animal life, scenic vistas and climate—provides a retreat from the disturbing noises of expanding American industrialism."

The hollow was freckled with sugar maples and honeycombed with caves, and peopled by simple mountain folk who hunted and fished and farmed just enough to get by, and seemed to want no more.

Well.

If such a place once existed, I told him, I wanted to go and see if it was still there.

Becker slouched in his chair, sweat dripping over the loose, mole-blotted folds of skin at his waist, and pointed a finger in the direction of his kitchen door—south, toward the Smoke Hole.

"Here you had what the nation was founded on—a population that was independent in all respects. And they still live that way, you can bet on it. They have standards for living and community that haven't changed since the American Revolution. They don't yearn and lather for material things. And they're living on land their forebears got when they were discharged from the Continental Army."

That night I took a small tent from my trunk and set it up by the Potomac, and by flashlight I found my way on maps. The tent smelled like a child's sleeping bag, a smell only a parent can love. The summer before I had taken my older daughter out for a night camping in a wide, dry canyon south of our town where she could see coyotes trotting gimpy-legged through the sagebrush and hear them howl. I suppose now she harbors within some inarticulate something about coyotes that no teacher or picture book will ever be able to dislodge—what it is, I don't know, perhaps just an emotional flicker of fear or excitement from that night. There was an abashed pang when I thought that she would like to be with me on this adventure. But I was traveling a different way, a measure removed from such pure experience, trying to bring words and the past up into the landscape. Unhappily, it seemed best to do it alone.

I traced my route to the Smoke Hole. I'd considered other destinations—coal mining towns on the Cumberland Plateau, for instance, or the defunct little river towns near Morgantown. But Becker insisted I'd find nothing in those towns but "people who float around, people who are not going to give you a valid point of view. All the hustlers, bigots, all the people with an ax to grind—they get all their ideas from television." Every sentence he uttered had spit in it.

Near my camp, the river was low and wide. It must have been three hundred yards across. In the moonlight, the brown rocks looked like the backs of migrating animals. I could imagine Becker's dilated eye looking at me, and through me. Something else he said: "Nobody cares about the goddamn past."

———

"It's right spread out, and it's mighty rough; but it's a damned good State for the shape it's in."
—West Virginia: A Guide to the Mountain State, quoting Moses Bennett

THERE were few road markers. You were simply expected to know your way, or what were you doing on this little road? Twice I missed turns and had to backtrack. In the end, I simply watched the roadside. The absence of familiar chain eateries told me I was headed in the right direction. The names of the old towns and landmarks began to tell stories: Blue Sea Gap, Crack Whip Furnace, Lost River, Potato Row . . .

I had come over the edge of the mountains and onto the Potomac Highlands, a series of ridges and narrow valleys running from the southwest to the northeast. Most of the rivers in the highlands flow north, unable to escape these valleys. The Potomac succeeds only when it joins the Shenandoah, and together they pierce the mountains and head east for the coast.

I dropped down to the valley of the Potomac's South Branch at Moorefield, followed the river to Petersburg, and then headed south into the Upper Tract Valley. It is from this compact, neatly farmed valley that the Smoke Hole canyon breaks away, taking, for a while at least, the river with it.

For days I had driven everywhere in the vehicular torrent of the capital. Now I was alone in the mist and rain on a winding road crowded by woods. Trying to anticipate its sudden curves, I missed the Smoke Hole turnoff.

By the time I realized I had overshot my mark I had crossed another elevation and was in a valley west of the Smoke Hole, looking up at a heavily wooded ridge topped by bare rock; the Smoke Hole, if I understood the map, was on the other side, to the east. The ridge was topped by Seneca Rock, a chunk of Tuscarora sandstone that has withstood weathering better than the softer sedimentary rock around it.

It was getting darker, and wetter, and I was too tired to backtrack, so I looked for a campsite. I stopped by D. C. Harper's establishment, which had the look and smell of an old dry goods store, and an order incomprehensible to anyone but the proprietor. Harper, a big, bluff man of about sixty, greeted me from the porch, which was decorated with fertilizer signs. I was standing on the ground below, and Harper reached over to shake my hand—and yanked me up beside him, in one motion.

I asked to buy some candles, and he said, "Don't you know how to rub two sticks together? Where you from?," jutting his chin at me. Inside, rummaging for candles, he claimed the Smoke Hole got its name not from Indians smoking meat, as I'd read, but from the moonshine stills that cooked in the canyon's many caves during Prohibition, and he proudly declared that a lot of federal government revenuers got shot up in those days. But his tales had a give-'em-what-they-came-for ring.

One minute he was telling me the U.S. Forest Service had built so many roads in the Monongahela Forest that the wild game was gone. But when I described to him the plentiful antelope in Wyoming, he quickly rejoined that there was abundant game in his area, and pulled out a snapshot of a startled black bear taken earlier that week. There was a picture, too, of a rattlesnake as long as a man is tall. I snapped an obligatory photo of Harper standing on the porch and bade him good-bye.

I set up my tent, making sure to zip the door against any slithering company, and slept intermittently to the loud lullabies of tree frogs. Their roar is so raucous it reshapes the words in your thoughts. I repeated to myself a nonsense verse I'd found in the folklore collected by the Federal Writers' Project at West Virginia University, which I wanted to master for my daughters:

> Kimo karro give to pharoah,
> Flemadoodle yellow bug.
> Turn a rap strap periwinkle,
> Breakdown, rap strap Barney Mishy Kimo.
>
> Kimee and kimo, strim stram,
> Stramee nicker lara bona rinktum.
> Rinktum, bona mitte, kimo.

But I could not hold the words or the rhythm against the surge of frog sounds. I woke in the dark imagining a single giant frog squatting at the tent door, belching with a maniacal smile. His name was Rinktum.

After a difficult night, I backtracked the next morning to Franklin, the seat of Pendleton County, which sits at the southern end of the Upper Tract Valley. There I found a coffee shop where I could order a two-dollar breakfast that included eggs, grits, sausage, and coffee. You wonder, eating bargain meals throughout the Appalachian South, if coffee shops were kept in the dark here about the inflationary 1970s. The newspaper I picked up, the *Clarksburg Exponent,* might well have failed to fill them in: It looked about one hundred years old itself, a broadsheet with an eight-column format, small type, and advertisements that could hardly be distinguished from the news columns.

The waitress, quick-wristed and terse, looked over my shoulder at the guide, but didn't ask me about it. I was reading a brief lexicon of word pronunciations particular to the Smoke Hole in the 1930s, and trying at the same time to decipher the conversation of a coffee klatsch at the next table. They were mostly older men, with gray hair and calloused, darkly freckled workman's hands, and I imagine they were setting the world right before the workday started, in the usual fashion of such gatherings.

I could not be sure, though, because I could understand very little of what they said. A bag is a "poke" and a chair is "cheer," said the guide—but what was "bearprassus"? I began writing down what I heard phonetically. "Eat bite addawkshun," I wrote, and "bleef ewebut" and "dounassus"—the table would roar with laughter and I would flinch, as if my scribbling had just been projected on the wall.

I looked over at the faces, which were not unkind, but not curious or friendly toward a stranger either. Most of what I found indecipherable came from the one young man in the group, a fellow who was quite round, with wet lips in a doughy face and a brown nylon shirt that hung out at the waist. My feelings were mixed. On the one hand, the strong accents assured me of a certain cultural obscurity here, just as the old guide described, just what attracted me; on the other, the meaning was as foreign to me as "flemadoodle yellow bug," and it had not been my intention to hire a translator.

I could finally stand it no more and waved the waitress over. I motioned her to lean down so I could whisper, but she did not lean at all. She actually leaned away, tucking her chin into her neck and retracting the coffee urn out of my reach.

"I wondered what they were talking about," I said hoarsely.

She looked at me warily and then seemed to relax. "You

want his pickup?" she asked. Without waiting for an answer, she walked over to the table and nudged the fellow in the nylon shirt. "You may not have to go down to Manassas after all," she said to him. "You got a buyer right here."

——

Deeply shadowed by towering walls, overhanging bluffs, and vaulted archways, the road and river wind their way through a sunless canyon; during one of the frequent summer thunder storms it has a wild and fantastic beauty.
—West Virginia: A Guide to the Mountain State

THAT first awkward interaction in the coffee shop worked out for the best. It took awhile to get it across that I was not interested in a pickup, but before the morning was over, I had directions to the Smoke Hole and the names of several people who knew it well.

I drove north from Franklin, following the flow of the South Branch of the Potomac, through an area occupied before the eighteenth century by the Delaware Indians. The Delaware, who were getting squeezed in Ohio, too, were angry enough to massacre a few dozen settlers in the South Branch Valley before retreating west; by the late eighteenth century the area had been left to American and European settlers. It's a beautiful valley, its narrow bottomlands mostly planted in corn, with family-size orchards near the homes, and a few hillsides cleared for livestock. By the road grew chicory and yarrow and goldenrod, and coming around one bend, near the Smoke Hole turn, a wild tom turkey showed himself.

Near the small town of Upper Tract, the South Branch of the Potomac takes a westerly detour down into the Smoke Hole. The writers' project guide calls this river piracy—the Potomac was stolen from its original route, down the Upper Tract Valley, and routed west through a canyon that had once been separated from it by a ridge. The work was done, "eons ago," by a little stream called Briggs Run. Briggs Run, collecting subterranean runoff from Little and Cave mountains, ate away the underlying limestone until it formed a cavern big enough, and low enough, to collapse the rock that separated it from the Potomac. The big river was kidnapped west, the roof of the cavern eventually fell in, and so we have today the steep-sided Smoke Hole canyon, running about twenty-five miles before returning the South Branch to its original bed.

When I entered the canyon mouth, the road narrowed and I was in shadow. The close rock faces that squeeze the river at this upper end of the canyon serve as portals, enhancing the sense of a world apart. There was a time, not that long ago, when a much narrower road clung to these cliffs, and during harsh weather a wagon or automobile trip out was virtually impossible.

The canyon was settled in the mid-eighteenth century by whites who came from Virginia, Pennsylvania, and Vermont and, before that, from England, Switzerland, Holland, and other parts of Europe. Many moved into the Smoke Hole after first starting farms in rich, tillable valleys like the Upper Tract. By choosing the steep confines of the Smoke Hole, they demonstrated their hunger for daily hunting or their distaste for agrarian domesticity. Population pressure elsewhere was only a small factor. In any case, they became mountaineers.

The mythology of the Appalachian mountaineer has its devotees and debunkers. It can at least be said that mountaineers preserved the style of frontier living long after the frontier had leapfrogged them to the west. In part this was because the topography of Appalachia defied civilized development. But the argument is often made, by the likes of Kentucky historian Harry M. Caudill, that the Appalachian mountaineer lived this way by choice, and viewed a primitive mountain life of subsistence hunting and marginal agriculture as "a golden age" of freedom from "even the mildest limitations on his liberty." Caudill wrote in mourning; the mountaineers of his region, southeast Kentucky, had long ago been compromised by jobs in the coal industry.

Because the canyon had no coal, had forests not easily timbered, and had slopes too steep for large-scale agriculture, no one interfered with the life of Smoke Hole mountaineers well into the twentieth century, long after this way of life had devolved in other parts of the Appalachian South.

I passed an old clapboard house, boarded up, as I started into the canyon. Across the river, which dallied below the road through long, slow pools, were several summer homes. The birches elms and maples were green and tangled thick, with vines here and there girdling the trunks.

The river follows an S-shaped route through the canyon, always with steep mountain slopes leaning in around it; then it emerges and picks up its North Fork and various small tributaries with colorful names like Zeke Run and Shoock Hollow. It becomes eventually the lazy, polluted flow that carries inedible fish into the Chesapeake Bay.

A few miles in I passed Eagle Rock, a sandstone spire which juts three hundred feet straight up on the river's north bank. William Eagle was a veteran of the Revolutionary War who was present at Valley Forge and at Cornwallis's surrender. He is more famous for his battle with another eagle, one which nested on the cliffs of the big rock over the river and occasionally dined on his chickens. Eagle, so the legend goes, dropped himself off the top of the rock with a rope around his waist and went after the nesting eagle with a knife. The angry bird fought back, ripping the dangling soldier's clothes to shreds as he spun and stabbed wildly at the air. The feathered eagle won. The soldier is now buried by the road, and at his gravestone I found a small American flag and a bundle of plastic orchids.

I drove farther into the canyon, and still I saw few signs of domestic life. There was here and there the roadside acne of beer cans and food wrappers, but hillside pastures that had once been cleared for livestock were growing in with cedar and oak, and cabins were boarded up. Becker had assured me these people would still be here—certainly more sedate and rule-bound than their forebears, but *here*.

At four miles, the road leveled near the river, and I came upon a roadside cluster of small cabins, one of which had a sign in the window saying MAYOR OF SMOKE HOLE.

The man in the cabin was Henry Kuntz. He was from Pennsylvania, and he laughed when I asked where I could find the old Smoke Hole families. His daughter had given him the "mayor" sign as a joke because of his frequent vacations here. He suggested I drive down to the end of the paved road and visit Sadie Kimble. "She's in her eighties," said Kuntz, rolling his eyes, "but she drives like she's eighteen."

———

In isolated instances the traveler meets, deep in the hills, picturesque individuals with the speech and social customs of the earliest Anglo-Saxon colonists. Perhaps it is a mountain preacher quoting tirelessly, hour after hour, from the Scriptures, with only a copy of Chaucer's Canterbury Tales *open in front of him (the book merely for show, whether he can read or not, his Scriptural quotations are culled from his capacious memory). Perhaps it is a railroading Negro, retelling stories of John Henry that the phonograph companies have not yet put on the records.*
These, it is true, are rare types, the passing of which is more to be regretted than hailed with provincial joy. They add their diminishing quota to the State's many contrasts, but are no

longer typical of the whole. With the longer-lingering family
reunion and country general store, they emphasize the distance the
State has journeyed since the time when such were the rule instead
of the exception.
—West Virginia: A Guide to the Mountain State

AT the end of the pavement there was a small store catering
to fishermen. There I turned left, up a short dirt track, past
some old trailers and buses with stovepipes in the roofs, to
Sadie Kimble's house. In front sat the automobile she drove
like a teenager, a green Ford Fairmont. Sheep grazed in a
pasture across the road, the first evidence I'd seen, besides the
store, of domestic pursuits. She lived in a white frame house,
well kept, with a fenced lawn in front occupied by a mixture
of real and ceramic chickens.

I was in the heart of the Smoke Hole now, and it was
beautiful country. But the Smoke Hole I had come to find—
the tight little families packed close on the hillsides in a
country teeming with game, the dialect and music and patterns of life perfected in isolation, the independent and
"undeviating, unflinching" honest folk that Becker had
described—seemed to have been reduced to one little house,
and one short, sharp-eyed octogenarian in a flower-print smock
with her hair snug in a net.

The front porch of the Kimble house was closed in, and
that's where we sat—Sadie Kimble in a wing-armed chair
with doilies on the arms, me on a straight-back chair by the
television. There were plastic flowers in a vase on a side table,
and the blinds were partially drawn.

In the 1930s guide to the Smoke Hole, certain family names
recur: Alt, Shreve, Judy, Kimble, Ayers, Shirk, and Self. Of
113 registered voters in the Smoke Hole at that time—all
Republicans, I should add—81 belonged to these seven families.

In the careful way of West Virginia old-timers, Sadie clarified that she was *not* a Smoke Holer, though she'd lived there over half a century; she was from the other side of the mountain, at Seneca Falls. "You would walk across the mountain, or take a horse," she said, recalling the trips to the Smoke Hole for socials. "It wasn't quite straight, walkin' the dog path, and I wouldn't know the way anymore. Them's questions that takes awhile." She looked up at me with a sneaky, toothless smile, then away. She hadn't been back to Seneca Falls since she married.

Sadie Kimble was a holdout. She had been taken to the hospital in Franklin during a spell of sickness and incoherence the year before, but when she got well, she came straight home. "Whenever I leave my house, it's going to be when I'm carried away, I reckon." Most of the other old-timers were gone, some of them to the rest home in Franklin where her husband, John, now lived, and none of the populous next generation had taken their place. "Part of it is that there's no jobs here, and part was through the women. When they married the boys, the women wouldn't stay down in here, so they just got scattered around."

I asked her how she and her family entertained themselves in the old days.

"Well, with children, you know, and then besides, a lot of work to be done, and you don't stay young all your life, but I stayed pretty good for quite a while. You know, sometimes people can work real hard and do nothing, and some can do nothing and it kinda shows like they done a lot.

"I had the post office in the beginning, and then we started up this little store. Finally it got to be too much for me. We had a garden and livestock, and we'd plow the old horse through, and get the hoe and get the weeds out. I took care of my husband and his brothers and his father, all living here." She looked at me conspiratorially, pulling in her

toothless upper lip. "That's why I took the post office—I
wasn't going to stay there and take care of all them.

"Sometimes we had little frolics, a little music around, but
I didn't go to them much. I had frolics at home—the children. We'd go to Sunday school over on Hermit Island, you
know, or something else going on. I'd take my children, and
we'd walk up there many a time. Just little frolics, not bad
things, just something for people to gather up on. There's
nothing like that anymore. Working was mostly the entertainment we got.

"They had some places out in the hills where they'd make
. . . you know. They'd drink it and go wild. Do anything,
say anything, or talk anything, or any other kind. I didn't
allow it, neither, around the house. I wouldn't want to mix
with it."

I asked her if it was lonely with her husband in Franklin
and most of the Smoke Holers moved away.

"Well, I've been on my own all my life. I always say if you
get a good tail, hold on. I don't do much eating or anything.
I fix me a little something. But it's kinda lonely like to be
by yourself and eat by yourself and stay by yourself.

"Sometimes when I get kinda worried about things, and
lonely, I get in my old car and take off to see one of the kids."

We went over who still made their homes year-round in
the Smoke Hole. A family of Shreves lived up the road from
her; another old Shreve couple ran the store down below. And
farther beyond the store, along the river, lived an old couple
named Judy. Of the old families, that was about it; the rest
were newcomers, tourists, mostly seasonal visitors like the
"mayor," who rented or owned the old trailers and buses
down the road from the Kimble place.

When I tried to determine her exact age, and the number
of children she'd borne, Sadie Kimble got flirty.

SK (small smile): How many do you think?

O'G: Let me guess. Five?

SK: That caught one bunch. Better go a little higher.

O'G: Seven?

SK (rolling her eyes): Not quite. Just almost.

O'G: Eight?

SK (big smile): Five boys and six girls.

O'G: I tried before to get you to tell me how old you are.

SK: Oh, dear me, and you're still going to try to?

O'G: You said you would tell me.

SK (laughing): I just carry on with people for a while; then maybe I tell them. Or I let them guess. Some guess, and I won't tell them. I'm eighty-four—I'll be eighty-five this coming March.

———

This same hardy self-sufficiency which had enabled their forefathers to withstand the onslaughts of nature and hostile savages was indirectly responsible for giving the Smoke Hole residents an unsavory and almost sinister reputation. Among their accomplishments was a well-developed ability to distill from grain an alcoholic liquor of smoothness, flavor and potency. . . . Certain outsiders . . . made a regular practice of buying it in quantity and reselling it at fancy prices. . . .
—*The Smoke Hole*

COMING out, I stopped briefly at Hermit Island, a four-acre plot that interrupts the river a few miles into the canyon, and the place chosen by one outsider to attempt to disprove the outside world's notion that Smoke Holers were "the lawless lot depicted by prohibition agents," as the guide put it. Here, on one of the few level spots of any size, the boys and men of the 1930s Smoke Hole played soccer, of all things—an inheritance from their Scottish, English, and Irish ancestry. Today the island is reached by a low-slung cement causeway that can accommodate vehicles.

Judge H. M. Calhoun came into the Smoke Hole in 1928 to set up a religious summer camp on Hermit Island. Calhoun left the doors unlocked at the lodge he built, and it became a gathering place for church, pie socials, and, of course, soccer. There was even a phonograph and a piano.

The log house that Calhoun built no longer stands, but the open playing field, one of the few flat spots in the Smoke Hole, is still there, now a lush Forest Service picnic ground. Standing in the middle, I could see the exposed rock faces high up on the surrounding mountains.

Locals who resent the intrusion of the Forest Service here claim the U.S. Congress was encouraged to make the Smoke Hole a National Recreation Area with florid, and false, descriptions of steam vents, of which there are none. The humid canyon, where the air is still and actually warmer than on the Appalachian Plateau to the west, generates enough mist to account for the name.

The geological wonders of the Smoke Hole, at least, have not changed, not in fifty years or many more: The cobweb of caves that surface on the hillsides above me attracts spelunkers from afar. And it is not hard to imagine the Indians smoking venison and bear meat in the caves, or the mountaineers heating their moonshine coils with green hickory and chestnut and other hardwoods. The smoke would find its way up through the fissures in the caves' ceilings, and from a distance it would appear to billow from the mountaintop—another rationale for the canyon's name.

In the 1860s Confederate soldiers also dug saltpeter from some of the caves, and they would boil this in iron kettles to reduce it for gunpowder. West Virginia was broken off from

Virginia—the only successful secession in U.S. history—to underline its pro-Union sentiment, but the counties on the eastern side of the new state were mostly friendly to the South. Not so the Smoke Hole. Pendleton County was the site of much guerrilla warfare, and a pro-Union group called the "Swamp Dragons" was formed as a "home guard" unit of the new state.

On the north side of the canyon, up on Cave Mountain, is Big Cave, and that was where the "peter monkeys"—mostly old men and boys—cooked down the nitrous dirt for saltpeter. The Swamp Dragons tore up the saltpeter works in 1865, driving the Confederates out of the Smoke Hole.

Becker's book on the Smoke Hole described how the canyon's inhabitants were, seventy years after the Civil War, all Republicans "except for one Democrat, and he got struck by lightning." Fifty years later the story still survives. Estyl Shreve, a Smoke Hole native now living in Franklin, whom I'd met the day before, told me his parents had been there when the lightning struck at a shooting match up on Cave Mountain.

"It started to thunder and lightning, and he hadn't taken his shot yet, and he said he was going to take it, in spite of the storm. And when he started to shoot, well, the lightning struck the gun and killed him dead." Shreve, a Republican, laughed good-naturedly.

——

Right on this trail, across the river and along a zigzag path
around the mountainside and over high cliffs,
to SMOKE HOLE CAVERN, *1.7 m. Some distance back from the*
oval-shaped entrance, overhung with large gray boulders, is a
circular chamber like an inverted hornet's nest, 14 feet in diameter
and 35 feet high. Lacking salt and other preservatives, the Indians

> *and early white settlers, according to legend, brought their meats*
> *here to be smoked and cured. Some early families found shelter here*
> *while building their cabins; the cavern is now used by sheep and*
> *hogs that run free in the woods.*
>
> —West Virginia: A Guide to the Mountain State

I DECIDED to stretch my legs by scrambling up to Smoke Hole Cavern, to let my imagination conjure the stills or the meat curing that once went on there. The quickest route was a straight climb up a dry creek bed.

The creek was steep and the footing was poor, but a long tumble was not my concern. Snakes were. Making the near vertical climb up the drainage, I remembered the six-foot timber rattler I'd seen in the snapshot at Seneca Rocks. Every time I put my hand up to grasp a handle of rock or grab an exposed root, it seemed inevitable that I would pull myself eye to eye with a coiled rattler.

I made my way up toward the ridgetop, ears and eyes focused on my immediate vicinity, sniffing for the particular smell of rattlers—something which I'd been told as a child to be alert for on my family's visits to the California mountains, but which I had never actually distinguished. I stopped once to look back across the canyon at the steep forest above the river, and I thought what a land of adventure this must have been for the young who played in the woods and the caves and the river years before me.

It was a stunningly beautiful place, then as now, but since beauty is relative, the youngsters may not have known that. They knew little firsthand about the world outside their canyon. Smoke Holers were so isolated they had developed a peculiar local dialect that transformed "climbed" into "clumb" and "ghosts" to "ghostes" and underlined significant words with redundancy, like "rifle-gun" and "ham-meat."

A child in the Smoke Hole lived an active life; it's a wonder they had the strength to play in the caves, given all their other activities. Much of it was work: carrying in water from the outdoor pump; chopping and fetching wood; feeding the livestock. After school and Saturday, Estyl Shreve remembered collecting and shelling walnuts, which they would then sell at the stores.

But the work was often fun. Hunting went on year-round, and for the men and boys there was no better combination of pleasure and necessity imaginable. In the fall families and friends would gather for apple peelings, moving from house to house, making apple butter. Church activities were popular, too, though not strictly for the hymn singing. Recalled Estyl Shreve's brother, Loy: "We would be having church activities at one part of the place, they would be very pious, and on the other side the young men were knocking the stuffing out of each other, getting rid of their feuds. Oh, it was always exciting."

I neared the top of the ridge, and the vegetation thinned, revealing a chunk of rock facing north just below the top, pocked like a skull with cave entries. Short of breath, I climbed up onto a narrow bench and took a step into the cave's darkness.

A cool breeze came up in my face, and by my third step I had lost my sight and was all ears. A fourth, a fifth step, with one hand on the crumbly wall. Then I heard an awful sound: the wail of a Grendel, echoing out of the darkness ahead.

Someone was throwing up. I heard panicked, overlapping voices. I backed out, surprised that I was not alone. Eventually the retching and moaning stopped, and I heard the voices again, down around the north side of the rock, at a lower entrance. Holding my nose, I started back in.

I'd brought no light, but I knew from the guide I was groping toward a large chamber with a thirty-five-foot ceil-

ing. For the safety of novices like me, several narrowing passages that spoked out from this lobby had been blocked with
boulders; tales are told of explorers getting lost for days,
searching for underground lakes in the caves of these mountains. Steeling myself for the slippery possibilities under each
footfall, breathing through my nose as little as possible, I
rounded a corner and saw the faint light of the chamber.

I stepped into it. A woman screamed. Startled, I yelped,
too.

In the dim light of the chamber, two women with their
pants down scrambled away from me, yodeling in terror. I
retreated again.

I climbed out onto the bench and looked hopelessly across
the canyon at the dense vegetation on the other side. Then a
foursome of Georgians came around the corner—one man quite
pale and sweaty, the two women giggling with embarrassment. In a moment they had me: I found myself snapping
their picture for them, and listening to a woman with bee-
hived blond hair and black eyebrows describe our encounter.

"There we were, just having a little *tinkle*, and around the
corner he *came*. He's the *cave* monster, boys!"

The four Georgians had come up by another route—a less
steeply pitched trail that allowed unhurried and plentiful
beverage consumption. I looked at them, bobbing against
each other in the camera's viewfinder, the pastels of their
sport shirts and pants, the bleached hair of the women, the
beer-rimmed eyes swimming in the smiling faces. I pur-
posely cut off their heads in the picture, returned the camera,
and started back down the creek bed.

Escaping as fast as I could, I heard their laughter behind
me. "Last one down has to pay for the bee-ah!" shouted one
of the shriekers. I slid out of control, grabbing for roots and
trees to slow myself. My heels thudded, the skin on my palms
was scraped raw, and fury thumped in my temples.

About halfway down, my left foot landed in a loose agglomeration of leaves and dirt; I heard a faint whir, and I looked down at a small timber rattler.

The rattler was not fully coiled. I grabbed a stick and flipped him off the exposed root he was on, and headed furiously on down the steep drainage.

———

In tabulating the census, a punch card is required for each individual. This means that at least 125,000,000 cards must run through the electric sorting machines.
—*Washington, Capital and City*

THERE were always the numbers. At some point, at every spot where I lingered on my way around the country, someone would look at me, usually over the top of bifocals, lift an important-looking piece of paper, and begin reciting numbers.

In Pendleton County it was Richard Harding. A solid, jowly man in his forties, he had lived in Franklin since 1976, and now served part-time as the Franklin librarian. His impatience and dismay with the county were manifest; he sighed as if he had been swimming against the sluggish current of the South Branch for eight years. He was prepared for the arrival of someone like me; he had the statistics in hand to show me just how backward the place is.

A selection: The average weekly wage in the county is $138; students at the county's schools are not taught physics or biology; the only substantial manufacturer is a shoe factory that employs about five hundred people, and wait until Italy gets through with *them*; the timber crews working in the surrounding national forest are usually hired from somewhere else; the closest hospital is across the Shenandoah Mountains in Harrisonburg, Virginia, and one of the county's three remaining doctors is about to retire; there is one weekly newspaper, no radio or television station, it rains thirty-two inches a year, there are twenty-seven Christian-denomination churches, three basketball courts, and 40 percent of the land in the county belongs to the federal government.

There you have it: the short course on Pendleton County.

——

. . . Contrary to the assertions of certain sensation-mongering writers, the Smoke Holer is not a cretinous fellow, imbecilic through intermarriage. He is tall, long of limb, ruddy of countenance, and clear of eye. He is a trifle shy, but hospitable. He is a courteous listener, but not necessarily naive. He is far from the sullen, suspicious mountaineer of the comic cartoons; he is mildly inquisitive concerning things new to him.

—*The Smoke Hole*

ESTYL SHREVE was a tall, trim man, with a wide mouth and gray hair, on the verge, when I met him, of retirement as an agent of the state liquor board—an occupation that, for a son of the Smoke Hole, has ironic overtones. While Estyl enjoyed digging up Smoke Hole memories—he'd always meant to set some of this down, he said—his wife, Gertie, would sit quietly, confirming details when he asked her and only occasionally adding her own recollections. She was a Kimble. Later, on a subsequent visit to the Smoke Hole, I interviewed Estyl's brother, Loy, so my description of the old life in the canyon is a mixture of their memories, supplemented by written accounts and conversations with others who lived there.

Like branches on a skinny tree, there were several distinct "villages" in the canyon—little clusters of related families in the different tributary hollows. Each of the major tributaries had its own schoolhouse, which meant no child had to walk more than two or three miles. The families would mix at church socials, or visit each other's homes for apple peelings in the fall, or sit on the worn benches at the little stores. The stores were several, located at the junctures where smaller hollows joined the river, and they mixed cash sales with barter for pigs, lambs, and moonshine, and later eggs. There were gristmills and small timber operations, too.

The children were educated in one-room schoolhouses, where students in nine grades shared the room. Loy remembered excellent teachers, some of them exiled to the Smoke Hole because their political beliefs (inevitably Republican) didn't suit the Democrats in power. Glady Wilson, a Stump who grew up in the Smoke Hole, said the smart kids "learned ahead when they taught the older kids," and it must have worked, because she went on to become valedictorian in her high school outside the Smoke Hole. Loy Shreve, who remembers his father and a Smoke Hole teacher as his most inspirational influences, went on to earn a doctorate in horticulture.

In the 1930s the canyon was reasonably self-sufficient; it had to be, since the narrow wagon road to Upper Tract was impassable much of the year. The Depression, then, was not of great significance to the Smoke Hole. The population was dense: Estyl, who now lives in Franklin, claimed it was the most densely populated rural area in the country back in the thirties. When I tried to check this at the U.S. Bureau of the Census, all I got were amused shrugs.

The Shreves grew most of what they ate; tapped the plentiful maples for sugar; kept some pigs, chickens, and cows; and milled their grain in the canyon. They would sell a few turkeys and lambs, and the walnuts the kids gathered, and use the cash to purchase staples. Itinerant peddlers would hike with sacks of wares from hollow to hollow, and usually at one of their stops, as nightfall approached, they would be offered a bed, a meal, and perhaps a little family circle music.

"We had a particular culture there," said Loy Shreve, who
has done a considerable amount of international traveling as
an expert in plant propagation. "Putting it simply, when I
was missing a sheep, I knew the histories of the families, and
I knew darn well who stole it. I've always wanted to come
home. Any place in the world, I've never seen a place I like
that well."

Prohibition and an improved road sparked the first outside
interest in the Smoke Hole. Outsiders were suspicious; there
were the rumors of imbecility and inbreeding, and the peculiar local dialect. Most homes were small one- or two-room
log cabins chinked with mud. Canvas was stretched over the
windows in the winter, and rusty, wood-burning stoves provided warmth.

The Smoke Hole had a reputation that attracted revenue
agents, and it was by most accounts well deserved. Smoke
Hole brew became popular outside the canyon during the
scramble in the 1920s to circumvent the Volstead Act. I could
find no solid evidence to the rumor that Smoke Holers actually
killed any revenue agents in those days, but everyone has a
tale or two about outwitting the still-busters.

THE Smoke Hole residents regularly held box socials, for which
the girls made up the box suppers, topped with fancy ribbons, and the boys would bid at auction for the boxes of the
girls they favored. But Smoke Hole life included a fair amount
of violence, too. Estyl recalled: "You never had a social gathering that I can remember where you didn't have a fight.
That was very routine. I had an uncle—he would get a few
drinks of moonshine in him and he would go into a crowd
and you'd happen to look at him, he'd probably walk up to
you and say: 'Hey, you looked at me, I don't think you like
me,' or he might just haul off and hit you."

Cornfield and road in Appalachian hill country.
Marion Post Wolcott.

Usually combatants were friendly afterwards, but sometimes real damage was done. A member of the Judy family gave me an old newspaper clipping, undated but from sometime in the 1920s, about one incident that still causes argument between two Smoke Hole families:

Along the narrow gorge of the South Branch, near the Grant line, in the county of Pendleton, there is located a store and post office called Ketterman named after the older people of that settlement. Here the folks of that section get their mail and do much of their trading. To them there is a world outside, but in the shadow of the mountains is the place they call home and nothing else matters much.

Grant Stump was the merchant and postmaster a day or two ago; today he lies dead at his own hands. A mind deranged took his life and shot a neighbor.

Gabe Judy went to Stump's store Tuesday morning to settle an account he had there. For some reason or other, Stump had some feeling against Judy, largely imaginary, and when Judy had mounted his horse, a boy behind him, to go, Stump came out of the store with a revolver and fired at Judy. The latter raised his left arm, which received the bullet above the wrist, and fell off the horse, the boy falling with him. They ran to the river and swam across, Stump having shot two or three times at him but did not again hit him. Judy and the boy got across the river and escaped further injury.

Stump, no doubt thinking he had killed Judy, shot himself in the chest with the revolver. His wife then took the revolver from him, as she also did a knife he had taken from his pocket in an effort to cut his throat. He then went to the store, got a box of cartridges and started to the river, his wife and aged mother trying to stop him. He walked about waist deep into the river and collapsed, either drowning or dying from his injuries. Neighbors were notified and his body was taken from the stream. No inquest was deemed necessary.

Judy came to town and a physician dressed his wound. He was able to walk around all right and told us of the shooting.

And told it in a certain way. The Stump version of the same story paints Gabe Judy as a heavy-drinking, violent man, who harassed Stump and then pretended to be mortally wounded, prompting a despairing Stump to kill himself.

———

Even today, many family reunions are held annually. The widely publicized Lilly Reunion raises questioning editorial eyebrows in newspapers from Washington to Florida, when attendance figures of over 50,000 are quoted by the Associated Press. At such affairs persons of no family connection welcome each other like long lost brothers, and fraternity rises to a peak at the barbecue pit and cider jug.

—West Virginia: A Guide to the Mountain State

I HAD been exploring the Smoke Hole and the surrounding area for some time when, at the invitation of the Shreves, I attended the annual Alt-Kimble reunion at the Old Judy Church. The church sat on a hill, and behind it there were log benches and an amphitheater. I arrived after the church service and before the picnic, driving on slick roads and listening to an evangelist on the radio talk about "salvaTION," hitting the last syllable hard. As I walked up the steep hill, a banjo and guitar began playing, and voices sang the reunion's theme song—"West Virginia Hills." I joined the hundreds of family folk on the hill and was invited to help myself to potluck dishes laid out on two long tables—biscuits and unsweetened cornbread, sugar-cured hams, fried chicken clothed in crusts thick enough to withstand harsh weather, chutneys and corn and scalloped tomatoes, and down at the end an army of pies. Brief welcoming speeches were made, and the West Virginia turkey calling champion demonstrated his skills.

It was a friendly and varied crew—elderly women wearing thick glasses who would rise crookedly from the benches and totter precariously until some relative involved in a conversation nearby absently took hold of an arm; a few young, earnest family historians, damp with excitement at the opportunity of the reunion; some outlandishly punk teenagers, brandishing peroxided Mohawks and nose jewelry; and, in large numbers, Estyl Shreve's generation, the last bunch of strong-willed, strong-backed West Virginians to grow up in the Smoke Hole. Shreve greeted me quietly: "You help yourself to some food, now. Here's some people you might like to meet." People would start off shy with me, but when another member of a Smoke Hole family swung into our conversation, the voices would rise. Stories, laughter, and genealogical inquisitions mingled with the light rain burring into the trees, and sometimes there were reminders of the quick-tempered times gone by. "Now who told you that about Gabe Judy?" said a Stump descendant to me, eyes narrowing. "You'll hear a lot of things. But people here know better what old Judy really was, and in the Smoke Hole it hasn't changed so much as you might think—a man here might knock you down." A spindly sixtyish woman pushed this fellow aside and took me by the arm, saying she wanted to show me some pictures under the awning up the hill. "You should just listen," she said, smiling and shaking her head. "Have you had something to eat?"

A group of kids sat on a rock at the top of the hill by the church to cheer and laugh as cars spun and spit mud, trying to make it up on a slick incline of wet clay in the rain. Nettie Kimble's driver was one who succeeded, and he disdained the parking area to plant her big red Grenada right in the middle of the gathering at the amphitheater. No one seemed upset by this obstacle; Nettie, the oldest in attendance at ninety-eight, opened her window halfway to accept the greetings of passersby in queenly fashion.

Attendance was down from the year before, when thirty-five hundred showed up for the fiftieth reunion. When the youngest grandmother in this year's crowd turned out to be forty—there is *always* one in her thirties, according to Allen Yokum, the reunion president—it was clear that the cold, wet weather had discouraged many.

I could not help feeling a little out of place, since I lacked the long, straight nose or the long, slanted mouth or the circle of chatting friends that marked most family members; surely, like the man in Lincolnshire who recognized the shape of my grandfather's head, these people knew at a glance that I was not family. I had had enough, too, of Smoke Hole stories that had become Byzantine in their variations and disputed facts. So I took a plate of food and went inside the church, a simple, one-room building with hand-hewn beams and a choir loft where children played out of the rain. There I looked over the genealogical work of young Mark Bowers, a Kimble, that traced the various families back into the eighteenth century, with the sorts of asides—illegitimacies, Queen Mary's stolen head-chopping ax—that inevitably embellish scant records.

When I departed, I was held up along with many other cars returning to Highway 220. The car of the punk teenagers, who had so clearly relished their conspicuousness at the reunion, was conspicuously mired in the creek that ran between the church grounds and the main road, blocking traffic. Walking up to see if I could help, I found Nettie Kimble's Grenada near the head of the line, her driver raging at the delay, and Nettie herself slumped in the back seat, looking a bit cross and sleepy.

*North of Ketterman {in the Smoke Hole} is an unbroken
wilderness of mountains and forest, for 20 miles impassable
except on horse or on foot.*
—West Virginia: A Guide to the Mountain State

I DROVE down into the Smoke Hole looking for Sadie Kimble. She wasn't home, nor was the Fairmont parked in front.

I decided to walk into the mountains west of her house, trying to shake the melancholy of the wet gray weather and the depopulated hollows. The gathering of these interwoven families from their new homes—many of them out of state— had only underlined the emptiness of the Smoke Hole itself.

I thought to hike the old trails and dog paths that Sadie Kimble once followed over North Ridge Mountain, and I drove a ways up the dirt road along Briggs Run beyond her house. A squirrel hunting season was just beginning, so I donned a brilliant red vest over a rain poncho, then pulled a gold-and-burgundy Washington Redskins cap over my head. A very unlikely squirrel began hiking up the mountain, stepping to the side of the ocher rivulets and into the dripping mustards and thistles on the shoulder.

I left the muddy road to the hunters and hiked by foot up a broad swath of open land cleared not for the travelers of old but for a buried natural gas pipeline that runs straight over the mountain. Rhododendrons, laurels, and sprouting chestnuts crowded the edges, restrained by whatever chemicals Columbia Gas uses to keep the path clear. The ground was soft, my boots slipped often, and I was forced to traverse my way up. By the time I reached the ridge I was soaked with rain and sweat.

The reasons for the demise of the Smoke Hole communities had gradually become clear. In part, the Smoke Hole lost its people because it became home to too many; the mountaineers' utopia of the 1920s had been hunted out a decade later. Finding a squirrel, much less a deer, was cause for rejoicing, according to Estyl Shreve. And many of the canyon's hillsides were barren and unproductive from erosion and single-crop planting.

The best of the young people were enticed away—for their fast legs (Estyl Shreve and others were "recruited" to play football in Franklin, with free lodging in a team booster's home), their good minds, their aggressiveness. Well-meaning improvement programs—like the Civilian Conservation Corps's construction of a new road into the canyon in the 1930s—had opened these attractive wilds to outsiders, and the visitors who came to hunt and fish introduced the inhabitants to modern conveniences and ideas. The CCC was another program that, like this writers' project, gave jobs to West Virginians, and the road gave Smoke Holers an easy way out as well as in. World War II showed many Smoke Holers a larger world, and if they still hungered for the close families and natural beauty of the Smoke Hole, they developed tastes for luxuries that the old barter economy could never provide. Today, with television to bring the world in and transportation to ferry the inhabitants out, life in the Smoke Hole seems . . . limited.

The bulk of the Smoke Hole is now public land, managed with the ecological know-how and ignorance of community culture that sometimes characterize the Forest Service. The hillside fields are filling in with oaks and walnut trees again; the bass and trout in the river are resurgent; the campgrounds are thick with RVs during holidays. But the few old-timers remaining no longer recite their stories with the vigor and regularity necessary to keep history in trim.

There was a thick, foggy cloud engulfing the ridge, and down the other side I could see no more than fifty yards. I knew there was a steep dip and then the rise of the Seneca Rocks, and I tried to imagine Sadie and her friends trudging up from below, and the peddlers with their junky sacks, making the circuit from hollow to hollow half a century ago.

On top of the ridge is a radio antenna, and standing near it, I felt a wave of heat on my left cheek, and wondered for a moment what sorts of messages were bounced off the tops of these Appalachian ridges—reports from CIA operatives in the Middle East, I imagined, or some pornographic video broadcast from an all-night New York station. I walked south along a jeep road, and came to the square, subdivided face of a microwave transmitter, pointed west. Again, a feeling of desperation assailed me. Not only were the people gone, but the invaders had scarred the landscape, too.

Beyond the microwave tower I slipped off the jeep track and into the woods, following a sag in the ground that was probably a game trail. I entered a hallway in the foliage that was thickly carpeted with fallen leaves. My boots were sloshing full of water, but the chestnut oaks and laurels and maples now buffered the rainfall with a gentle, hissing deflection. The clouds and fog made a false twilight, and as I moved deeper into the canopied wood, I found the golden leaves beneath my feet were giving off more light than the sky was.

I walked along that witchy, illuminated trail, smelling humus and moss, and I heard the strangling laughter of a wild turkey to my left. I stopped for a moment and crouched, looking into the gloomy woods and down the steep slopes that fell away from the ridge. I imagined myself with a shotgun, and when I stood again and began walking, down the sloping ridge toward the Smoke Hole, I found myself peering into rock cavities, half expecting to see the crude paraphernalia of a still—the tin drum with the fire crackling underneath it; the copper coil twisting up and away; the earthen jug where the precious liquid falls—craggy men with straight

Mountaineers hauling wood with a sled and a mule.
Marion Post Wolcott.

noses and long mouths standing by; guns leaning against an oak trunk.

Off down the mountain into the Smoke Hole, into the mist and the smell of moldering leaves. It would be nice to find, down near the river, a stove-warmed home with venison stew cooking, a slab of bread with apple butter for a stranger, a sip or two from somebody's jug, and, when chores were done, a ready fiddle player.

Places that live only in memory are frequently distorted and mythologized, and like the story of the Stump shooting, there is no way to rescue them from dispute. But the surviving landscape and grave markers bring one version or another to life for succeeding generations, and the way of living embedded in those stories, fleshed out with remembered detail, cannot be found much of anywhere now. That's reason enough to preserve what memories survive, distortions and all.

I collect stories the way a traveler does, hurriedly and haphazardly; someone whose imagination is fired by blood ties to the old way of living might linger longer and dig deeper. What is surprising is that no one had ever asked the Shreves for their story before.

I left the Smoke Hole and continued my travels in other directions, but I did not consider this first trip quite completed. And so I found myself sometime later wandering back into the Potomac Highlands, back along the Potomac tributaries, looking at the pacified towns and countryside, and arriving finally at Franklin. I drove again into the Smoke Hole, looking for Sadie Kimble; her house was empty. I went to the library to pick up some statistics and then walked down by the river to an old swinging bridge that hangs low over the water, where I interrupted a couple of teenagers embracing under a birch. Farther downriver, where the steep topography is briefly relieved and there is room for a football field—always a siting problem in West Virginia—I went for a run. Later, I drove past the school, and finally pulled up at the modern nursing home to which many locals refer proudly.

It was, like most nursing homes, low-ceilinged and weakly lit. A harried nurse doubling as a receptionist waved me by without asking who I was or what I wanted. Wheelchairs were parked in the hallway. Voices from other places, other times emanated from the hunched figures in the chairs. "I wouldn't take that no more, I said," said a woman with hair white and fine as gossamer. "Hey, hey, hey, hey," shouted a man from his bed. He would not stop. But there was no foul smell here, as I've encountered in other nursing homes, and two women chatting on a couch greeted me with kindly and apologetic smiles.

"Is Sadie Kimble here?" I asked one of them.

"Why, sure, sure," said one. "That's her, just a-walking down there."

Light from a windowed door at the end of the hall silhouetted a small figure, slightly hunched, leaning on a cane and moving away from me. She wore a dark blue dress with a neat black belt, and her hair was more tightly bound up in a bun than the last time I'd seen her.

"Sadie? Sadie Kimble?" I said, coming up next to her.

She looked up and gave me a familiar sly smile, but her eyes searched my face uncertainly.

O'G: I came to see you down in the Smoke Hole awhile back, you remember me?

SK: Last year, maybe, seems like longer, lots happens. I reckon I do. You're a young fella. Where did you say you was from?

O'G: Wyoming.

SK (laughing): Wyoming! Seems like it was more than a year. Seems like bunches!

O'G: When did you move up here?

SK: Oh, my daughter, she thought it up, awhile back, didn't want me alone and all that and so forth.

O'G: You're with your husband here. That must be good. How is he?

SK: He's sick—John's sick off and on. Don't know much. Can't talk to him much.

O'G: Seems like a nice place.
SK: Wyoming! That's off a bunch.

Her manner was more subdued. Her grooming showed considerable care. I didn't have the courage to ask her, standing in the hall with the shouts of "hey, hey, hey" pouring down on us, why she, who had once told me, "Whenever I leave my house, it's going to be when I'm carried away, I reckon," had surrendered her home in the Smoke Hole.

Point of Departure

New York City

WHENEVER I make a stop in New York, I hang my hat in the lower 100s of the Upper West Side, the area once called by the Dutch "Bloemendael," or vale of flowers, according to the writers' projects' New York City guide, in "patriotic remembrance of a town near Haarlem in the old country," rather than the New World's first department store.

I traveled to New York in early spring, and brought with me from Wyoming some ugly gray clouds and cold temperatures. My daughters, still a little foggy about the reason why their father kept disappearing for weeks at a time, had picked up from my wife a kind of protective flippancy—sniffly tears mingled with sarcastic cheers as I took off for the airport. I said to my oldest daughter, "You would be bored traveling with me," and she answered, "I *am* bored."

By the time I arrived at Newark International, my head had begun to ache and I was sneezing sufficiently to infect

Third Avenue and Forty-second Street in New York City.
Marjory Collins.

about eight rows of passengers around the wing exit. I headed
quickly into the city, bound for the comfort of a friendly
apartment.

On the uptown subway, passengers spread their legs wide
and placed satchels and newspapers on the empty seats next
to them, filling the spaces where I might have sat, and with
spaced-out obsequiousness I simply stood, surrounded by my
lumpy bags full of books and clothes and potions for my cold.
I disembarked at 104th and Broadway, where an arctic wind

blew through Bloemendael and penetrated the thin, French-tailored jacket I wore to appear fashionable. "The city becomes an emblem in remote minds," wrote the writers' project authors of *New York Panorama,* and in recent times that emblem is less alluring than the flask of perfume from Saks or a Harlem band playing "Young Woman's Blues" mentioned in *Panorama,* a book of essays that supplemented the *New York City Guide.* Today a remote mind is more likely to think of the reptilian subway of Bernhard Goetz or the peacock penthouse of Donald Trump.

I tiptoed around slushy gutter ponds and kept a wary eye on a few bundled bodies in doorways. No one was home at the apartment where I hoped to drop my bags. I stood shivering on the street and large, soft gray plops began landing on my shoulders. Either someone was pouring soggy cold cereal from the top of the roof, or it was time for the meteorologists to think up a new term to describe this phenomenon.

I walked back to Broadway. More broken umbrellas than I had ever seen in one place at one time littered the pedestrian islands that divided uptown and downtown traffic. The cars and buses whizzed recklessly, north toward Harlem on one side, south toward Times Square on the other. On the west side of the street the vending trays of compact produce markets bulged into the sidewalk traffic. On the east side of the street a young man in a knee-length black coat of fake leather peddled an armload of umbrellas on the sidewalk, with great success. I got stuck between the two traffic lanes, and a taxi heading uptown splattered my knees with soggy cereal.

In a locker downtown I stored my bags, bought a trench coat in a small store, and began wandering back up the West Side.

A place as large as New York can endure many visits without revealing much of itself; there is too much to sort out,

from the aging terra-cotta ornamentation all along the avenues to the costumes that flag particular neighborhoods. A
visitor has to acknowledge each time back that there is plenty
still to discover, and the writers' project New York City guide
is helpful that way. Buildings that were fresh and new in the
1930s now have a grimy survivors' visage, and the people
once in them are mostly long since fallen. But reading the
guide excites you nevertheless: "Papa Strunsky still rails at
the tenant in arrears in his West Third Street building—and
at times lets the promising writer or painter stay on, the bill
unpaid." Or: "Whenever a heavyweight boxer in Madison
Square Garden . . . takes too many right-hand punches, or a
circus trapeze performer misses his safety net, or a rodeo rider
falls under the hoofs of a steer, the victim is carried across the
street to POLYCLINIC HOSPITAL." You get a sense of the rich,
dense lives once lived in this cacophony; a visitor's ear becomes
tuned for echoes of that old life.

    This is the magic of all the guides. As I walked up the
West Side, I dog-eared pages describing quirky places I had
passed often enough before but ignored. The monuments along
Riverside Drive, for instance: How often had I jogged stonily
by Joan of Arc without knowing that fragments from Rheims
Cathedral and the Tower of Rouen trembled at my passing
footfall? I would have to go back this time, look Joan of Arc
in the eye, apologize.

    Many of the old buildings whose histories are encapsulated
in the guide still stand, thanks to their public usefulness and
preservation efforts that began in the 1960s. The gabled Dakota
Apartments at Seventy-second Street, ill famed since the
shooting of John Lennon, showed little of the yellow brick
described in the 1939 guide, but the courtyard and its foun-
tains remain. The New York City guide has the same opinionated tone as the Washington book when it comes to
architecture. It decries the "pretentious" Roman style of the

Roosevelt Building at the American Museum of Natural History. There I watched a woman juggling three small children up the front steps; when a black man in a dark suit and a tweed cap tried to assist her by lifting the front rim of her child's stroller, she looked for a moment panic-stricken. Only when she heard his colonial African accent did she smile gratefully.

In the West Eighties I had to pick my way through the milling, prosperous crowd on Columbus Avenue among the boutiques and restaurants, avoiding towering ice cream cones—never mind the weather—in the hands of gesticulating promenaders. I rendezvoused with a friend on Broadway and we charged along that busy thoroughfare to a crowded bar farther uptown. A smallish woman, my friend dressed strong: padded shoulders and dark eye makeup. An actor friend of hers in jogging clothes joined us. He ordered Perrier, and asked for a glass of "ordinary" water as well. When the drinks arrived, he gulped down the glass of tap water hurriedly. Then he settled back and took demure little sips of the Perrier. He crowed about getting an acting job in a commercial about cookies. I could tell my friend was jealous; her acting career had never taken off, and though she was a successful editor at a magazine now, she was restless.

Their chatting went on, and I slipped away to a pay phone to call the apartment where I'd be staying the next few days. As I dialed I watched the tables around me—the confident asexual touching, men and women having forceful "professional" talks, the mildly conditioned bodies and faces. The variety of dress and race was no cover for the swarmy fraternity sameness in the room, from the shared slang to the exclusory cost of a drink; returning to my seat, I almost didn't catch the little eye signal my friend gave the actor, precipitating his immediate departure. These arrangements were unfathomable.

We walked back to her apartment and had some more spirits. It was sparsely furnished, but I recognized a quilt. It had once been draped over her sofa in the small California town where I'd first met her. "I think of moving back there," she said. "I've got no desire to be living alone in New York ten years from now, and that's how it's shaping up."

In California, where she'd gone to college, she'd held herself in a hunched, defensive posture, and wore a perpetually startled look that was distinctly her own, and lovable; older people invited her into their families. She was made of sterner stuff now. "You can be living alone in a small town ten years from now, too," I said, "and you might like that less."

"I want to be someplace cozier."

"Where's your family?" I realized that if I'd ever known where she was originally from, I'd forgotten.

"Deceased," she said, with finality. "California's home, really, more than any place."

"Because you liked it there."

"I suppose," she said, lighting a cigarette, and laughed. "I get this way whenever I'm looking for a new apartment." She moved every couple of years within New York, and she was about to again. I tried to picture her in a small town— she who so enjoyed the professional warfare and private vices of the city. "So, what about Wyoming?" she said. I raised my eyebrows uncertainly, and she said, lightly, "I expect I acquire some special status just from knowing someone from Wyoming. Do you ride horses and all?"

But I was from California—that was on the birth certificate, wasn't it? I told her that the cowboy with the weathered face and mustache who rides the range in Marlboro ads owned a spread near Lander. She swigged, and was off into a chortling fantasy about recasting Marlboro commercials with women. The subject never got back to Wyoming, but she'd gotten me thinking about my family, missing them, and I got up to leave. Out the window, snow was falling. As I stood by the elevator, my friend popped out of her apartment in a long coat and said she felt like walking me to the corner.

Outside, a thin layer of snow had settled on the sidewalks and front steps and the sills of iron-barred windows, and large, cottony flakes sifted in the streetlights. Through the windows of the smooth-sided apartment buildings a few remnant Christmas lights still glowed, and when we reached the corner, she loosed my arm, kicked a little crown of snow from a fire hydrant, and skipped back down the street toward her building. I couldn't see her face, or imagine what it felt like to go back there alone.

I took in a late-night movie, and picked up an early edition of the *Daily News* as I walked up Broadway to 106th Street and then west, in the shadowy, early-morning snow, to the apartment where this time a key was waiting with the doorman. After a few hours of fitful sleep I was on the street again, unsettled and thrilled by the thought of innumerable mysteries hatched by the round-the-clock life here.

There was close to a foot of snow, and the walk up to Grant's Tomb along Riverside Drive was a slippery, tentative one. I entered the tomb alone, circled slowly around the central room, and looked down over the marble railing at the red granite sarcophagi where Grant and his wife lie. The cloud cover outside dimmed the light through the high windows of orange glass and made the scene moodier. The New York City guide quoted Henry James's description of Grant's Tomb: "A great democratic demonstration caught in the fact. . . ." James wrote elsewhere that he adored the monument for its simplicity and openness; it is indeed even simpler than it was originally designed to be, with little of its once-planned statuary, only a couple of Greek types above the entrance, sitting with their backs against the motto: "Let us have peace."

Perhaps because I visited on a winter morning, like James,

I felt the *Presence* he wrote about, something beyond aesthetics—the monument is not particularly beautiful—that had to do with the "true hard light" and the mutual indifference of the tomb and the city around it. ". . . few New Yorkers have visited the tomb," said the guide, "and no visitor has ever missed it." For the half hour I was there no one entered, and I left alone; outside, I walked entirely around the tomb. Five rows of trees lead away south from the entrance, and there is an open square on the east side, the dropoff to the river on the west, and a small park to the north; in other words, they have allowed the general a deferential space. Around the monument runs a low-slung bench with wild, colorful mosaics; the sinuous line of the art at first seemed to disrupt the ponderous gray blocks of the monument, but only for a moment. As I walked, I began to like the mosaic more—it was added in the 1970s by Pedro de Silva and neighborhood artisans—and see it as a nice concession to the neighborhood, a concession the tomb could afford to make, because it had, against all things, that inviolate "Presence" James wrote about.

I slopped south along Riverside Drive, looking for Joan of Arc, but couldn't find her. Down a narrow path under the Henry Hudson Parkway I found my way to the walkway that runs right along the water. All alone—how astonishing, that I could look upriver an endless distance and see no one!—I leaned on the rail and watched a huge Nissan ship move downriver. Across the water there were docks, apartments, and new condos being built like stairsteps down to the water. Looking north, I saw an unshaven young man in a peacoat walking toward me, slowly, and felt an old chill. It seemed impossible that he, like me, had no more reason than meandering whimsy for being here: He was looking for a solitary tourist like me, separated from the city by the traffic and the park and snow, in this soundless strip of loneliness. Still, I

waited and felt him pass behind me, then shivered as he stopped
a short ways beyond and leaned on the rail. But he did nothing—only looked out at the water as I was looking. Finally I
raised myself up and walked past him, and stoked with bra-
vado by my own foolishness, I asked him if he knew where
the Joan of Arc statue was. He looked at me carefully and
said no.

So I walked back under the parkway, among trees bowed
with fresh snow and a miniature streetlight, and up the curving path into the sliver of park between Riverside and the
parkway. Things were busy there with a surprising phenomenon: children. Men and women plunged this way and that,
losing their footing again and again as small children in puffy
snowsuits plummeted ahead like drunken penguins in the
fresh snow. A dog or two had been unleashed as well, and
the canines bounded as the children rolled. I could see a few
hands pop out of gloves and the reddish burn of the chill on
delicate cheeks; there would be a price to pay later for this
frolic. But it was the happiest of scenes, and I felt no shyness
about asking, again, "Do you know where Joan of Arc is?"

One woman did, indeed, and pointed the way. She saw
my writers' project guide and told me she collected guides to
the city, and recommended another one that identified and
informed about all the statues in the city. I backslid my way
up through the park to Joan of Arc, and there she was, facing
the Hudson upright on her horse, with snow all down her
front just as if someone had thrown a meringue pie.

Maybe in a few years those tumbling children would be
stealing cars along Riverside here—that still happens regularly, a doorman warned me—and maybe the old man who
walked by me at the statue holding a book in Polish in front
of his face would be mugged within the hour. The woman
who directed me to the statue had asked where I was staying,
and when I told her, she said, "Oh, up there on the *border*,"

with a raised eyebrow, implying, I thought, the fringe where gentrification meets poverty and crime . . . but then she laughed. Borders are exciting places, of friction and change. The emblem of New York in remote minds—fear of talking, of eye contact, of people just walking along—had fallen away. Joan of Arc had set her conquering eye on New Jersey, and she got a load of snow in the face; that was the direction in which I was headed, too.

Destination

Barre, Vermont

Thoroughfares leading to the water front meet with a chaos of side streets that cross and interlace, forming odd-shaped islands upon which squat equally odd-shaped structures. Skeletons of abandoned buildings stand crumbling in the shadow of newer factories, humming with the roar of machinery.
—New Jersey: A Guide to Its Present and Past

*I*T was late at night when I caught a bus out to Newark International for a cheap car rental. The snow had quickly turned ugly in the city streets, and now, a few days later, there were only a few gray remnants slumped against the shady sides of buildings. I was tired, but nettled by an agitation that seemed to come from nowhere in particular, so I decided to hit the road for Vermont. But before that I needed coffee, and as I wound through the interchanges around the airport, I kept my eye on a distant Howard Johnson's sign.

The landscape became more disorienting as the cocoon glow
of the airport faded behind me. Hulking old factory buildings were everywhere, age-grimed and ghostly in a yellowish
fog. Along the upper stories were long rows of clerestory
windows, painted, broken, hollow-eyed; above them, lifting
out of the light into a charcoal sky, were the smokestacks, so
faint at their summits that I couldn't see which were adding
to this granular atmosphere.

The streets down which I drove would narrow and twist,
become rutted with old freight rails, and dead-end at a brick
wall or fence. The fences were often topped with barbed wire,
and surrounding parking lots were full of cars, which meant
there must have been people in these buildings—grinding
machinery that never stopped, hissing pipes and faces bathed
in the yellow light. Soaps, pencils, cans, mouthwash, cigarettes, macaroni, meats, electric elevators, pinless diapers—
these are some of the products, according to the New Jersey
guide, that emerged from these municipal caverns. Old gas-
works and transformer stations, where metal spires held aloft
dense tangles of power lines; cranes overhead like grappling
insects: I was lost in a cheap science fiction movie. Did drivers wander lost here until they ran out of gas, and then disappear forever into one of the buildings, where they stitched
together pinless diapers for an eternity?

Then I saw a billboard that said: ALL NATURAL, GRADE A
TURKEYS! and below it the beady lights of cars on a freeway.
I turned onto a narrow, unlit road curving off in that direction and accelerated . . . then braked and spun around, as
headlights came speeding toward me. I backed out to a big
factory lot, where a young uniformed man with an Afro sta-
tioned in a security cubicle said, "Hey, man, you almost did
yourself there!" He laughed—it was the only entertainment
he got—and explained I'd entered the Pulaski Skyway in the
wrong direction; he gave me directions to an on-ramp.

Eventually, I made my way onto the New Jersey Turnpike going north, and past the Lincoln Tunnel I pulled off at a turnpike "island," daring once again to dream of coffee, and deciding this would be a good time to call my wife.

In the fast-food restaurant there were some men loitering in the front hall by the map machine and rest rooms. One was nodding off on his feet; another kept leaning over the drinking fountain and taking short sips, then snapping erect and staring around. Two black women, one overweight and graying, the other a short-haired teenager, were behind the counter, and two highway patrolmen wearing dark glasses were sitting at a table. Sunburned bags of french fries waited under a hot light on the serving counter, and a couple of wrapped burgers sat in slots facing the dining area. A tall black man with his shirttail out stood at the condiments table, looking angrily at a pile of sugar packets. I smiled a grateful smile at the highway patrolmen, who may or may not have looked back at me from behind their glasses.

I ordered and sat down, and a minute later the older woman, behind the grill, picked up the piece of paper my order was written on and squinted at it.

WOMAN AT GRILL: What's he want here—a burguh? A cheeseburguh?
WOMAN AT COUNTER: Yeah—we got one up here—how long this been here?
GRILL: I dunno. You didn't give it to the dude with the red shirt?
COUNTER: He still lying out there.
GRILL: No shit.
COUNTER (giggling): In that bush. They gonna turn the sprinklers on, and he gonna drown.
GRILL: He don' want no cheese? I put cheese on this thing.
COUNTER (to me): You care about cheese?

MAN AT CONDIMENTS: I don't care what! And if she go be
with her sister, that sister gonna see Mr. Stick here.
O'G: Cheese is okay.
GRILL: I gotta clean this grill. Shit.
COUNTER: Give me that. Here's your burguh. What you say
you wanna drink?
O'G: Coffee.
CONDIMENTS (to COUNTER): I'm gonna show *you* Mr. Stick.
COUNTER (laughing): Jee-sus, what you doin'? You wanna
get arrested?
    (The Highway Patrol departs, ignoring everything.)
CONDIMENTS: Foh carryin' a concealed weapon.
GRILL (angry): You zip up before you get *in* something.
COUNTER (laughing): You'll get cooked up like a french fry.
CONDIMENTS: I got a phone call to make, call her myself—
and Mr. Stick has a few words to say.

So it would not be an easy matter to call my wife, with
Mr. Stick next to me at the other pay phone. I ate my burguh, drank two cups of coffee, and headed back to the car.
The men by the drinking fountain and the rest room were
still there; Condiments was relieving Mr. Stick by the pay
phone.
    It was 2:30 A.M. Had I called Wyoming, it would have
been midnight, and I would have seemed as mad to my family as these folks seemed to me.

——

{Woodstock's} instinctive reaction to change is negative: it has no
factories and wants none; it saw its railroad discontinued without
regret; it tenaciously cherishes its old covered bridge, picturesque but
hazardous, at the west end of the village. If Woodstock sometimes
places sentiment above progress, if it is—as its rustic neighbors

say—too smug in its own well-being, it is perhaps by these very
tokens a microcosm of the State to which, culturally, intellectually,
and politically, it has contributed so much.
—Vermont: A Guide to the Green Mountain State

THERE was just the dimmest hint of rouge on the eastern
horizon when I pulled into the far corner of a parking lot
next to another fast-food restaurant, in Connecticut now, on
Interstate 95 where it runs along Long Island Sound. I flattened back the seat as best I could and covered myself with
my trench coat.

When I awoke, it had begun to rain. Exhausted and edgy,
I drove north, feeling acutely sensitive to the discordant noise
rain makes striking against windshields, asphalt, or even air.

Considering my condition, it would be hard for me to
pinpoint when the change began. Slivers of shrubbery and
open field began to invade the town house rows and gasoline
alleys as I drove north into Massachusetts. Knots of hardwoods interfered with the asphalt landscape. I got off the
interstate for good at hilly Brattleboro, and by then the culture of fast-food joints and shopping malls was faint, and
time backslid a little as I meandered north toward Barre.

Vermont on a map looks like one of a pair of boots stored
away, tucked efficiently upside down against its right side up
mate, New Hampshire. The roads I took, State Highways
30, 100, 11, 106, wind like shoelaces down the boot's neck.
Two things about the Vermont map differentiated it from
the many other state maps I'd perused: first, the large number of roads designated "scenic," and second, the number of
ski areas—more, by my count, ski areas in Vermont than
there were sizable towns of any kind in, say, Nevada. Vermont is more and more a provider of snow and scenery for
richer, more urbanized neighbors from the south; it's the back

door out of which they slip to get a breath of fresh air.

But "they" were not much in evidence during my visit. The autumn leaves, which lure thousands up every year, now decayed in soggy mats beneath the snow. The snow was

past its skiing prime, discolored and icy. I was here just in
time for . . . the mush.

Vermonters reputedly take pride in their Yankee independence and taciturn ways with outsiders; this is part of what

Bringing butter into
Woodstock.
Marion Post Wolcott.

draws visitors, who think a lack of warmth, or better yet outright rudeness, is the surest sign that the expedition has reached an extremity untainted by tourism and hype. Even in the 1930s the Yankee pose had an element of self-parody; one can read Dorothy Canfield Fisher's introduction to the writers' project Vermont guide as either incredibly smug or a witty put-on: "We do not in the least claim to know what is the matter with the roaring, money-making industrialized world, or with the share-cropping misery of rural life in one-crop regions. . . . We know that our ignorance of, our lack of instinctive 'feeling' for those modern industrial and mass-life problems makes us seem to you like your great-aunt in curl-papers, but we are helpless before our tradition of not pretending to know more than we do, of not being other than what we are." Quite a marketing ploy.

It was raining the afternoon I reached Woodstock, a village snugged around the Otauquechee River on Highway 4. The town is beautifully preserved and reeks of history. I parked my car, circumnavigated the green, and ducked into the library, a churchlike nineteenth-century Romanesque building, where I read about nearby covered bridges, the world's first ski tow, and the four church bells cast by Paul Revere. Much of the town is on the National Register of Historic Places.

Signs were modest to the point of obscurity. I went into Young's Cheese Shop, the only place I could find for an ordinary breakfast and ordinary coffee at ordinary prices. Even there I found myself among folks whose John Deere caps were spotless and whose wool scarves tastefully matched their wool skirts.

I suppose it is too obvious to point out that it's oil money that has spruced up this town; one cannot explore here without finding the Rockefeller fingerprints everywhere. Minus such philanthropy, Woodstock would likely be cheapened by loud signs and poverty such as we find elsewhere everywhere, and perhaps we would still be hearing the disturbing hum of the defunct woolen mills up the road, at Quechee.

Those mills, which operated in the 1930s, have given way now to town houses and condominiums erected by the Quechee Lakes Corporation. You can play polo or ride hot-air balloons there, if you like, and then retreat to Rockefeller's exquisite Woodstock Inn. Altogether a wonderful place, if you can afford it, to lower your blood pressure in a dream of an earlier America that never exactly was. Woodstock is Disneyland's Main Street with the National Commission for Historic Preservation seal of approval.

The hardest thing to do in Woodstock is to find a gas station. Perhaps it was hidden in a restored livery stable, but rather than empty my tank searching back and forth along the road, I took off east, figuring I could make it to White River Junction. Up the road I went, flooring it and then coasting whenever I could, scrutinized critically by the crisp new town houses up along the ridge.

———

Born here on an isolated farm, Joseph Smith spent the first 10 years of his life in these hills. It was as a farmer boy of 14 that he had his first visitation while wandering in the forest near Palmyra, New York. From there he moved to the Middle West, and, in Nauvoo, Illinois, founded the Mormon Church. More than any other Vermonter, Joseph Smith spread far-reaching influences, whose impact affected the lives of many thousands.
—Vermont: A Guide to the Green Mountain State

I MADE one more stop on the way to Barre. Up a steep road near Sharon, Vermont, surrounded by aspens and birch and smooth lawns, stands the tallest cut piece of Barre granite ever erected, an obelisk almost forty feet high. This monument was erected in honor of Joseph Smith, the founder of the Mormon Church, who was born in Sharon in 1805. That may surprise even a few Mormons. Brigham Young, who succeeded Smith as head of the church, was also born in Vermont.

Smith got out when he was ten years old, and the Angel Moroni chose to visit him in New York rather than his state of birth, so it is understandable that Vermont does not loom large in Mormon lore. Nor does it attract latter-day Mormons: There are only twenty-five hundred of them living in the state, and the monument gets only about twenty thousand visitors a year. A kindly white-haired caretaker, Dick Mendenhall, himself a refugee from Utah, let me into the visitor's center, where I stood before a diorama showing Smith—who looks a little like comedian Martin Short—writing at a table. A voice, Smith's voice, told me about his first religious vision, while airport music played in the background.

Then I walked up some steps behind the visitors' center to the monument. I had been preparing for my visit to Barre by reading up on granite, and because of that, I knew to appreciate its hardness, its exceptional durability, its resistance to streaking or discoloring, and the enormous work that goes into cutting it.

A single piece this big is highly unusual, an accomplishment of great magnitude. But if you didn't know that—if you just looked at it as a piece of rock, smooth and straight and pale gray, stuck on a little base ringed by flowers and hedge—well . . . you might not be all that impressed. Granite is an igneous rock, a mix of quartz, mica, feldspar, and other minerals stirred together in a molten stew. Granites can come in rich blacks and gentle pinks, but Barre granite is a quiet bluish gray, and if you aren't schooled in its advantages (hardness and consistency), you would see merely a dull, grainy rock.

The Smith monument has little color, no moving parts, and no ornamentation at all. I stood before it in the rain, trying to appreciate its excellence, but wrestling within against treasonous thoughts about the more seductive softness of marble statuary. The love of granite is not an easy thing, as my later investigations would confirm.

There is no room here for extended discussion of Mormonism, the Angel Moroni's tendency to repeat himself, a significant but tongue-twisting stone named Thummim, or the delightful parody of the King James style in the Book of Mormon. Just a final word about the obelisk: While in jail in Carthage, Illinois, on what his church now sedately calls "false charges," Joseph Smith was taken by a mob and either shot or hanged. He was thirty-eight years old. And that's why the monument is 38½ feet high.

Barre lies in the depression formed by two branches of the Winooski River, the Jail and the Stevens. Above the town to the south rise Cobble and Millstone hills, the two massive granite humps which have given the town life for 170 years. Cobble is a desiccated rubble heap now, its many small quarries converted to large tubs of water. The only major quarrying operations today are on Millstone Hill to the west. There is a wide interstate, U.S. 89, that comes north from the New Hampshire border and swings near Barre, but I took a prettier, less traveled route along the Second Branch of the White River, on Highway 14. Small, neat farms dot this valley, which is steep and forested toward the north end, and then you climb out of it to the small town of Williamstown, just shy of Barre, which might be called Typical Vermont,

The Wells-Lamson granite quarry, near Barre, Vermont.
Jack Delano.

with its green hills, deep-porched clapboard houses, and steepled church.

I cut east and pulled in at the Rock of Ages granite quarry. It is the largest granite quarry in the world, and a look over the edge sets the blood churning, and immediately erases the pastoral image of the Second Branch Valley only minutes before. Approaching the quarry, I first noticed the bare knobs of grout, little hills of discarded rubble pulled out of the granite quarries, the older grout stubbled with trees. Then I saw the huge fir arms of the quarry derricks sticking meanly up into the gray sky—big beams that lean out high above the quarries and lift up forty-ton slabs of rock. I pulled up next to the quarry amidst huge akimbo chunks of granite, discards set out by the road in case a passerby wants to buy a five-ton piece of rock. It was like entering an ancient Greek city after a bombing.

None of these sights was as affecting as my first look down into the quarry. The rim was fenced off, but there was an access point where you could walk out on a promontory and look in. I am both thrilled and wobbly-legged when I arrive on a mountain peak, and it happened to me here, too. The vertical faces of the quarry hole were bearded with ice, and way down near the bottom I could see ants—a few men, moving about in the ferociously cold depths of the pit.

The chiseled sides of the quarry drop more than three hundred feet almost straight down, broken up by narrow horizontal ledges that mark the seats from which granite slabs three times the height of a man have been removed. The visual effect of these ledge seams is like the lapped scales on a reptile's back. Snow clung to the ledges and the rungs of long ladders that spidered their way up from the bottom of the pit, from ledge to ledge. The granite faces were stained with dark water streaks and hung with ice falls.

Cantilevered shacks suspended above the pit housed the

hoist engineers who raise the granite slabs on cables suspended from the huge Blonden derricks. Like giant mantises,
the arms of these derricks rise above the pits and hang there
silently, waiting to lift or swing the granite. The guy wires
that keep the cranes in balance run every which way above
the pits. Even as I watched, a derrick was dropping down
a cable with a bucketlike structure attached to it.

The ladders rose along the sides, seemingly unanchored,
patching a haphazard route from the bottom of the pit to the
crest, precariously footed on the icy ledges and sagging against
the granite walls. It was easy to imagine myself frozen halfway up one, swaying dizzily, hands locked on a rung.

This time of year the quarrymen rarely work. From Janu-
ary until March there is very little production; it's too cold.
In the spring the pumps chug nonstop to drain accumulated
rain and springwater from the quarry.

Rock of Ages now dominates the quarrying end of the
granite industry in Barre, producing about eight hundred
thousand cubic feet of granite a year from several quarries.
The company, which was recently bought by a New Hampshire family, is expanding its quarry operations on Millstone
Hill, but locals live in fear that Rock of Ages will be shut
down by cheaper granite from Georgia or Canada.

The bucket began rising from the depths of the pit, with
a couple of men in it, talking and gesturing. The derrick
swung them around, away from me. One of them appeared
to wave. They looked so minute and adventurous, and I made
a mental note that I'd like to try it sometime.

———

*Main Street, an extremely long thoroughfare, is paved with granite
blocks and lined on either side with close-set places of business,
dingy buildings masked by colored fronts, gilt signs,
and show-windows. To enter this long narrow stretch from the open*

*countryside is to come suddenly upon a virile little city transplanted
from some busier section to the heart of rural Vermont.*
—Vermont: A Guide to the Green Mountain State

COMING into Barre is nothing like visiting Woodstock. Where
Woodstock looks as if every component down to the waste
receptacles were carefully chosen to match the town's appointed
historical mise-en-scène, Barre looks as if the parts of several
unsuccessful cities were dumped off the granite hills into the
valley and left to lie where they landed.

I came off Millstone Hill on twisty, narrow roads, passing
through the small satellite towns where quarry workers used
to live, before the automobile. One of them, Graniteville,
forms a small colony of white cottages sharing a common
foundation, neat as a military camp. It appeared that someone had recently painted and repaired them.

In a West Virginia coal town this would be the place the
rich man builds his house—at an elevation appropriately
superior to the town, and providing a panoramic view. But
living on the top of the hill in this part of Vermont means
you're up among the old quarries and grout heaps. I didn't
find them bothersome. Conifers like white pine grow in the
acidic granite soil, and most of the old quarries are wreathed
in trees and filled with water, making them attractive swimming holes. Perhaps not in March, though.

The granite industry on Cobble and Millstone hills really
came to life in the 1880s, when over a decade the population
of Barre grew from 2,060 to 6,812, mostly Scots and Italians
and Spaniards bringing stonecutting skills from Europe. A
track was installed to carry by train the big stone slabs from
the quarries down to the stonecutting sheds in town, and on
weekends it became something of a party car, loaded with
workers from these little settlements heading down the hill
for some high living in Barre. Barre was indeed quite lively:

there was a racetrack where the high school stands today, grappa flowed from the many stills in the Italian section on the north end of town, and there was an opera house, well attended.

Roadside artifacts today couldn't tell me all that. But the community still flows along the same lines: The broken rock on the top of the hill gives way, as you descend, to first residential, then commercial buildings, and finally, at the center of town, a long main street backed up against the stonecutting sheds—the heart, then and now, of Barre's economy.

Poorly planned and pretty shabby-looking it was, and in the early evening the traffic crawled along and often stopped on Main Street. On the valley floor, South Main Street jogs left through a bottlenecked intersection in front of the granite-faced Aldrich Library, and then you are, for all purposes, downtown. Main Street was long and narrow; there were drugstores, clothing shops, office supply stores, of the usual nondescript sort, strung out on one long street ahead of me. Trucks crowded their way into the narrow street, and traffic was further slowed by the crosswalks, which were abundant.

The City of Barre is encircled by the Town of Barre, and just a few miles up the road is the state capital, Montpelier, which is very small for a state capital, with only about eighty-three hundred residents. I drove all the way through Barre on its Main Street, and toward the north end the road widened and the shops congealed into shopping centers. Once I was out on the Barre–Montpelier road the traffic moved at what I'm inclined to call a more contemporary speed, past a Howard Johnson's and a Wendy's and the kinds of businesses, like car lots, which most comfortably fit the format of the strip.

When I was close enough to see the broader avenues of downtown Montpelier, I turned around and returned to Barre.

There I turned east off Main Street—to the west was the river and the stonecutting sheds, which would be closed now—searching for a speedier way across town. I did move faster, but I found myself going up and down and all around. Barre, because of its hills and the river and the frantic pace of its early growth, is not laid out on a grid.

Eventually I made it to the south end of town, where the pinch of hills widens briefly and there is a flat area, centered on a park populated with dying elms. The houses in this part of town were mostly large but tired-looking Victorians, many of them broken up into apartments, painted in pale colors, similar to each other. I pulled up before the exception: an enormous, rambling old Queen Anne with an entry vestibule and a long side porch, painted a foggy blue with white and red trim. That would have been my description. Bob Somaini, the owner, describes his 1883 house as having vanilla trim and cranberry shutters.

If the exterior of the Somaini house seemed to raise its voice a tad above the whisper of its pale, quiet neighborhood, the inside of the home babbled loudly with a thousand tongues. The first room I entered, a small sitting room, was crammed with a round marble table, a Glenwood stove, mahogany chairs, a blanket chest, antique pictures and an old snowshoe on the walls, and three hanging ferns with fronds that sagged from their containers like dreadlocks. There were three floors in the house, and each was as busy as the first with antiques and "collectibles" of every stripe.

I call it Bob's house, though he shared it with his wife, Terry, and their daughter, Katie. A large man with a mop of dark brown hair, he was the domestic center here, buying and restoring the furniture, cooking, and doing most of the worrying. The world outside was a large attic to him—he entered it in search of old photographs, chairs, and such—but it made him nervous. He liked staying home.

The Somainis were very active in the Assembly of God Church—Katie went to a church school—and a missionary about to depart for South America was visiting upstairs, so Bob, talking all the time, put me in a room where the plaster wall had been freshly stripped, hoping I didn't mind, and never pausing to find out if I did.

———

"Before tailors, before tentmakers, there were granite cutters. I know it's a shame to have machinery displace so many men engaged in this ancient industry, but machines work fast and cheap, and we have to fill the demand."
—Interview with Birnie Bruce of the Granite Association,
1940 (Federal Writers' Project)

IT was a short walk along elm-lined streets from the Somainis' house to an odd intersection where South Main jogs left and becomes North Main. Here, forming a triangle, were three excellent vantages on the stonecutting world that had defined Barre. One corner of the triangle was the Barre Granite Association's offices, another the eighty-year-old Aldrich Library, and the third a granite statue of the Scottish poet Robert Burns.

A library is a sensible starting point when you know nobody in a town. Pat Belding, a librarian and writer who often collaborates with her photographer husband, understood intuitively what I was after, and gave me directions. She introduced me to a collection of taped oral histories stored upstairs at the library and began bringing by interesting people to chat with me. Later she would lend me her husband.

This was wonderful, but I began to feel, sitting at a long table upstairs, listening to tapes and receiving interviewees, like a self-appointed auditor going through some company's books. So I slipped out one afternoon, and crossed the little triangular park that sits across from the library under the watchful gaze of Robert Burns. "Robbie," evidently a favorite of many Scottish stonecutters of Barre's early days, was erected on the hill by the old high school to the south in 1890. The statue was actually carved by two Italians.

Across the park, I entered the offices of the Barre Granite Association to chat with Milton V. Lyndes, the association's longtime executive vice-president. Lyndes's association is primarily made up of granite "manufacturers"—the companies which take the quarried granite chunks and cut them, carve them, and polish them. Primarily, these companies produce gravestones, but they also tackle projects like the Vietnam Veterans Memorial, the black granite panels of which were fabricated here.

Lyndes is a Vermont native who moved to Barre after starting a public relations career in New York. He wanted to raise his children away from the big city. He looks about sixty, with a strong jaw, a crease down the middle of his forehead, and, atop the crease, a small tuft of hair.

The granite industry is still central to Barre's economy, said Lyndes, but it is no longer the dominant employer it once was. Machinery has replaced some jobs, and competing granite-producing areas, particularly Alberton, Georgia, have cut into Barre production. There are about fifteen hundred jobs in Barre's granite industry, said Lyndes, and another five hundred in dependent industries, like trucking.

Georgia granite is "inferior," according to Lyndes and everyone else in Barre, but it's cheaper to quarry. The climate there is gentler, cutting utility costs, and "right-to-work" laws allow nonunion workers. The European immigrants who populated Barre's granite sheds in the 1880s brought union fervor with them, and the unions still dominate the industry.

What Barre has going for it is good management, excellent workers, and the best carvers and sculptors ("there's a difference") in the country.

No one with any memory is going to knock the unions in Barre; it was the unions, in the 1930s, that forced the companies to install dust reduction equipment in the sheds. This came too late for many of the great immigrant sculptors who came to Barre early in the century. In Europe they had chiseled stone by hand, but in Barre they were handed revolutionary pneumatic tools. Pneumatic tools made carving faster and allowed bigger projects, but they raised a dust so fine that "on a sunny day you could not see fifteen feet in a granite shed," according to Achilles Belucci, whose father was a stonecutter. I met Belucci at the library. "It would be solid dust," he said, "and these guys worked in there ten to fifteen hours a day."

As a result, many of them were dead of lung diseases by the time they were forty. They had provided well for their families, imbibed the opportunity and newness of America, and, coughing and hoarse, warned their children not to follow them into the stone sheds. The stonecutters' union built a sanatorium where the victims of silicosis could die with dignity, and Bob Somaini remembered visiting there. "As a little kid, that word, 'sanatorium,' had a kind of death aura to it," said Somaini. "A man went there, and he died." Somaini's father, who began polishing stone in the sheds after lifesaving suction devices were installed, is healthy and still at work forty years later.

Those who could afford it sent their children off for a better education. If they became doctors or lawyers, they rarely came back. The ones who did were usually members of families that owned a granite manufacturing shed, so they came back not as wage earners but as managers. According to Lyndes, ownership in the sheds has changed little in the last fifty years.

What has changed is that you can no longer get into the business. In the 1930s a family that collected a good stone-cutting wage, and perhaps sold home-brew grappa on the side, could scrape together the money to start a shed of its own, and often did. Today too much capital is required. Similarly, few new Barre granite quarries are opening; it's just too expensive to remove the overburden, whereas in Georgia it's relatively easy.

Lyndes emphasized that Barre is not your typical Yankee town. "It's a friendly place, but it's quite argumentative, which has to do with the heritage of the people," he said. "This is a melting pot society here, and people are not stay-at-homes."

Since Lyndes originally moved here because he thought it would be a good place for his children, does he expect them to stay? "I've encouraged them all to leave. For two reasons. Living in different parts of the world is an enriching experience, and I want my children to do that. And in their chosen fields, they'll have more opportunity outside Barre. There's not much here. But I'd hope they'd move back here someday. Presuming I'm still around."

———

. . . it takes an hour to saw four inches into a granite block.
Steams of chilled shot are fed under the notched blades, and a
constant flow of water is required to prevent both the shot and the
saw from melting in the intense heat of friction. . . .
—*Vermont: A Guide to the Green Mountain State*

ONE of Lyndes's cohorts, Bob Stuart, manager of member services for the granite association, took me on a tour of some manufacturing plants. It was immediately obvious why this is now an expensive business to get into: Your equipment, which now includes such marvels as diamond teeth saws, costs plenty, and you have to upgrade frequently to keep pace with improving technology.

Still, I could see something of what it must have been like in the old days at the Grearson Brothers plant, a business that dates back to 1894. The dust no longer hung in the air, thanks to suction machines, but the long frame building, lit partly by clerestory windows, was still organized the way it was in the beginning, with stone moving at a pace determined by workers, not machines. Granite chunks were moved with a traveling crane and blocks, starting at the south end, where a wire saw cut the rough dimension of a piece. I watched what I think was a miniature Roman Doric column in the making. After the saw made the first cut, stonecutters hand chiseled the rough edges off to create an "approximate" cylinder. The stone was mounted on a lathe, where steel disks smoothed it as it turned. Abrasives and successively fine grades of steel shot finished the job. Capitals would be carved elsewhere.

At the other end of the spectrum was the Anderson-Friberg plant, a state-of-the-art operation which smelled like a dentist's office. There production began with a full-size detail of the design, created in a roomy drafting department. In a huge workroom, chunks of granite were lifted by crane and moved about on roller conveyors from station to station in a kind of assembly-line process. Big saws with hard diamond teeth were programmed to cut speedily the exact size of slab needed, and contour planers with silicon carbide grinding wheels shaped the stone further. Stones disappeared into polishing machines that looked like large airport metal detectors, where they were worked over with steel shot and a variety of abrasives, and given a final buff with tin oxide. A carver would use a sandblaster to cut out letters, and a sculptor would produce the fine work, using a pneumatic hammer with a carbide chisel.

Sculptors often take work space in a manufacturing plant— called "banker's space"—in exchange for being available when the plant owner needs some carving done. They work for the manufacturer, but they also pursue their own projects. Those who consider themselves sculptors are sometimes derisive about the cemetery monuments that put bread on the table, and eager to show a visitor their more challenging work.

——

"Our shed is pretty cold and damp in the wintertime. The floor is dirt and the wind blows through the walls. I've got a hernia that bothers me bad sometime. If it wasn't for my family I might start hitting the bottle like some of the boys do, and letting everything slide. But they keep me going all right, and I'll work as long as I can. I don't want my boy to have to work like this all his life."
—Interview, 1940, Federal Writers' Project Collection,
Manuscript Division, Library of Congress

AT ONE of the manufacturing plants a short, dark fellow wearing a hat made of newspaper put down his tools and came over to us. His hat was the folded pyramid type that children make, and it was stained with sweat. I could read the logo: *"Corriere della Sera."* His hand, when he shook mine, and his red-checked sleeve were lightly coated with whitish dust, and when he looked at me, he uttered a short, grunting laugh. This was Alcide Fantoni, a sculptor who came to Barre from Carrara, Italy, and I had heard of him.

O'G: How long have you been in Barre?
FANTONI: I came in 1966. . . . When I was in Italy, I had been kind of scared to come over, because I know you don't

go to some other country unless you are good. Not to brag. First thing I do when I come over: I go to the cemetery and see what kind of work they're doing. I say, if you can do something like this, you can stay, otherwise you better go back. And I say: I think so.

O'G: But why do the good sculptors still have to come from Carrara? Why aren't they trained here?

FANTONI: Okay. The idea is this. Here, you start late. Like my son is getting too old. He's sixteen.

STUART: You gotta start about twelve.

FANTONI: What I would suggest to these people is this. They have art in school, right? Instead of making, like, cutting paper dolls, why don't you take some of these kids that are interested in art and given them credit for what they do, send them to the shed directly? Give them contact with the real art.

STUART: And the real world.

O'G: Because that's the only way they'll make a living.

FANTONI: Sometimes you get people that are very educated. They know everything by the book. They come to touch the stone, and they are lost.

O'G: How about someone like your son? Is he likely to go to college?

FANTONI: He don't know.

O'G: I know you can't control these things.

FANTONI: Today isn't like years ago anymore that, hey, the father says you gotta come down to the shop and you gotta help, because if I feed you, I want something back. Today, when they are the age of eighteen, they say, "Oh, I go out on my own now. I go out and rent an apartment." You don't hear things like that in Europe. No way. "You are my son, you live in my house. You are a part of a family, I don't see any reason why you should go out."

O'G: Things have changed a lot. The Italian community here

isn't as close, from what I hear. Do they still make grappa, and wine?

STUART: Well, everybody used to sell wine.

FANTONI: Okay, but they weren't supposed to. You can make wine for yourself, but you can't sell it—

STUART (laughing): I know, sure, and they used to bring one hundred and fifty carloads of grapes in here—was that just to drink for yourself?

FANTONI: If you sell, you get in trouble, for selling wine; if you drink it, you get in trouble, because you get drunk.

STUART: He makes good wine, too.

FANTONI: I gotta bring another bottle for you. You gotta taste this new white wine.

STUART: Did you let it age this time?

FANTONI: Sure, yes.

STUART: The problem is he makes it, good wine, but he has to drink it before it ages.

There is in fact a Barre Stone Trade School, I learned later, which gives high school kids an opportunity to work in the granite industry while they're still in school.

———

"I worked {in Concord} until a letter came from a good friend of mine, working in Barre, telling of the coming of the Scottish cutters there; saying the stone was by way of being the best ever, and just the stone for a carver like myself to work on. Fine stone with a fine grain, hard but not brittle. So it was to Barre we came. . . ."
—Interview, 1940, Federal Writers' Project Collection,
Manuscript Division, Library of Congress

SERIOUS stonecutters refer somewhat derisively to what they call "Sacred Hearts" and "cemetery sculpture," but it's what they mostly do, and it feeds their families. In every shop I visited, Madonnas and Christs struck the same sorrowful poses on half-finished gravestones, and the interchangeable crosses, flowers, and hearts went on forever.

When the thing you're carving in granite is an unoriginal copy or cliché, you might call it a "Facowi." Frank Gaylord, one of the most renowned sculptors in Barre, was working on a "Facowi Columbus" the afternoon I dropped into his studio. The term "Facowi" popped up a few years ago, when work began on an Italian-American monument in Barre. The monument is a belated attempt, some would say, to equal the 1890 Robbie Burns statue over by the library.

"Facowi is a tribe of Indians out in the Phoenix area, I believe," said Gaylord. "Some Italians from around here visited there and heard the name Facowi, and they said, 'Jeez, there are Italian Indians out here.' Indians often go like this"— Gaylord shaded his eyes with a hand on his brow and peered into the distance—"and the Italian-American monument was a man wiping his brow. Well, it *looked* like an Indian, so they called it a 'Facowi.' Or maybe it looks like an immigrant just stepping ashore, saying, you know, 'Where the *Facowi!*' So that's our new word for cemetery sculpture, and our Columbus here is a Sacred Heart dressed up like a Columbus—a Facowi Columbus."

Though Gaylord could tell a funny story, he had a disheartened air about him, as if he were tired of refereeing his own talent, the bouts between real art and "Facowi" stuff. He is also a proud man, and in some ways a little of a showboat. Where Fantoni wore a crude newspaper hat, Gaylord is decked out in a beret as he burrs away at the stone. He is short and muscular—the men who work in granite have to be strong—and has a pendulous, pouting lower lip, which I imagine serves him well in the theatrical productions he performs in.

Clearly granite is a tough medium, and while not all these

men were artists, they had to be artisans. That perhaps contributed to the gulf many felt existed between Barre's sculptors and the gallery world of modern art. Gaylord ridiculed
influential art collectors like Nelson Rockefeller, and ironically applauded the "promotional job" that had been done for
a piece like Claes Oldenburg's five-story clothespin in Phila-
delphia. He wouldn't be above sewing the emperor some new
clothes himself, he said, and then he would "have a wonderful time, living in Florida."

But Gaylord is too dour for that kind of scam, and too
self-aware. "Here I am in Barre, Vermont, the remote northeast corner of the country, sparsely populated, trying to set
the world on fire, and feeling a little foolish."

He had no plans to leave. "I'm here because the stone is
here. I love the stone. Granite has its limitations—it's very
hard, it's gray and it has spots in it, and it doesn't reflect
light as well as marble—but you can use that to advantage.
Barre granite is a beautiful granite, but it's in all the cemeteries, and that cheapens it. It's like blue jays. *One* blue jay
is beautiful."

He invited me to come back on Friday, when the town's
young sculptors, many of whom apprenticed with Gaylord,
stopped by for beer after work. As I made my way out, he
kept stopping me to point out another project. One was a
relief of Shakespeare, holding a quill to a globe of the earth
held in his right hand. It was commissioned for the Old Globe
Theater in San Diego, and as I looked at it, Gaylord's deep
voice boomed behind me over the sound of the stonecutter
tools:

> When, in disgrace with fortune and men's eyes,
> I all alone beweep my outcast state
> And trouble deaf heaven with my bootless cries
> And look upon myself and curse my fate. . . .

"The story of Barre granite," {Mayor Duncan} mused.
"Which side is it you want, the proletarian or the bourgeois?
Yes, of course, you want both sides if you want the true picture."
—Interview, 1940, Federal Writers' Project Collection,
Manuscript Division, Library of Congress

THE Europeans who populated Barre around the turn of the century brought with them more than their skills working with stone: They brought the ethnic clannishness that ward politicians thrive on.

They also brought radical political ideas that were agitating Europe, and when they met in their clubs and at the Socialist Hall in Barre, they were as likely to talk about syndicalism as about women or grappa. In 1903 a meeting at the Socialist Hall got out of hand, and a sculptor named Eli Corti—he did the lettering on the Robbie Burns statue—was killed by a Socialist. "He got excited—and he shot," recounted an old-timer interviewed by the writers' project researchers in the 1930s. "Crazy for a minute and sorry all the time after."

The daughter of Garreto, the man who shot Corti, recently died, and there are residents of Barre living today who can remember going to the funerals of Nicola Sacco and Bartolemeo Vanzetti, anarchists who were executed for murder in the 1920s in South Braintree, Massachusetts. The debate over their role in the murder and robbery of a paymaster continues to this day. At the time immigrant Italians saw them as innocent victims of the Red Scare, and they wept and rioted after the funeral. A Socialist mayor was elected twice.

Things are considerably more peaceful in Barre politics today. The Socialist Hall is now used as a tomato packing shed; the ethnic clubs play bingo on weekends, and if you can mumble a little Italian or Spanish, you're in. The mayor's mother was Italian, and his father French-Canadian; the latter would have cost him votes fifty years ago, when the Canadians were ostracized as strikebreakers. He is a mild man in an argyle sweater vest, a far cry from the Socialists who held the post in the 1930s. He worries about the drain of industry and would like to see the City of Barre consolidate with the surrounding Town of Barre. I had heard City Council meetings could get pretty heated, but the night I attended it did little more than pass a resolution to prevent entertainers in the opera house from tap-dancing above city offices during working hours. The only fun was a man named Victor Masi, who kept throwing up his arms and saying the city had no money.

Masi, a large kettle of a man, was the city clerk and treasurer, but his bellowing voice had long been heard at meetings of the council, where he owned a seat from the Little Italy district until they put a limit on consecutive terms. He was a caricature of the owl-faced ethnic alderman, his eyes popping and his fleshy head jerking around. A self-confessed "man of the people," he was moved to tears by his own modesty. Homilies popped like straining buttons; he was a grammatical loose cannon.

His political career began in the Italian neighborhoods at the north end of town. His father was a stonecutter, and he described the man's work with a tremor in his voice: "If he made a face, the only thing it wouldn't do is speak; if he made a rose, the only thing it wouldn't do is smell." That was typical Masi. Like so many stonecutters, the senior Masi was dead before he was fifty.

The politicians all bemoan Barre's dependence on granite, but they have failed to lure much new industry. Some old stalwarts outside the granite field are losing ground, too:

Spriggs Electric went to Florida, and Bombardier has cut back its work force. "If the quarry closes, we have an empty hole here," said Masi, and he doesn't mean the quarry. Ironically, there is no open space within the city limits for industrial growth. And though the narrow, long Main Street looks

The Whitmore and Morse granite quarry
in East Barre, Vermont. *Jack Delano*.

busy now, there is talk of a shopping center on the road between Barre and Montpelier.

"Mark what I tell you," said Masi, who has never been wrong. "A shopping center in Berlin [halfway between Barre and Montpelier], and the people will be going up there. Somebody is going to suffer."

Masi has campaigned for tax cuts (successfully) and for improved water treatment (it failed by twenty votes; another Barre resident told me voters had to choose between a new water plant and a refurbished opera house, and chose the opera house). Perhaps because he championed the tax cuts, the City Council decided Masi's salary was an appropriate place to apply a knife to the city budget.

Masi claimed to hold no grudges. "You see, my success has been the workingman," he said. He gestured; he breathed heavily in my face. "I started on the ground, and I stayed there, no chip on my shoulder. These new guys, I tell them: 'What I forgot, you will never know.' But I'm not the type to knock them down."

ONE afternoon I took a walk around Hope Cemetery, up on a hill northeast of Barre. This is where Alcide Fontani came to size up the competition among carvers and sculptors in Barre, and it is a gallery of monumental sculture, visited by tourists and artisans alike.

Tombstones here come in many styles: There are the traditional "bleeding heart," Victorian sculpture, Art Deco, and the unclassifiable. I have no special knowledge of sculpture; when Frank Gaylord mockingly described an art patron who knew Claes Oldenburg but hadn't heard of Ivan Rostrovich, he knew from my hesitant laughter that he had to explain: Rostrovich ranks with Michelangelo and Rodin in Gaylord's pantheon of great sculptors.

Cemeteries have always caused me discomfort, not because I imagine ghosts or spells, but because I have never been able to walk through one without imagining the decay taking place under my feet. Under a glowering sky, I walked the loops of Hope Cemetery's roads amidst some of the most impressive memorial sculpture in the world, stepping over snowbanks, writing down names and dates. Occasionally, a car would hum by; the afternoon chill was not enough to discourage sightseers. Cameras clicked at the Catto Memorial, three very modern-looking pillars of light granite that bend together at the top like wilting asparagus spears. More common were the Marys and the Jesuses, the "bleeding hearts." Simpler tombstones often had a ribbon of roses or stand of calla lilies cut into the stone, and these, when you looked closely at the fine detail of leaf and petal, were clearly not hackwork. The granite lived up to its reputation for resisting weathering or blemishes; the carved oak leaves and flowing script on the grave of Assunta Di Bona (1882–1912) were as distinct as newer work.

Sometimes a family overreached in its effort to memorialize a relative, but purple poetry and crazy, cluttered carvings were the right medium, I thought, for this last stand against mortal decay. Paul Martel, who died in 1978, will be forever remembered because his family chose—who knows why?—to erect a granite cube, standing on its corner, as his memorial. Each face immortalizes a trait: There is a rose for "love," linked rings for "together," a "tree of life" with his children's names, and, delightfully, a briefcase for "salesman."

The most outlandish piece of granite memorial sculpture produced in Barre now sits in a New Jersey cemetery. It is a full-scale carving of a 1979 Mercedes-Benz four-door sedan, right down to the letters on the license plate and the tread of the tires. It weighs thirty-six tons, and sits behind the former owner's mausoleum. No one is going to steal the hubcaps off this one.

One of the most famous memorials in Hope Cemetery, and my favorite, is Elia Corti's, carved by his brother. I had begun to feel a certain affection for Corti, as I heard his story told again and again from various perspectives. The memorial has what they call a "shell rock" finish—the rock around the figure is rough and scalloped. Corti is carved in relief, seated with his hand on a broken pillar. Sculptors often say they enjoy feeling a piece "emerge" from the rock, paraphrasing Michelangelo, and an observer gets exactly that feeling looking at shell rock sculpture.

My biases played a role again: I often find standing sculpture pompous, and aggressive, and much prefer seated, reflective figures, such as the Lincoln Memorial, or the John Marshall statue at the U.S. Capitol. The life-size Corti sculpture impresses many for the exactness of the folds in Corti's coat, his shoe buttons, and other such details, but what I liked best was the posture of Corti. He sits, leaning his elbow on his knee, slightly bent forward, with his hand on his chin, and his tools at his feet. His gaze is level, not over our heads at some noble abstraction.

The Corti figure seemed all the more attractive to me because behind it, rising out of the snow, stood a very different kind of tribute to the dead. A smooth phallic pillar soared upward maybe thirty feet, with an ornate frieze atop the pillar, and then, riding an abacus, an urn that seemed to demand worship. My eyes kept coming back to Corti, and each time he seemed a warmer presence. His name is cut at a slant into the rough rock behind him, and even the choice of lettering, simple and uneven, was moving.

It's impossible to divine the true nature of a man eighty years dead, especially when neither he nor his relatives wrote

memoirs. But the writers' project interviewers left us a por-
trait of Corti in the form of an interview with an "old Italian"
on a park bench in City Hall Park.

"Corti I knew well. We were friends. He came in my store
a lot. Quiet, he was. Just a small, thin fellow. People talk
more about him now than when he was alive. Lots of times
they do that way with a man." This impression harmonized
with the Hope Cemetery sculpture, so I read on.

Garetto, the man who shot Corti, was a high-spirited and
generally happy fellow, but like the politics of many immigrants, his were passionate. The publisher of a socialist newspaper in New York, known for his criticism of anarchists,
was late arriving for a speech in Barre one night in 1903. The
anarchists and socialists began yelling at each other. Corti
was just standing by the door, staying out of it. Garetto
pulled his gun and fired two shots, and Corti was hit in the
stomach. He lived long enough to name his assailant.

The "old Italian" was interviewed by someone named John
Lynch, and the interview was "edited" by Mari Tomasi
and Roaldus Richmond, who were known to do a little creative doctoring of these oral histories. Whether it is an accurate rendering or not, the old Italian's tale has a nice
ending.

"All the day before Christmas that year after Corti was
shot, I worked in my store. That night we heard that Garetto
was sentenced. I left the store just before midnight. I was
going to a party at a friend's house. I walked up that street
you see goes by the Burns Memorial on the left. It was snow-
ing and not many people were out on the street. When I got
close to the statue [of Robbie Burns] I saw a man there. It
was Corti, plain as day I saw him. Just standing there, his
head down a little, and looking at those panels he carved.
Sad, he looked, standing there in the snow. It seemed natural

he was there. I had been thinking all day about him in the store."

Corti was thirty-four when he died.

———

"It's so like France," {said a Frenchwoman visiting Vermont}.
. . . "That is, like the French people {Vermonters} instinctively
and invariably think of the individual in the frame of his family,
not isolated from his past."
—Vermont: A Guide to the Green Mountain State

I WAS exhausted that evening, but Bob Somaini was cooking a big Italian dinner. His kitchen is narrow, and Bob is wide, so nobody could squeeze in to give him a hand, and he happily worked up a sweat over the steaming stove, creating a pasta dish. As we ate, and ate, he began talking, and because he kept talking, I kept eating until I was ready to burst.

The ethnic groups that came over at the turn of the century stayed separate and clannish, partly because they often had no common language. Somaini's grandfather—his *nonno*—spoke almost no English. When the grandchildren visited his north side home, "He was a scary person—bald. He would sit on the opposite side of a porcelain table in the kitchen—all the Italian families had a table like that, I don't know why—and pat his cheek. And he would pinch us.

"My father moved to a house across the street, and the first house *we* bought was there. You could have thrown a stone and hit any one of them."

On Somaini's mother's side, his Irish grandfather drove wagons for a lumber business, and always carried a knife or a gun to be ready for the Italian "mob." His Scottish wife—they met at a dance at the Socialist Hall—was by reputation "a little hell" when she was young, though Bob remembers her as a sweet grandmother.

But the next generation mixed with the other groups in school and in the sheds, and shared a language, English. It became possible, if still a little venturesome, for an Italian man to marry an Irish woman. The child of such a union saw the similarities, not the differences. "On both sides of the family, food was so important," remembers Bob.

The Italian side seemed to hold more memories. "In Little Italy I could go up and down all of those streets and tell you everybody that lived in those houses, and had lived in them for years," said Bob. So that night we got in the car and went for a drive. We drove through his old neighborhood, and there was *nonno*'s house, looking sturdy and well kept to me, smaller and run-down to Bob. The patch in front where the garden had been was now well-trod lawn; you simply did not cross a neighbor's "sacred garden" in the old days.

East and below this row of houses there once was another row, but now there's a big highway there, beyond which stand the granite sheds, some fragments of residential blocks, and a high rise.

The north side had always been broken up by two sets of railroad tracks, which brought granite to and from the sheds. The tracks, though, did not really fence off neighborhoods, being so integral to the livelihoods and lives of people there. A row of houses even stood between them, on Railroad Street, where Bob's father was born.

The multilane highway that runs through here now, and helps travelers from the interstate get around Barre's congested downtown, has been, to Bob's mind, an engine of destruction to the old community. Looking beyond the zipping headlights of the highway, he pointed to a high-rise apartment building on the other side. It provides low-cost housing for senior citizens, and it gave a lot of older north side folks the opportunity to sell out. Thus it played a role in robbing the north side of its old character, but even Bob would agree it was good to provide for the old folks—many of them former residents of *la strada delle vedove,* whose husbands had died young of silicosis.

That evening Bob could name very few people living in the houses in the north side. Many of them now are French-Canadians; the houses are inexpensive, and the residents are more transient.

We drove past the shady hulk of one of the last of the old granite sheds, down by the Stevens Branch, where the industry is still centered. Sheds used to be built in the shape of horseshoes, with a derrick in the center yard so granite slabs could be hoisted and moved around to different parts of the shed. The newer sheds are somewhat nondescript—long metal buildings, where the slabs are delivered by truck and rolled along conveyors.

We drove up Gospel Hill, Trow Hill, and Cobble Hill, and Bob never stopped talking, pointing out landmarks that were little more than shadows in the dark. He told a long story about making grappa with his father at the north side house.

"The houses down there were somewhat close together, and old Mr. Catto lived off at an angle up a little higher from our house. He had a garden that came down to the brook and then our property started; Mr. Catto said he owned the brook over to our side, and we said *we* owned the brook. After we'd made the grappa, Dad would take the pulp—peaches, plums, whatever—down to the brook and dump it. Talk about pollution. Old Man Catto came down when we were doing it, screaming in Italian. They'd certainly know when the Somainis were making hooch. Mr. Catto would be hollering, and all this stuff would come floating down in the brook."

When we got back to the house, I stumbled in and knocked

an antique ladder mirror awry. I was tired and felt feverish, and the hanging light fixture in my room, which had five light bulbs on curvy mounts, looked spectral. I stumbled to the bed, and when Bob asked through the door in his sing-song way if I'd like some more food, I pretended not to hear him.

ALL this talk about families! I went to bed under the big down comforter, and thoughts of my own came to me with fierce intensity. What usually gets left out of travel writing, in the glory of passing landscapes and faces, is the enormity of time alone a traveler must spend. There are books, and sometimes new friends; but there may only be one time in life when traveling alone comes naturally, and that is the brief interlude when you have shucked your parents' embraces and not yet done too much embracing of your own. When there are loved ones waiting for you somewhere, you feel deprived during the empty hours of traveling, and against all reason you may even pity yourself. My wife knew by now to expect a few plaintive phone calls from me when I was on the road, and with sensible calm she would urge me to get on with my journey so I would be home the sooner. The children listened attentively during phone calls to whatever I had to say, and when I would pause to give them a chance to beg me to come home, they would say, "Dad, are you going to bring me something?"

Throughout my life the best cure for loneliness has always been a tramp in the woods, a night under the stars, but here it was cold and muddy, and I had brought no equipment. So I read voraciously in the empty hours— -and there were many of them, even when I spent twelve hours a day interviewing people and exploring Barre.

In a dull objective way I understood my rationale for traveling. It was not to see some distant shrine or natural wonder. It was to change myself, or rather to find out some things I didn't yet know about myself, and might never discover if I didn't venture into the borderlands, where the senses are assaulted and something new is demanded. Many travelers go in search of antecedents—the tracks of a black sheep uncle or an obscure and antiquated architectural form. Even Aeneas, in his attempt to fulfill prophecy, was searching for his history . . . only it was history that hadn't happened yet.

It is a much commented-upon aspect of journeying that you begin coming home the moment you depart. The search for history is certainly that kind of journey, and it is hard to imagine any interesting writing about travels that is not cast out from and ever tugged back toward home. I felt that night as if my snooping into other people's homes had carried me so far from my own that I could not reach back when I needed to.

Bloated with rich food and tired from all the talk, I lay on my back and stared at the ceiling. The biley taste of old insecurities began to assail me. What reason at all did I have for being here?

The doubts of the moment gradually became the doubts of a lifetime, the little failures of nerve and imagination that can take place in a buffeted airplane or at a junior high dance, and live with you forever. The notebooks I had been keeping—I thumbed through them hurriedly from page to page—were little consolation: The words I wrote seemed not to fit together. There was no map to this project to set me right. It had no more shape than curiosity itself, which had led me this far and then turned on me with pitiless, devouring eyes.

Shadows from the ceiling light played on the remnant snow outside my window, overlain by the movement of a wispy

curtain. A smell flared in my head—the smell of a room
where I had spent a night, years ago, with snow outside the
window and the same play of light . . . one night, when I
was a small child in someone else's house, and I had wondered, as most children must at some moment: What if I
never get to go home again? That brought tears to the child
I was, and the tears brought a comforting thought: that for
every tug of loneliness I felt, my parents, my grandparents,
my family, even the house I missed were tugging back on
the other side. And when I stared then out the strange window at the snow, I imagined the shadowy patterns playing
there reflected great elastic bands of feeling stretched around
the world, between parents and children and all those who
mattered, and I slept. But recalling that moment more than
twenty-five years later, in Barre, I sensed, in an awful, worldly
way, that it was just a child's comforting fantasy.

I put my head back and stared at the ceiling and waited
for sleep. It would come, I knew, when the pressure of my
thoughts could grow no worse, with a feeling in my chest
like a twig breaking. Even sleep, though, was no refuge on
this night. There were dreams set in barren landscapes; twice
in dreams I would open the door of my car to find one of my
children curled in the back seat, forgotten there for who knows
how long, blank-eyed with deprivation, shallow-breathed. I
would jerk awake, and each time there was a moment when
I didn't know where I was, who I was, what time it was,
which way was up. Vertigo made me reach out and clutch at
the bed. Yet still it was not time to go home.

———

*. . . it is true that {Vermonters} in normal health can, by their
own efforts without cash, to some extent make their environment
and daily life more to their taste. . . . He is not, that is, no*

matter how poor, in the nightmare helplessness of the modern wage-earner, gripped fast (so we understand) in the rigid, impersonal framework of a society organized uniquely around money. . . .
—Vermont: A Guide to the Green Mountain State

IF my sense of humor had been in working order, I would have had a laugh on myself the next day, when I decided the cure for my discomfort was to go traveling—get away, that is, from Barre, which felt claustrophobic. I called a couple of people I had planned to meet that day and canceled appointments, then hopped in the car and headed north through Montpelier and west around the Northfield Mountains. I stopped in Montpelier only long enough to drink a cup of coffee over *The New York Times* and note that snow covered the Vermont Capitol steps (the legislature was out). Superficially, a least, Montpelier appears to be as different from Barre as everyone says it is, with its wide thoroughfares, people in suits and Gore-tex parkas, and traffic lights that chirp like birds when it's time for pedestrians to enter the crosswalk.

I drove around the ridge that separates Barre from the Mad River, and up State Highway 100 along the river. This valley felt several degrees warmer than the Barre side of the Northfields, and the highway, which runs the whole length of the state through some of its prettiest country, was busy but unhurried. Along the river, gentle, open foothills alternated with forestlands coming down off the mountains. Maybe fifty miles up the valley the river thins and one crosses a low pass and into the White River Valley, flowing south. This is the home of Mad River Canoes, a favorite place for paddling, cycling, skiing, and other healthy outdoor things. There are tasteful little shopping areas with rustic, undemonstrative signs, orbited by clusters of new-looking chalet-type homes. On this route you can see aplenty the new face of Vermont.

In the 1930s the little towns along here were lumber towns, and the town of Rochester, where I stopped for the night, had won some sort of "Model Town" prize, and was admired for its "industrial virility," according to the FWP guide, turning out bobbins, talc, grist, and dairy products, adjusting itself with alacrity to market demand. It's a smaller and quieter place today, to judge by the lack of shops, but it has a lot of handsome old trees and houses.

Valleys like this have grown in some. There are fewer working farms in the Northeast, and trees tend to move fast into fallow fields. In its early days of settlement three-quarters of Vermont was cleared and planted. Now that is the percentage covered with trees. If they're not cutting trees the way they used to, and not tilling the land, how do the people here make a living?

Certainly, the encroachment of wilderness has been a boon to other once-beleaguered species. Deer, beaver, bobcats, wolves—all were hunted to near extinction in the nineteenth and early twentieth centuries. Mountain lions and wolves never did recover—though there are rumors, as there seem to be in most places relapsing into wilderness, of cat cries in the Green Mountains today—but short hunting seasons and improving forage have made deer almost too populous today. The rural population, at least the folks who fence fields and kill predators, is declining here, just as it is in Kansas and West Virginia, and certain kinds of game are filling the void. I saw no deer, but I'm pretty sure I spotted a coyote crossing the road; coyotes are newcomers.

Diminishing light had begun to tighten the weave of dark evergreens on the hills when I arrived, tired from the fitful night before, on the doorstep of a bed and breakfast near Rochester. It was run by a couple who had tossed aside graduate degrees and gilt-edged résumés to retreat to the country. Now they mixed in occasional paid work with raising chickens and other subsistence activities. I stayed up late that night with David, drinking the strawberry wine he brewed in the cellar, reinvigorated by his enthusiasm. He had a curly beard and the kind of sputtering energy that you expect to exhaust itself suddenly and leave him snoring under the table, only it never did.

I asked David if he ever missed the joys of urban life, as I sometimes did. He answered that he enjoyed the adventure of a "getting by" patched together out of found materials. "In the city," said David, "you get in one freeway lane, and it becomes yours. You *make* it yours." He leaned forward, as he did whenever he made a point. "And all the people in the lane become your people. That's it for you."

That lane was his metaphor for specialists, people who filled a niche in some large economic machine. He himself had a specialist's degree, but he was a practicing jack-of-all-trades, and a pack rat, very like some of the old Yankees he has— let's make him a hermit crab, too—succeeded. "I could never tear anything down. No, when I need a space for something different, I just add on."

A friend of his dropped by and shared a drink. The friend was trying to get a small manufacturing operation going— another college grad exploring the lower echelons of economic development. He reminded me of friends in Wyoming, and I wondered, because of the way friends there had departed: Where would he be five years from now? Back in the city, or adding on a new room in rural Vermont?

I slept that night on an antique brass bed in a restored second-floor bedroom. David, at least, seemed to have found his place. You have to work hard for small wages, and then, because the wages are too small to redistribute, you work hard at fixing the house and keeping chickens and doing other such things to survive. He was outgoing and skillful enough to be useful to his neighbors here.

Perhaps this will be the new face of rural America: second homes and ski resorts and bicycle paths for the weekending urban wealthy, neat new bungalows for the army of "vigorous retired," and then shambly old homes repopulated by the poor who provide services. This last category includes many impressive résumés—aging hippies or latter-day dropouts. They get their start in the country with perhaps a small inheritance, or the savings of a few years in a high-salaried city job. That dwindles, and life narrows. Some see it coming, and flee back to that hyper, fragmented life with the good salary. Others take solace in becoming part of a "new economy" of barter, and dream of some sort of apocalypse that will leave them better prepared for survival than the rich second-homers down the road. Others just fade away, allowing their minds to atrophy and their bodies to bend under the real labor that their new caste requires.

THERE were five young men sitting in Frank Gaylord's studio when I arrived Friday night. Several had worked for Gaylord, and some still did. There were Eric Oberg, Stanislaw Lutostanski, Jerry Williams, John Hanna, and Hanna's brother.

We drank beer, and drank it fairly fast. My companions were still in their workclothes, and one said how good it felt, at the end of the week, to cut the dust that had been glomming in the throat. For me, it was a chance to stop thinking so hard; the tape recorder and the notebooks stayed out in the car.

Granite was hardly mentioned, though Gaylord did lead a little group exercise in academic bashing. As I recall, the subjects ranged from Arthurian legend, to yoga, to Rock Springs, Wyoming. At one point we got talking about snow leopards, and John Hanna's brother revealed that he was just back from a trip to Nepal. The brother was long-legged and had a dark mustache, and he smiled a lot. He had given up a career carving granite years ago, and now he seemed awfully free, ready to go anywhere, if, for instance, a snow leopard in the Bronx Zoo caught his fancy, or a guru in the Far East beckoned.

Whereas John Hanna seemed not to be free at all. Hanna had Gaylord's build, but more height—a little pudgy, but strong. He had a long, straight mouth and a very direct gaze. While his brother told adventure tales and Lutostanski told bad jokes that he translated in and out of Polish, Hanna sat hunched forward and smoked, watching people closely as they talked.

Finally I asked him about his life in Barre. He said, "I left for a while. I went back home to try some things. I left when I'd had enough; I'd been helping Frank out."

Hanna had been Gaylord's "bull," his number one assistant, helping Gaylord off and on for a decade. Gaylord designed pieces, and Hanna would execute. It was a grueling way of learning the trade from a master. But he seemed to have learned more than just Gaylord's skills; he had also taken on the older man's craving for serious art and recognition. Now, sitting with a bunch of young sculptors yukking it up, he was preoccupied and nervous, thinking of escape.

He had gone back to Wisconsin the year before, he said, to the town where he was born. He went back, he said, to try new materials and to see if he could get his serious work in the galleries. He went because his house in Barre had burned, and he sensed it was time to "test the dream."

"You see," he said, "Barre, it'll eat you up. The monument business is everything here. Granite is such a hard stone. You have to work so hard to get anything out of it, and then we make these." He gestured at some Sacred Heart work in

Gaylord's studio. "They say artists have to create pain in themselves to make themselves produce. We don't have to search out pain—not doing this work."

———

It is in the field of monumental stone . . . that Barre granite
excels, because of its beauty and flawless texture. The granite comes
in two principal shades, with many variations: the "light" is
nearly white, and the "dark" is a soft blue-gray that takes a high
polish. . . .
—Vermont: A Guide to the Green Mountain State

I STAYED on in Barre, hoping still to ride the bucket down into the pit of a granite quarry. The new owner at Rock of Ages, John Swenson, said no, it was too cold this time of year, and the risk was too great. He was a young man, but his family had been in the granite business since 1883. "People who are in this business," he said, "they never seem to get out of it. They try other parts of the field—they become brokers, or something else—but they stay in granite, some way."

Frustrated, I went for a walk with Jack Belding, up on the hill where the old quarries were. He explained that the air up on the hill stayed cool because of the air spaces in the cobble piles, which moderated temperatures generally; the leaves up here were the last to turn in the fall. We went for a walk around the old quarries on Cobble Hill. Belding used to work for the Vermont Fish and Wildlife Department, and one of his jobs was to explore these hills looking for signs of the gypsy moth, a deadly pest. It had been awhile since he'd hiked up here.

He took early retirement, and these days he is a professional photographer. In addition to his own work, he has been working to salvage some glass plate negatives of the granite trade at the turn of the century, the time of the big boom, which many consider the liveliest era of Barre's history. His years in this area seem to have spawned a special affection for the beauty of granite in the landscape. For instance, he likes to shoot in the spring, when ferns and shrubs and trees begin to leaf out, and he can catch the light greens against the gray mass of the grout piles.

He is not unappreciative of Vermont's fabled fall colors, either, but he sees them in a granite setting. As we sloshed over an edge of snow to the rim of a small quarry, now full of water and surrounded by forest, he said, "You can get nice shots here in the fall. You see the way the white birch, the paper birch hangs out over the quarry; you get a nice reflection, with blue sky, red leaves, and gray walls." It was from this quarry, he said, that quarriers took the slab that became the Robbie Burns statue.

The slushy roads we hiked looked as if they got little use anymore. Railroad tracks, too, have been buried or pulled up on the hill. But several of the quarry ponds were beautiful— "alpine lakes in a hardwood forest," said Belding, laughing—and a few had sandy strips at one end or the other. I mentioned what fun it must be for kids to come up here and swim, but he, like most other Barre people, didn't respond to that image. It happens, as evidenced by some old beer cans, but it is not a particularly innocent adventure.

We hiked through Websterville, once a stovepipe village, and worked our way over to the Wells-Lamson quarry. This quarry is so old that it has islandlike four-hundred-foot spires of granite rising from the center of the pit, holding old derricks that must have once stood on the edge. I could think of climbing friends who would love to work out on these—in warmer weather—and I confessed to Belding my interest in taking a ride down to the bottom of a big quarry. If it looked so spectacular from above, I said, it would be interesting to change perspective and look up at those sheer walls. And like a good acrophobic, I thought it would be a thrill to dangle in a little bucket over the big hole.

Belding laughed and said, "I'll show you some old pictures of guys climbing up and then swinging from cables hanging off the towers."

That night, with Pat Belding and Pace Nicolino, we looked through some of the old pictures.

Nicolino's father left Italy in 1910 to avoid the draft. He wanted no part of war, and hence his daughter's name; there was a brother named Ateo *("atheist"),* and Pace married a fellow named Libero, not just for the pleasure of being introduced as "Peace and Freedom." Houses were going up like crazy during her childhood. They tended to be alike, because of the hurry, and you can still see today the little adjunct room on the back of many—that was the outhouse. It sounded like an extraordinarily merry place, despite the hard work. There was a trotting track, and the opera house was packed. "My father would come home after all day in the shed, drop his clothes at the door, get dressed, and go to the opera." Kids would be sent down to the sheds to bring home their fathers on payday, to keep them from taking their paychecks to the booze places all over the north side.

But Pace's father was dead at fifty-five of lung disease; he died the year they installed the suction machines. And the dances at the Socialist Hall were often benefits for the widows or the sanatorium. So it wasn't all fun.

Pace and Pat began telling stories about Barre today—a quieter town, to be sure, but with its own merriment. They laughed about the increasing number of senior citizens and the commensurate hairdressers. And we talked about a couple of street people whom I had seen. The two women knew each one, and could tell a little about them, and it was clear that townfolk found ways to provide for them. They told stories about a transvestite who worked up at Rock of Ages and came to their poetry group, and how things came to a head when he began wearing see-through blouses to work. We laughed and laughed.

What I was thinking, as I left to return to the Somainis', was something Jack Belding had said as we stood on the hill looking down at Barre in twilight: "You can see it's not a very big town. The attitudes are still pretty small-townish."

In the best sense, yes.

I DROVE across town to the offices of Jones Brothers, which operates, rather faintly, the only ongoing quarry operation not controlled by Rock of Ages, Wells-Lamson.

Morris Kelley, a bald, birdlike little man of ninety, sat behind a big desk and shook his head no. I could not go down in the quarry, and I could not, for that matter, run that damned tape recorder in his office.

"I once had a salesman who kept begging me to let him go down, and I said no. But he kept on and on, and finally I gave in, and they put him in the cart, but they didn't get the chain all the way around." Kelley laughed. "So there he went, and he was just hanging on, shaking like a leaf, hoping it wouldn't fall open. Never asked again. But I can't let you go."

He wouldn't let me take notes either. He talked for an hour, about granite sculptors, about unions, about the industry, about playing golf in Arizona with a Wyoming sheepman I happened to know. He said the biggest problem in the industry was quality: "These buyers don't recognize the quality of our granite. You can take horseshit, freeze it, and they'll buy it today."

The granite under Barre runs ten miles down, and the deepest anyone has gone is about four hundred feet, at Kelley's quarry. The deeper you go, the more inward pressure on the rock, and the risk that pieces will "pop" inward. Nevertheless, there is a century's supply of accessible granite here.

I dropped by the shed where John Hanna was working, carving a Madonna on a large tombstone, leaning against his hand-held pneumatic drill. He smiled and greeted me, throwing back the plastic shield that protects his eyes. When he got off work, we went and had a beer.

The year in Wisconsin was not a failure, he said. He had just "ran aground on what hadn't changed." He had tested his illusions, and worked in other media, particularly mahogany, walnut, and oak. But he found the artists he knew there in his college days were still there, and struggling more than he was. Many had surrendered to academic careers, "trying to make points with the college, doing the same stuff they did ten years ago."

He sipped his beer. "I had to blow the dream image," he said. "Then, just as suddenly, I decided to come back."

He works for six or seven granite manufacturers, doing the bleeding hearts and Facowis, and he continues, at home, to produce art. He has some nerve problems developing in his hands that many granite sculptors ultimately develop after years of powerful vibrations, but he is financially more comfortable than he's ever been and he's learned how to disappear when he needs to.

"I've settled down in Barre, but it's not home. I've tried not to make too many friends. I probably don't have too many friends at all. I've shouldered some of Frank's negativity."

He came back for the granite. "When I first got to Barre, I was a punk. Then I found granite, and I found something that was tougher than I was, and I fell in love with granite. I like to see the form emerging, but it's the process of carving that got to me."

On my way out of town, I drove back down Main Street, and suffered again the hopelessly poky traffic. It was poky because, in this rough-and-tumble town, people stop when they see a pedestrian anywhere near a crosswalk. I could have taken the bypass, the one that knifes through the old Italian section and goes by the high rise full of senior citizens and up around Millstone Hill. But I didn't.

Point of Departure

New Orleans

"WILD and fast and hot with sin!" That's the grinning description of New Orleans in *Gumbo Ya-Ya,* a racy compendium of high life, lowlife, and other-life written by the Federal Writers' Project's Louisiana team. The phrase promises a kind of moral free zone for the likes of the conventioneering urologists who disembarked with me at the New Orleans airport late in the summer. Seekers of the foreign, we sniffed cautiously at the wet air as we stepped squinty-eyed out the glass doors at the airport. The Gulf Coast obliged with tangy, overcooked bayou smells and Cajun cadences, and if the Louisiana that greeted us seemed a little spruced up, even stylized, I enjoyed it anyway, and blamed the packaging on the frantic promotional efforts of state tourism officials.

The guidebooks turned out by the Louisiana Writers' Program were promotional, too, in the sense that they worked hard to pass along the special and peculiar qualities that make

Intersection in the Vieux Carré. *Marion Post Wolcott.*

the Gulf Coast different from any other region of the country. *Gumbo Ya-Ya,* despite that beckoning line, delivers something quite different from what conventioneers seek: swamp haunts and violence and witchcraft, the legends and dark magic found a few thin layers beneath the cosmopolitan surface. The Louisiana writers, led by the accomplished Lyle Saxon, pulled the layers back by incorporating the jazzy vernacular of the streets in their writing: "the pimps and the imps and the shrimps," "Higher than a cat's back," "Saute crapeau, to chieu va bruler!"

The urologists and I had timed our visit to coincide with the opening of the New Orleans World's Fair, an expensive attempt, in the words of the Louisiana governor, to "show the world what we've got." The busy bureaucrats whose jobs it is to diversify the state's energy-dependent economy see tourism as the next best thing to oil wells. They gave me a press pass so I could see what Governor Edwin Edwards had gotten for the state's $350 million investment in the fair.

On my first night in a cramped, low-ceilinged upstairs room near Tulane University, I opened a window to the smell of bougainvillaea and lay back with a map in hand. Breathing in the sweet sweat of the city, I planned my travels south, down the dangling sixty-mile peninsula that follows the Mississippi River from New Orleans out into the Gulf of Mexico. First, though, there was the famous city to see, the fair to enjoy, and some New Orleans people who knew the delta well to look up. Perhaps I would get lucky and stumble across a back street that was still wild and fast and hot with sin.

The next morning I rode a streetcar up the shady, humid streets, and because I was newly arrived in the South, race was particularly conspicuous, from rheumy-eyed blacks, to tan leather Creoles, to whites, mostly looking soggy and tired. I entered the fairgrounds beneath the buttocks of a plaster mermaid; higher overhead, shiny new gondolas bobbed above the river. Twenty-four hours from the fair's grand opening, there was an awful lot of scaffolding and wet paint still about. Promoters were panicky. They had begged a last-minute ten-million-dollar loan from the state, and had begun stressing the "residual" benefits of the fair, downplaying the importance of actually making money off gate receipts.

At a gala welcoming ceremony for the hordes of international press people, Peter Spurney, a veteran "event manager" who had masterminded the 1980 Winter Olympics at Lake Placid, dared to dream that this event would produce a major innovation like "the ice cream cone or pizza on a stick." Dozens of television crews were here to get the scoop, and, failing that, had taken to interviewing each other ("They don't have daiquiris in Japan, do they?").

The fair was packed up against the waterfront just east of the Greater New Orleans Bridge, below Magazine Street and only a short walk from Canal Street and the famous French Quarter. A map of it looked a little like a pig facing west: A long promenade ran along the sow's back, lined with a tangle of kitsch and refreshment stands called the "Wonderwall." In the pig's stomach were the Louisiana exhibits, and down below, like teats dangling at riverside, were international emporiums for countries like Egypt, the Philippines, Australia, and China. Atop the animal's head, scratched by Tchoupitoulas Street, were a jazz and gospel tent and an Italian village, and mounted on its back were more concessions and the Vatican Art Exhibit. The animal's rear end housed the petroleum industry exhibit, featuring the giant aquarium stocked with serene fish weaving amidst the pilings of an offshore oil rig.

In the 1930s the riverside here was lively in a different way, according to the writers' project's New Orleans city guide. Longshoremen shouldered banana bunches and carried them from the ships to the railroad cars; hogsheads of tobacco, raw food products, automobiles, and coffee added to the cacophony of commerce. "Old Negro women, fat and wearing snowy turbans on their heads, move about in the crowd selling sandwiches and sweet cakes." But the big boats have been gone for years, to ports upriver and elsewhere on the Gulf, and when the idea for the fair came along, it was seen as an opportunity to spiff up New Orleans's half-dead warehouses, railroad yards, and waterfront for the 1980s. After the fair, the development would be handed over to a company renowned for converting blighted waterfronts into a salad of toney boutiques and frappe vendors. The little gondolas that dangled over the river would eventually, a disingenuous guide told me, provide relief for traffic on the bridges and ferries that carry commuters back and forth across the river.

I had been reunioning with journalist friends over crawdads and beer for several hours before I heard someone mention that the theme of the fair was "The World of Rivers: Fresh Water as a Source of Life." It came as a surprise to most of us. The rivers theme had failed to get a mention from Spurney, Governor Edwards, Dick Cavett, or Al Hirt, though a few exhibitors were gamely trying to get in sync with the theme: The women's pavilion was called "Women in the Mainstream," and I was told one entered the Afro-American pavilion on a Disneyland-style slave ship, though it was not open yet. I wandered toward the big Mississippi, down where the pig's front foot would have been, in the shadow of the bridge, and there I found the exhibit of the U.S. Army Corps of Engineers, an agency that could really put its heart into a theme like "The World of Rivers."

The corps' exhibit was housed in a superannuated paddle wheel dredge boat, cramped quarters compared with, say, Chrysler's enormous pentagonal exhibit. It was a "dustpan" dredge, the kind that sticks its wedge nose into sandbars and sucks muck, then pipes it away. The *Kennedy* (named after an engineer) was built almost a hundred years ago, and used to work the Mark Twain stretch of river between Cairo, Illinois, and Hannibal, Missouri.

The corps simply lives to doctor rivers, doing everything from simple pulse taking to major bypass surgery. No other

exhibit was as apt for the fair's theme. But from the way the
corps' guides rushed toward me, it was clear they were not
getting many visitors.

With Janis Mosier, a corps public relations aide, I walked
up a canopied ramp to the boat, where the exhibit began with
a sculpted miniature of the Mississippi River Basin, followed
by a zippy cinematic trip down the river from its source in
Minnesota to the Gulf. A walk-through display explained
how the corps handled major Mississippi floods, routing the
excess water through the Old River "flood control structure"
near Baton Rouge into the Atchafalaya Basin, a more westerly
and direct route to the Gulf than the Mississippi normally
follows. This is in part to prevent another flood like the one
of 1927, which spewed water and mud over about twenty-six
thousand square miles of southern Louisiana, and killed
hundreds of people. The bypass to the Atchafalaya was still
under construction when the writers' project Louisiana guide
was published, but it got a mention as "an additional precau-
tionary measure." The corps now dumps about 30 percent of
the Mississippi's annual flow into the Atchafalaya, and the
rest of the river would apparently like to follow, having grown
weary, after about a thousand years, of its present course.
Corps officials minimize that danger—that the river would
completely reroute itself, leaving New Orleans high and dry—
but water experts elsewhere say the river very nearly did so
in 1973, when the Old River structure, damaged by an earlier barge accident, was tested to the limit by a major flood.

When I remembered how the Potomac River in West Virginia had jumped its old channel for a new route, the possi-
bility seemed real enough to me. The impact would be
enormous: river shipping traffic at a standstill; the delicate
Cajun swamp country swept clean by a deadly tide of river
water; the delta, the old Plaquemines Delta, sinking away
into the sea without the river mud to replenish it. In fact,

the Mississippi has several times changed its course in the eons before man's settlements lined its route.

Janis Mosier laughed nervously and confided that the subject had come up during briefings the corps held for the young student guides who would stand around pointing the way for fairgoers. Corps officials described for the kids the flood control system up near Baton Rouge, and discussed their efforts to shore up the structure, which was undercut by scouring during the 1973 flood. One of the student guides piped up with a question: If someone were to set off, say, a small bomb up there at the locks, what would happen?

There was a pause . . . perhaps while the officials envisioned two million cubic feet of water per second roaring down the Atchafalaya. Then the question was answered smoothly and reassuringly. But after the briefing was over, corps security men approached Mosier and the other briefers, asking for help in identifying the boy who asked the question.

I had a late lunch with an old New Orleans lawyer, whose name I feel obligated to withhold because he believed, despite my attempts to convince him otherwise, that he was dining with a young alumnus of the college he'd attended forty-five years before, and thus spoke with chummy freedom throughout the meal. We ate seafood in a crowded bar and restaurant in downtown New Orleans, a few blocks from his office. He drank iced tea while I ordered a beer, and when his glass shook as he lifted it, he looked down at his hand with contempt.

He was a shambly, cross man, skilled at storytelling and knowledgeable about the delta. He recalled the days in the 1940s when a group of Louisiana businessmen railroaded back and forth from the Plaquemines to New Orleans on weekends, towing an ice car with fans to blow the cool air forward; often, barrels of ducks and geese, provender from the almost limitless waterfowl populations down the delta, traveled on the same train. He remembered drinking orange wine with delta girls who had blue eyes and dark hair, and he rolled his eyes at the memory.

That was in the days when the wild country at the very end of the delta belonged to a wealthy Chicago grain merchant, Joe Leiter, whose guests rode the train from New Orleans to his mansion in the marshlands. Leiter, the story is told, later offered his place to the most powerful oil dealer on the delta, Judge Leander Perez, for three dollars an acre, and was refused. Now the U.S. Fish and Wildlife Service owns and protects the Delta Wildlife Refuge, and restricts hunting, shrimping, and fishing. As a U.S. attorney the lawyer fought successfully to keep drilling rigs out of the game refuge. Poachers, who aren't quite as conspicuous as oil rigs, are plentiful in the area, he said.

Then we talked about the Perez family. Of course, I knew the Perez family? An interesting bunch, said my lawyer friend, speaking in a voice loud enough to be heard several tables away. Had I met Lea Perez, one of the judge's sons? I said no, members of the Perez family would not talk to journalists. Now his tired, jumpy eyes came around sharply. "The Perez family *is* the Plaquemines Delta. You better know *those* sons of bitches."

I knew a little about Judge Perez and his sons, enough to measure my ignorance and keep quiet. The story of the delta since the 1930s was in large part the story of the Perez family's rise and fall. And this gray-haired lawyer with the deep lines in his face would know a great deal about them, because he had fought with a courageous team of federal attorneys and judges to tear down Louisiana's race restrictions in the 1960s. Judge Perez was a loud segregationist voice in that debate, and he did not restrict his opinions to the Plaquemines. Yet the man eating gumbo with me was praising the judge's son, Leander Perez, Jr., who had taken over the Perez machine after the judge's death. The younger Perez was a charming man, a man of good manners, he said, and that mattered. "The mark of a gentleman is not how well you get along with people you like," said this lawyer, looking above me. "It's how cordial you are with people you don't like. That's what keeps society going."

I asked him about the tumultuous 1960s. He told me that this period had cost him his marriage and many friends. "I've got a very short fuse, you see. This fella, this fella came up to me at a party and sassed me about the work I'd done, he kept asking me what the hell I was getting out of it, this desegregation work. Kept right after me, sayin' he knew *something* was in it for me, he was sure. Well, finally I turned on this man, got right up to his nose, and said loud as this, 'Yes, by God, the NAACP is going to make me an honorary nigger!' "

The lawyer laughed until his eyes watered. He rubbed them tiredly, and got to his feet. Outside, we said good-bye on a street corner, and he looked at me again, hard. "What do you think of it, really—do you think it ought to be?"

I didn't know what he was talking about. He had told me as we finished lunch that the answers no longer seemed to him so black and white, and it seemed to me that loyalty to southern brethren of his own race and class now burned brighter in him than his service in the desegregation movement. He looked at me closely, then turned, flapping one side of his sport coat to cool himself. "I just don't like it. I don't think they should let them in. I'm old-fashioned. Why would you change something that's been as good as it was? But I don't know what you younger folk think."

I said, "I don't know." Inside, I began to recoil.

"I guess I'm just against it," he said, and then uttered the name of his Virginia alma mater, which he presumed to be mine, too. "Why bring in the women, really?" The college was going coed, one of the last southern institutions to break that barrier. I started to answer, but he interrupted me to say good-bye, and hurried off with a worried look on his face, and I stood awhile on the corner, relieved but saddened. Relieved that this old man had not given up the convictions of his braver days; saddened that a man who had shown some courage and who had hung his career on a delicate web of alliances with other crusaders had not been taken care of. He would return to his small office and go back to work on divorces and property deals and whatever else walked through the door.

Only once during our lunch had I seen any light break through in his face—when he talked about life down on the delta. I walked over to the big river, just a couple of blocks from the restaurant. It swirled in a fat U around the heart of the city, a tawny surge sucking the senses out toward the warm and perilous Gulf.

That night I threw a small bag and a couple of guides in my rented car, and drove downtown, through the French Quarter, and then along the riverfront, where the world's fair was now in full swing. The fluttering inside which I had felt whenever I began another leg of my journeys began only now, as if the merchandised comforts of the fair had not been a part of the adventure at all. I headed for places where I would be unexpected, unprovided for, and perhaps unwelcome.

My first task was to find a way onto the Greater New Orleans Bridge, which passed a few hundred yards above me. I drove with the windows open, letting in the wet air and the street noise, punishing the car on the narrow, potholed streets—Arcade and Carondolet and Dorsiere—near the waterfront. The streets were crowded by sagging two-story houses and dingy neighborhood stores with wrought-iron bars on the windows. The value of this real estate, the fair's promoters had assured us, would skyrocket following the waterfront's rejuvenation.

Out of a small doorway in front of me reeled a stubble-faced man in a torn shirt and pants shiny black around the pockets and seat. A black kid ran up behind him and grabbed his shirttail, and the stubble-faced man spun wildly, cursing. He held a hunting knife, and his hair hung in a stringy mop on one side of his face. There were many people in the street, taunting him and throwing rocks from a safe distance. A bottle struck him on the shoulder, and he spun my way, forcing me to brake. He bounced off a parked car and fell on the curb, still shouting: "Chickenshit! C'mon! Chickenshit!" A rock brought him to his feet again. The hard faces around him were laughing now; blood from his shoulder began to soak through his shirt. He held the knife out in front of him and staggered on down the street, more dangerous to himself than anyone else. I saw a sign for the bridge, turned right, and was gone.

Destination

Plaquemines Delta

Among the earlier settlers of Mechanicsham was a justice of the peace who not only issued marriage licenses and performed marriage ceremonies by day, but cheerfully accommodated elopers, largely from New Orleans, at any hour of the night. As the years passed the name of the town gave way to "Gretna" after the famous Gretna Green, in Scotland, along the English border, for centuries a haven for runaway lovers.
—Louisiana: A Guide to the State

NEW ORLEANS has kept at least the facade of its old character—the tight streets of the French Quarter, the tree-shaded boulevards, the cramped neighborhoods scaled more to walking than driving—but its satellite towns, like Gretna, just across the river, and Algiers, have lost the sleepy riverside look of the 1930s. The dry docks and truck farms have gone. The runaway lovers must run somewhere else.

Louisiana, for all its uniqueness, has not eluded the New America of fast food, heavy traffic, and malls. I landed in the midst of it when I came off the bridge from New Orleans. The lumpen, disposable architecture that typifies our metropolitan fringes appeared randomly in Gretna, replicating amidst poorly signed, poorly maintained streets and unfinished overpasses. The result when we graft the automobile onto an older community landscape has never been pretty. Eventually I worked my way clear and found myself speeding down Highway 23 on the west side of the river, through the old plantation town of Belle Chasse—where you can open an account at the "Mississippi River Bank"—and on out toward the Plaquemines.

The geographical boot of Louisiana has an unstitched sole dangling into the Gulf, a long, pencil-thin peninsula called the Plaquemines, pronounced with three syllables, like "placable," which the residents generally are not. It holds together the last landlocked run of the Mississippi before the river hits the sea, and along the banks are small towns like Empire, Buras, Venice, and Pilottown. Here live, said the Louisiana guide, Yugoslav oystermen and voodoo practitioners and makers of orange wine. The Belle Chasse Highway would carry me away from New Orleans and its suburbs, and then I would drive south alongside the river until the roads simply stopped, in marsh or swamp or at the Gulf itself; after that, if I could find a boat, I would go farther.

Once I cleared Belle Chasse, I was suddenly free of the homogeneous commercial bric-a-brac. The road became an uncrowded four-lane highway, where my reveries were interrupted only by the occasional hoot from the river. I would look left and the bridge of a freighter would pass in disembodied majesty above the hump of the levee bank. The green, moist air smelled faintly of fruit and salt and rot. A young black couple in loose clothes walked by the road, going

Louisiana muskrat trapper. *Marion Post Wolcott.*

nowhere fast, striking the tall weeds with sticks.

The delta topography is horizontal; its "mountains" are the fifteen-foot levees that fend off the river on one side and the marshes on the other. Highway 23 is lower than the Mississippi's crest. The houses behind the levees are mostly raised on stilts, but the green strip in which they stood was well groomed and dry. To the west, over another levee, was a maze of bogs, soft grass flats, canals, and marshes of saw grass and wild cane, fading from fresh to brackish the farther you went. I drove along the top of this levee, and followed a little ridge road of broken shells that ran west to small groupings of stilt-borne cabins and docks. Where the salt is not too bad, cypress and oak trees grow, and down among the grasses and waterways, a vast assortment of birds and reptiles and furred animals call and slither and eat one another.

———

Extending from Magnolia to Venice, a distance of 37 miles, is the "Orange Belt." Here and there, especially beyond Buras, citrus groves line the roadway. Citrus-growing was begun here about 1750, but it was not until about 1917 that large-scale operations were undertaken; since then growth of the industry has been phenomenal. In the spring and early summer blossoming orchards perfume the atmosphere here for miles around, and in the late fall and early winter the trees are heavily laden with golden fruit.
—The New Orleans City Guide

THIS was busy and diverse country in the 1930s: The Freeport Sulphur Company was refining and shipping sulfur, orange orchards spread away from the road on both sides, there were wax myrtle bushes supplying a small candlemaking industry, and the oystermen and trappers were busy year-round. Nutria and muskrat and alligator were their prey.

Sulfur is still produced today—high white mounds sit waiting to be loaded on railroad cars at Port Sulphur—and the Dalmatians and Slavonians arrive from Yugoslavia, generation after generation, to tend family-held oyster leases. But the orange groves are mostly gone—victims not so much of the hurricanes, which have become more frequent, as of the freezes, which are alarmingly frequent. Germaine Curley, a fiftyish woman who serves on the Plaquemines Parish Council, remembered how surprised she was by her first hard freeze, when she was eighteen. "Now it's pretty regular," she said. "It's strange the way the weather has changed." Her parents kept orchards, sold groceries and furniture, and ran a marina.

Such an array of endeavors is not unusual in small and remote communities throughout the United States.

I drove all the way to the end of the blacktop, to the town of Venice, aptly named since it lies below sea level, seventy-three miles southeast from New Orleans. The delta continues beyond, but from here you can go only by boat. Venice today is a busy town, thanks to the enormous growth of the oil and gas industry offshore, though it suffers the vacillations of the world energy market. It is from Venice that the oil companies dispatch their boats and helicopters to service the stilt-mounted rigs that dot the rim of the continental shelf along the Gulf. Parking lots, jammed with the pickups and late-model cars of the rig workers, are everywhere.

It was getting late, so I backtracked north to Fort Jackson, which sits along the eastern levee between Empire and Boothville. Next to the fort is a small backwater off the river, shielded by half-submerged willows, where a few dilapidated houseboats and skiffs were tethered. The cone of a porch light on a houseboat inspired a dervish of damselflies and mosquitoes. Through the window I saw a squat, shirtless figure moving in the kitchen, and wanted to knock, but I couldn't think of a way to introduce myself.

I parked up on the levee, and then explored a high cement fortification that once seated cannon. The small cells within the structure smelled of urine, but on top of the fortification I was higher than the levee, looking out at the river. Mullet jumped in the shallows. Perhaps because it was summer, and the kids who might have parked among the tall, droopy trees behind me were out fishing and oystering and shrimping, there was no one around. I decided to sleep on the levee bank, where I could watch the red and green port and starboard lights of the passing boats, and listen to the lap of the big river beside me.

———

According to a picturesque account, {Alvarez de} Pineda in 1519
discovered the great river, to which he gave the name Rio del
Espiritu Santo. At its mouth he found a large town, and for a
distance of six leagues upstream counted forty villages inhabited by
giants and pigmies wearing ornaments of gold in their noses and
ears. All that was lacking in this beautiful and densely populated
El Dorado, where the rivers ran to the sea heavily laden with
gold, was the Fountain of Youth, for want of which, perhaps, the
Spaniards thought the country not worth conquering.
—New Orleans City Guide

FORT JACKSON is one of a pair of forts that face each other
across the wide river at a steep S-turn about twenty-five miles
from the Gulf. On the opposite bank is Fort St. Philip, on
the edge of Bayou Mardi Gras, the first spot in the Mississippi River Valley to get a non-Indian name. The bayou was
named by Pierre le Moyne, Sieur d'Iberville, who camped
there in 1699, inaugurating the French colonization of the
Mississippi River region. The fort played an important role
in the Battle of New Orleans, when it held the British fleet
at bay, and in the Civil War, when its fall to Union troops
led by Admiral David Farragut signaled to many the beginning of the end of the Confederacy's struggle.

In the fading light I could see only thick vegetation across
the river. The fort is two centuries old and reportedly infested
with snakes and vines and some sort of hippie cult. I had seen
a newspaper photograph of it, taken in the 1960s, with Judge
Leander Perez standing on the stockade wall. The wall, in
the picture, is ringed with barbed wire; Perez has a cigar in
his mouth and wears a dark suit and a wide-brimmed white
hat. He is stout, and his mouth is set in a firm line, but he
has less of the cracker cruelty in his face than you might

expect, and his hands hang by his sides, vulnerably. He has vowed, according to the picture's caption, to place within the stockade any civil rights "agitators" who stray into his parish.

In my travels so far historical hindsight had allowed me to see how the writers' project guides often prefigured the changes of the subsequent fifty years. But there was no clue in the Louisiana guide that Plaquemines was destined to be ruled and—to hear his enemies tell it—robbed for decades by a segregationist boss. Perez seems nevertheless to have been, along with the likes of George Wallace and Lester Maddox, a predictable expression of southern post-Reconstruction indignation. He built a powerful political machine and spouted thinly rationalized racism. "I think it's brain capacity," Perez once said, trying to explain the black inferiority he was so sure of. ". . . a Negro child at the age of about ten or eleven developed normally, but after that time in life his brain was stunted. . . . That business about Negroes being held down. That's a game, you know. . . . The Negroes, of course, are largely emotional. EEE-MOtional! And UN-THINKing!"

Fort Jackson is now a park, with large playing fields, picnic tables, and a cinder running track used by athletes from the desegregated Plaquemines schools. But the Perez machine, run by his sons since the judge's death in 1969, had only just begun to loosen its hold on Plaquemines Parish in the 1980s, and I had no idea whether a solitary traveler like me would be viewed as an "agitator." With no experience in the Deep South, my notions were a pastiche of W. J. Cash and *Easy Rider*.

Cautiously, then, I flattened myself on the bristly slope just on the river side of the levee, out of view of the roads within the fort. The light of the stars was fat and soft through the river haze. I awoke after a brief nap with an irrational fear that a river so big might simply rise and gulp me down in the dark. I retreated to the car, where I closed the windows and flattened the seat as best I could. I tried to imagine how I would explain myself to the mythical southern sheriff who would awaken me. He would hold his flashlight inches from my face, and ask with a snarl what I was doing sleeping on his levee, half clothed.

The parish police did, at about 2:00 A.M., aim a patrol car spotlight at me—but they just waved, and I waved back to show I was all right. The air in the car was hot and exhausted, so I opened the window a crack. Then I met my real tormentors.

They came in like an army battalion and, in the British fashion, marched at me in droves, unafraid of death. They were small, subtle bugs. You couldn't feel them light upon you, and by the time you noticed and slapped, a pouch of blood spattered the upholstery. I tried to follow the gentle buzz and grab them out of the air. It made no difference. Another regiment came marching up to replace fallen comrades. When I closed the window, it was too late; a legion had set up camp inside.

There were welts all over me by morning, and I felt ill. Yellow fever was once the busiest undertaker in these parts.

FORT ST. PHILIP . . . *accessible only by boat, was erected in 1795. . . . During the World War {I} it was repaired and a watchman kept there until 1923. Shortly after its abandonment the property was sold at public auction. Later, government agents learned that the historic ruins were serving as a hiding place for smuggled liquors, and the property was confiscated. Fort St. Philip is also overgrown with weeds, grass, and trees, and does not invite exploration.*

—Louisiana: A Guide to the State

THE man I'd seen in the gray houseboat invited me over that morning. He had eyes like king-sized marbles, draped with muddy-colored lids, and he called himself Smokey. Smokey took me on a tour of his houseboat, the upper part of which was a restaurant that never opened, though there were red tablecloths and place settings on the tables. He wore a tattered bathrobe and underwear, and smoked a cigarette. Finally he said, "You must be goin' to the fo't. She be here any minute now." He led me back to the houseboat porch. "You come back and I take you out by the rip. There we gonna catch some fish."

A lean, dark-haired woman in a black skirt and blouse hailed Smokey in a boisterous voice. She was undoing the bowline on a small motorboat next to the houseboat when we came out. A muscular man with curly blond hair struggled to pull-start the engine.

"He wants tuh come ovah, been waitin' for you," Smokey barked, pointing to me, and in minutes we were out on the river, cutting across at an upstream angle. The woman, Veleja Christos, in the bow, held the wheel, I sat in the middle, and the man, Uriah Christos, sat in the rear.

We shouted above the outboard as we crossed in a chilly upriver wind. Then the boat slowed, and we slipped into an opening among the cypresses and willows which grew out of the water along the east bank. The trees canopied a shallow passage to a rickety plank dock. While Uriah refueled and secured the boat, Veleja and I walked up over the levee bank. Behind it was a clearing, green but dissected by spokes of muddied paths which connected various buildings. Nearest to us was the "Suneidesis Cultural Center," an enormous old pump house with a Quonset roof.

Veleja's hearty talk belied her pale and fretful face. I thought it would be easy to explain to her why I was traveling about, but it wasn't. The more miles I covered, the less able I was to describe what I was looking for. She listened without showing interest, then warned me, "You can really hurt us. People write such distorted things. And we've worked hard to get along with people here. They didn't know what to make of us; it's hard to convince them we're not so different, not strange. I don't talk to delta people about meditation, and its power, that would be too much. I do talk to them about forgiveness. Archanna says . . ."

Stories had circulated on the delta about drugs, sex, and occult rites at Velaashby—their name for the fort—and Veleja and Uriah had waged a normalization campaign. They took regular nine-to-five jobs in Empire, and hung out at blue-collar coffee shops. Veleja watched my reactions carefully; Uriah sat silently in a crouch by the engine housing, looking everywhere but at me.

Still, I tried to show what a nice guy I was, nodding cheerfully at the New Age buzzwords as Veleja explained their goals during our walk to the main house, Timberlane. It was a sturdy, thick-walled building with a heavy tin roof. Secretly, I just wanted a good night's sleep, for free—I had spent most of my travel money in New Orleans. Nearby were two smaller, dilapidated houses, and all around us, extending farther south than I could see, were the ramparts of the old fort.

I met Tasha, a woman about Veleja's age with a small baby; Niko, a boy in his teens; and Paul, a twelve-year-old. Parentage was not discussed. I was put in the care of Darda, a striking, moonfaced girl of fifteen, for a tour of the fort. She wore shorts and a loose-fitting shirt, and when mosquitoes struck, she would let them drink their fill, while I slapped wildly. We circled the ramparts, ducking under leaning cypresses, then walked the grounds inside, among free-roaming cows and chickens and the occasional egret.

The older women would boast to me later that this girl, when tested by the public schools in Plaquemines Parish, proved better educated than schoolchildren her age. Her composed, mellifluous exposition of the history and rituals of Velaashby seemed to confirm her intelligence. But as Darda walked light-footed along the rough cement rampart, unbothered by the mosquitoes, I found it difficult to dislodge her from a mechanical recitation of Velaashby history. She would not say whose child she was—what an awkward question!—or where else she had lived in her life. I imagined a father somewhere who was missing her transition from child to woman, who would peer hard at a luminous stranger whenever they met again. At Velaashby, those questions were inconsequential at best, perhaps even subversive. She deflected my attempts to find out about her interests outside the fort.

I asked her to identify some of the birds and flora along our path; I had seen a redwing blackbird, egrets were everywhere, and I thought I spotted a bittern in the salt marsh behind the fort. She was no help with the wildlife, but she could tell me about the successes of their domestic garden and the tending of their animals, and what they had learned by trial and error since they arrived here in 1978, in great detail. We walked around cannon mounts, by a disabled tractor, amidst groves of cypress trees, and by a chicken coop. We circled the house where, off limits to me, Archanna Christos lay in bed.

Sentences at Velaashby often began with "Archanna says . . ." He was the one who had brought them here to live, surrounded by water and marsh, cut off from their pasts. They said he was in poor health and could not be disturbed.

I ate that night in the main house, which is equipped with a big kitchen and a long hardwood table, and talked with Velajah and Tasha about Archanna. Tasha labors mightily to put the group's vision into a newsletter. It describes healing the world through a worldwide "silent ministry," and the creation of a "Light Center" for the Gulf Coast at Velaashby.

Tasha was reserved that night, and Velajah filled the void with her boisterous talk.

The children, who had undoubtedly heard it before, kept busy with their homework. Uriah, who had said about two words since my arrival, watched a small black-and-white television as he ate. I kept nodding, smiling, and trying to keep my eyes open.

Archanna was weak and had difficulty breathing, the women said, so he rarely received visitors. He ate in his bed and never left his room. He was tended by Jautau, another serious-faced woman in her thirties. He read and meditated and rarely slept, they said. He was participating less in the community. Now he liked simply to watch his followers from his window, still and quiet because breathing was difficult. I was a little surprised, then, when late in the evening I was invited to meet him.

We walked a damp trail in moonlight. A light wind blew, and the stars shone brightly. We climbed a rickety stair to Archanna's room. He lay under a ragged blanket on the bed, knees drawn up, smiling through a graying beard. He might have weighed eighty pounds. He had a beaky nose and long, untended hair that was pulled to one side of his forehead, and his handshake was soft. Occasionally he had to interrupt his own talk and suck the difficult air. He drank coffee. He looked familiar, but I couldn't place him.

He told me a little about his life, which he began as Louis Hubert Casebolt. A manslaughter conviction as a street ruffian in Indiana, the destruction of his lungs by shrapnel during World War II, his days as a traveling evangelist. He told me about Nathan, one of several apparitions he spoke with; Nathan, he confided, was not very bright. He told me of lying on his back with the children, teaching them how to make clouds move, change shape, or disappear.

His life, he said, had been a search for the bridge between

logical and spiritual thought. And he had found it, right
there in anybody's head: intuition. You don't need leaders,
you don't need gods, Archanna said. . . .

For a man with very little lung remaining, he proved a
remarkably dynamic orator, and I found myself egging him
on, quoting vaguely remembered Spinoza and arguing about
philosophy. Tasha and Jautau listened solemnly; Veleja occasionally rephrased Archanna's ideas, apparently excited by the
rapport she sensed developing between the old man and me.
The children wandered in and out, without formality, did
some homework on his bed, or asked questions. Though
Archanna said repeatedly that he was not a leader, I thought:
What a nice solution to his chaotic life he had found—followers, innocents, who will tend him to his grave, idolatry
fostered in isolation. My reading in religion and philosophy
was sketchy, so by taking me seriously, Archanna exposed
the shallowness of his sophistry.

The sixty-acre property that includes Fort St. Philip
belonged to a Louisiana oilman. Archanna Christos and a few
followers took a skiff over to the island in 1978, and began
fixing the hurricane-battered buildings, clearing away the viny
overgrowth, and planting. This was about the time of Jim
Jones's disintegration and destruction in Guyana, and the
oilman had his doubts. But he was impressed by their hard
work, much of it done with primitive tools, and he let them
stay.

I must have been more exhausted than the ailing Archanna,
because I was the first to say uncle; I had to sleep. Tiredness
had made me meanhearted, too, and I was wondering what
relation these people had to the past or future of the delta.
They were refugees from another world, the dropout culture
that flourished in the late sixties and then seemed to die of
hard work and hard play. Uprooted, they washed up on this

shore, where they subsisted on a meager fare of borrowed ideas.

But I felt a little rotten inside. I was here for a free bed; I was a voyeur having a peek at life in a cult. The imaginary father I had created for Darda could as well have been myself; fathers find all sorts of reasons of their own to be separated from their children.

As I˙rose, the old man took my hand and looked at me with critical, agitated eyes. He said, "You've got a glow, you know. I feel something good coming from you." I looked past him at the old pillowcase, the rough-paned window, and the mosquitoes outside hurling themselves against it.

———

In Louisiana local government units, known elsewhere as counties, are called parishes. Originally they were ecclesiastical units set up by {Count Alexander} O'Reilly, Spanish provisional governor of Louisiana (1669–70), in conjunction with 11 administrative districts. As Louisiana developed, it was found that the districts were too large and that the smaller religious divisions were more suitable. . . .
The government body in the parish is the police jury, composed of from 5 to 16 members elected for four-year terms. It acts in a legislative, administrative, and quasi-judicial capacity. . . .
—*Louisiana: A Guide to the State*

BACK on the west side of the river, I visited some politicians. Most of what is new in the delta, whether it be an oil patch worker or a new bank or a newly elected pol, you'll find housed in trailers. The double-whammy hurricanes of the 1960s, Camille and Betsy, impressed on many the impermanence of building. Ernest Johnson, a parish commissioner, works in a trailer in Boothville.

Johnson is no polished politician: His handshake is limp, his eyes are evasive, and his speech is a shy mumble. Except for his considerable size, you would not take this man for a political giant killer. Yet he can take credit for toppling the Perez machine after forty years of entrenched rule.

Some say it could never have happened if the judge had still been around, and if his sons—whom he had installed as district attorney and president of the parish Commission Council—hadn't had a falling-out. Judge Perez died in 1969, at seventy-seven, after a series of heart attacks that began with one at his hunting camp in Tiger Pass. His friend George Wallace wore dark glasses at the funeral. Though Perez had been excommunicated by the Catholic Church when he opposed the integration of parochial Plaquemines schools in the 1960s, it was announced that the old man had secretly reconciled with the church, and a requiem mass was held. "Make him a companion of your saints," said a priest over the judge's casket. Five Catholic theologians wrote a letter to the archbishop calling the service "a disgrace."

With the judge gone, Ernest Johnson seized the opportunity. While the judge's sons still controlled the parish, they seemed to have less stomach for intimidation than their father. Johnson, a construction and oil industry worker, filed a civil rights lawsuit in 1975, claiming that the Commission Council, which runs the parish, effectively excluded black participation by electing its five members at large. For seven years leading up to the 1982 elections, there had been no voting at all. U.S. District Judge Frederick Heebe agreed with Johnson's attorneys that the Plaquemines system denied representation to black voters. He broke the parish up into nine districts and said each would elect its own council representative. Johnson, fittingly, was the new commissioner from the mostly black Boothville area.

In the meantime, the Perez machine was falling apart of

its own accord. Leander Perez, Jr., the district attorney, known as Lea, had a grand jury investigating parish corruption, with his brother Chalin as the prime target. The centerpiece of the investigation was a charge that royalties from parish oil and gas leases had been diverted to Chalin and the Perez-owned Delta Development Corporation. Lea suddenly dismissed the grand jury when stories circulated that he, too, was about to be charged. That dismissal led to his indictment for malfeasance.

Old Perez loyalists on the Council then turned on Chalin, ousting him as council president. He announced that the fight was not over, but he refused on principle to run for Council office again under a new system that a federal judge had "forced on the people." With lawsuits pending, the Perez brothers now keep a low profile.

Germaine Curley was one of the white mothers whose children attended the Our Lady of Good Harbor School at Buras in 1962, when the Catholic Church opened the school to blacks. Perez called on whites to boycott. For most of that school year, the priests and nuns sat in near-empty classrooms, waiting for students who never came. In 1963 someone doused the school's roof with gasoline one night and lit it. The damage was repaired, but parish officials would not grant a repair permit, and the electricity could not be turned back on.

Curley has a voice as deep and dawdling as marsh water. She is among the most popular of the new council members. Through the courts, the Council is attempting to recover mineral royalties from oil and gas development in the delta, which today's council members claim were diverted illegally to Perez family corporations.

It worked like this, according to documents filed by the parish in the lawsuit. In 1936 the Grand Prairie Lease District gave the Perez-owned Delta Development Corporation oil and gas leases in the delta for three hundred dollars; Delta then sublet the oil and gas to Gulf Oil, for five hundred dollars and "other valuable considerations." Gulf then conveyed a one-fourth royalty to one A.S. Cain, who in turn conveyed it to Delta. The short road to riches, by way of "other valuable considerations."

"Along about when I was fifteen years old, I got to go places with the school pep squad," said Curley, a hefty woman who laughs a lot. "All my life I'd been hearing about what a rich parish we were, you know? We'd go over to Lafourche Parish and I'd see playgrounds and running water and streets and I'd come back and I'd ask: 'If we're so rich, why don't we have all of that?' . . . I really believe the people in this parish should be very rich today, but they're not."

The crusade to recover those revenues, and to clean up the inequitable parish payroll, has resulted in some threats to the new commissioners. The Perez family still has loyal friends in the parish, I found.

Curley, whether she was racing through meetings at her office or socializing at home, seemed to be having a good time. She laughed especially hard one night when she told me about Mitchell Jurisich, a Yugoslav oysterman with whom she grew up. She described him cracking Christmas ornaments over people's heads, rushing onto the Tulane football field pushing a wheelchair, and brawling in the French Quarter. His craziness, she said, intensified when he spent weeks at a time working in the oyster beds out in the bayous, and almost none in school.

"They're here for hard work and hard dollars," said Curley. "That's their Yugoslav heritage."

———

*First, the oysterman obtains empty oyster shells and transports them
to carefully selected breeding grounds; these must have water of a
certain degree of saltiness so that the bivalve may "spat" (spawn),
"set" (attach themselves to some object—usually a larger oyster
shell), and grow to maximum size. Here the shells are scattered
carefully, so as to prevent overcrowding. Then, after 2 years, the
new crop is gathered up, the very small oysters re-bedded on
the same grounds, and the larger oysters carried to a bedding
ground nearer the sea, where they may fatten and acquire the
delicate flavor for which the Louisiana oyster is noted. After a
period ranging from a week to 2 months the larger oysters are
tonged up again, to be taken to clean grounds, usually located close
to the oysterman's camp. . . . Several hours before the freight
lugger arrives they are tonged up again. . . .*
        —Louisiana: A Guide to the State

THE work of oystermen has eased considerably from the days
of lifting, sifting, and raking the oysters by hand, but it is
still more than most of us could take, and it comes in seven-
days-a-week bursts. Oystermen dredge now, instead of using
hand-held tongs, and that process has increased the volume
and made the business more profitable. "My grandfather used
to ship out about two thousand oysters a year," said a young
Yugoslav with a thick accent, Tima Tomasovich, whom I
met over breakfast at Miljaks, a restaurant-bar in Empire.
"Now, with these dredges, I can do that in two weeks."
Yugoslavs hold most of the oyster bed leases around the delta,
and they rejuvenate their population here with a steady stream
of recruits from the Dalmatian coast, which, they say, has a
climate like the delta. It started when some Yugoslavs jumped
ship here in the 1840s, and now they pretty much control
the oyster industry. "There's more people from Dubac here
than there are in Dubac," said Dave Cvitanovich, a former

Unloading oysters in the Plaquemines Delta. *Russell Lee.*

oysterman who now guides oil companies through the bayous. "In the old days a man would come over here to Olga [a
town across the river] and not go home for twenty to thirty
years. He'd arrive home in Yugoslavia and find he was a
grandfather . . . and he'd never seen his *children.*"

Some Yugoslavs return home, but others, like Cvitanovich, whose father arrived here (after a stint in New Zealand)
in 1931, would be hard to pick from a police lineup if placed
among the young American tourists who prowl New Orleans's
French Quarter. The Yugoslavs who still live in Plaquemines
declare themselves a tough bunch, and crazy, and most close
observers will, like Germaine Curley, vouch for that. Stories
about Mitchell Jurisich were piling up. I heard that he once
held a priest upside down by the ankles at the blessing of the

shrimp fleet, and that he fired his rifle at a helicopter of wild-life biologists because he thought they were from one of the oil companies. (Jurisich's version, when I asked him about that: "I just thought he was a big duck, man.")

Jurisich has a splendid iron-gated home now. Gruff and red-eyed, he greeted me in a dirty T-shirt. His hair was going white, but his iron grip and barrel-chested build indicated he was still working hard. In the thirties, during his long outings in the bayou when the rest of the kids were in school, Jurisich surveyed new marshes for oyster beds, and ultimately he made a fortune, and a few enemies. His admirers say he can walk barefoot on an oyster bed.

Jurisich turned me over to Cvitanovich, who took me in his Lafitte skiff outside the levees to explore the camps and bayous where Mitch made his fortune. As we motored out past Dramand Island and into Bay Adams, he said, "Nobody would come back out here now; everybody's used to the tele-phone, automobiles. To be in the bayou every day—no." That's half true. Almost everyone I met liked to shrimp or fish, and many, even those who had moved to New Orleans, maintained camps that they visited regularly. It reminded me of the mountain country of Wyoming, where the remote mining towns and timber camps are mostly ghost towns. There, too, the descendants of the men who worked there come back often, and many think of those visits as their only time "at home."

Forty to fifty Yugoslavs lived half a century ago in the bay Cvitanovich and I explored. Now there were none. The peo-ple have changed, and the bayous are not the same either. We visited camps (a camp is a cabin, basically, usually with-out running water or electricity) that had been on solid ground ten years ago. Today the stilts which once lifted them off dry ground—to protect them against hurricanes and tides—dis-appear into water.

As you move away from the Mississippi, out beyond the protection of the levees, you often see dead white cypress trees, like clutching hands reaching up out of the marshes. Salt has killed them, salt borne inland by oil companies' canals and the gradual sinking of the delta itself. Some of the trunks are on dry land, and some extend up out of the water in the bays and inlets along the peninsula's edges. There are also thinner, man-planted sticks, wagging in the tides, to mark the oyster beds, so shrimpers can avoid dragging their nets over them. The occasional poacher appreciates the sticks, too.

In some ways, oystering resembles raising cattle (and there are cattle on the delta, by the way, shifted about by barge). Just as you move beef from high to low pasture, into and out of the paddock when they're calving, so you have to shift the oysters around. They start their lives in salt water; they fatten up in fresh. You can't look into an oyster's eyes the way you might a steer's, but oystermen have a lifelong relationship with the oyster that a shrimper or fisherman could not imagine.

These days the oysters are sucked up by dredges, moved from bed to bed, and blown out again. Oystermen grade oysters for size, rake them, cull them, and move them to a clean bedding ground. They'll take the old shells and toss them in Bay Adams to form a reef where new oysters can attach; then, as the gang begins to grow, they'll break off the dead ones and toss the living back. The seed oysters come from the east side of the river, where there is a protected freshwater sanctuary for oysters. Bay Adams is on the west side, and this is where an oyster grows up. It's a pretty spot— clear, salty water, sliced by sunbeams, dotted with little windblown islands, elevated cabins, and a few fig trees.

Oysters are "planted" in September. That's when oyster-men stay out for weeks at a time, often enduring some of the worst weather the delta can offer. The oysters mature for eight or nine months—old-timers used to give them up to two years—and then are harvested, sorted, and sacked for the trip to the shucking houses. You pay about two dollars an acre for a lease, according to Cvitanovich, and an oyster operation may lease a thousand acres. You can pull in 250 sacks a day at harvesttime, and sell them for twelve dollars or more a sack.

But 70 percent of the oyster beds have been shut down because of pollution. The canals that service the oil rigs throughout the bayous haven't helped any. Nor have the flood control levees and the deepening of the Mississippi River's channel. Those efforts, which have protected upriver and delta homes from flooding, and which have given the big ships a deep channel up to Baton Rouge, have also allowed the delta lands to sink. The river's annual overflow used to spread a new layer of mud now and then (and sometimes take homes and lives in the process). Without new layers of silt, these camps and the land they stand on are simply dropping down into the ooze. And the salt water is moving in.

When I got back to Empire, I called up the Corps of Engineers in New Orleans. It keeps a deep channel open out into the Gulf as far as the edge of the continental shelf. The sediment that used to fan out and settle over delta lands during floods is just dropping off the shelf into nowhere. The corps had plans to deepen the river's channel further to allow bigger ships and tankers.

The corps people promised to send me some information— promised repeatedly. There were plans, a voice on the phone said, to divert some mud into the delta lands that needed it. Various phone voices said they'd send me material, too, about the corps's effort to keep the river from jumping its channel and switching to the Atchafalaya.

I'm still waiting.

This {new flood control} system will not be used, however, until
high river stages threaten to break the first-line, or main levees,
along the Atchafalaya. . . .
At such times, excess waters entering Atchafalaya River from Red
River and through a connection (Old River) with the Mississippi
River would top the low or "fuse plug" levees on each side of the
Atchafalaya. . . . These levees would give way entirely, of course,
once any considerable volume of water began flowing over them.
Permanent, controlled spillways under the general flood control
plan of the U.S. Engineers are expected eventually to supplant these
emergency "fuse plug" levees.
—Louisiana: A Guide to the State

I DROVE up to Baton Rouge, and stopped on the way to look
at the Old River flood control structure, which was pretty
nondescript to the untrained eye. Little boats patrolled on
the lookout for runaway barges that might strike it. Should
it ever give way, most Americans would hear of the deaths
and destruction in the Atchafalaya swamp country caused by
a runaway river, and about New Orleans, a port city of half
a million people with its waterway reduced to a trickle. But
the Plaquemines would surely be doomed, too, without the
river. It would simply sink slowly into the Gulf.

While the corps had failed to produce much written material on its effort to keep the Mississippi in line, officials have
testified before congressional committees that the agency's
various Mississippi endeavors—shoring up the Old River
structure, deepening the channel, and installing a deepwater
port just outside the delta's southwest channel—would amount
to the corps's most ambitious undertaking for the rest of the
century.

Corps officials express confidence; experts at Louisiana State

University (LSU), and private consultants, are a lot less sure
that humans can keep the river from doing what comes naturally. What has come naturally in the past is a lot of movement. About seven thousand years ago the Mississippi Delta
lay way to the west. From above what is now Baton Rouge it
ran more directly south, emptying into the Gulf near what is
now Morgan City, about 150 miles west of its present outlet.
About forty-five hundred years ago it swung to the east,
dumping its cargo mostly in St. Bernard Parish, east of New
Orleans, and pushing out toward what is now the Breton
National Wildlife Refuge and the Chandeleur Islands. Those
islands, in fact, are what's left when an old delta gradually
sinks.

The river found its present course about a thousand years
ago, and for the first eight hundred or so years the delta
didn't expand much farther out into the Gulf than where
Empire is today. The extension of the delta, which provided
terra firma for Buras, Triumph, and Venice, among other
towns, has taken place within the last two hundred years.

In other words, fast.

Sherwood ("Woody") Gagliano first discovered that this
growth was reversing by looking at old maps. He was an LSU
professor, and interested in coastal archeology. "Every place
I went to that was on the old maps was eroding," he said.
"Not only are we losing wetlands, we're losing ridge lands,
and the people that live on them, at an even faster rate."
Gagliano left the university and became a consultant to Plaquemines Parish, the Environmental Protection Agency, oil
and gas companies, and other entities, and a thorn in the
corps's side. His "life expectancy" maps of the delta show
that, at the rate of land loss over the last thirty years, much
of the Plaquemines delta will simply disappear underwater in
the next century. The invading water will come not from the

river but from the Gulf, which surrounds the delta. His studies indicate that where Cvitanovich and I crossed open water
the week before, there was "a veritable carpet of unbroken
marshes" in the 1930s.

The land is dropping because it's in a geological trough.
There's no bedrock underneath the delta, so it sinks like a fat
man sitting in a sprung chair. Periodic flooding used to build
up the sinking land by layering mud over it—Gagliano esti-
mated that river silt had created five million acres of new land
in Louisiana over a five-thousand-year period—but that
building process reversed around the turn of the century. And
now, said Gagliano, "I think I'm measuring the collapse of a
major system."

Gagliano is small, bald, and round-shouldered, with a deferential but sly smile, sort of what you would expect a consultant to look like. We talked in a conference room with no
natural light—wood paneling and maps, a large empty table
between us. It was a little hard to imagine him hobnobbing
with the brawny Yugoslavs down on the delta. In fact, he's
spent a good deal of time with them in the wild country he's
trying to save.

Gagliano has proposed solutions, but they would cost a
lot. They would also require that the corps shift its emphasis
away from flood control and navigation—the heart of its existence. He would limit levee protection to towns and cities,
allowing the river to flood and muddy rural areas. He would
divert fresh water from the river to the marshes to reduce the
salinity. New land would be created in little subdeltas, or by
dredging.

But first the ideas have to be sold. "It's an intricate game,
and everybody likes to play," said Gagliano, smiling at the
ceiling. "In this system, you can go in one day and talk to
an oysterman on his boat in Lower Plaquemines and to the
governor later on. They all play politics here. They relish it."

———

*In 1923 air mail service was established between New Orleans and
Pilottown at the mouth of the Mississippi River to connect with
outgoing ships, and to expedite delivery at New Orleans of mail
from incoming steamships. This service, discontinued in 1934,
was the third air line to carry foreign mail in the United States.*
—*Louisiana: A Guide to the State*

TO Lower Plaquemines I went, again, on a sunny day when
the gulls were screeching above the Venice loading docks.
The ponds around here were choking with water hyacinth;
the docks of Venice were crowded with boats and money.

Two young men were readying a huge powerboat named
the *Joyce,* which runs workers back and forth to offshore rigs.
They were rock musicians from Florida, and they wore
Hawaiian shirts and dark glasses. They worked slowly, with
a kind of preening indolence. I remembered Mark Twain's
description of apprentice river pilots, who "could not help
lolling carelessly upon the railings of the boiler deck to enjoy
the envy of the country boys on the bank." I asked to hitch a
ride downriver to the outpost of the real river pilots, the men
who steer the big ships around the shifting shoals of the Mississippi. They agreed to give me a lift.

We motored for a few hours, past a stranded ship caught
on a sandbar. Then we swung by the dock at Pilottown, and
I hopped off. Hitchhiker's luck would have to get me back
to Venice. The dock connected to a cement walkway about
five feet wide, which ran the length of the town. The stilt-
mounted buildings were connected to the walkway by plank
piers, like branches to a trunk. There were two large buildings, for two associations of river pilots, and numerous homes.
A shallow film of water ran from the river under the entire
settlement, and out into the marshes beyond.

A Louisiana heron, bluish black, squawked at me from the

overgrown willows and cypresses. Harvey Carr, wearing a brilliantly colorful short-sleeved shirt, came walking along. He didn't seem surprised to meet a stranger. He was sixty-five and retired. His black hair was greased and combed straight back. He said that life in Pilottown was radically changed by the two hurricanes of the 1960s. Camille and Betsy blew down buildings, changed the land, and broke spirits. In the aftermath, Pilottown lost most of its year-round residents, and much of the game—nutrias, alligators, rabbits, and deer. "You used to walk clear on across," said Carr, pointing east. The water that flowed under the town, shallow but fast, continues now for miles across stubbly flats. A distant stand of trees marked a branch of the river. "You used to walk to that other pass. Now you try to walk and you go clear up to your neck."

Tom Smith lived at the north end of Pilottown. I walked by several collapsing houses and some empty ones (there were lawn mowers on two porches) and an empty schoolhouse to his pier. He built his house of cypress in 1927, and remembered those days as if they were last year. Pilottown then had a big store, two bars (the Bungalow and the Bumblebee), and more than a hundred citizens, including families with children. He remembered the excitement when big boxes of bananas arrived. The schoolhouse was built in 1952. It has been empty since Camille.

Behind Smith's house was an elevated plank leading to an outhouse that towered high over the marsh. The house to the right of his had a fenced, raised bed for a vegetable garden, but it was overgrown and succumbing to erosion by the river's overflow. Smith had stayed through every hurricane, and he pointed to the water mark on his second-floor door to illustrate Camille's force. He was a frail man, but he had no intention of leaving. "This house will take plenty of wind. You'd have to lift it up over the pilings. One hundred miles

per hour ain't so bad, but when it goes up to two hundred
. . . The trouble is you get so much water, and big things
will hit you."

He waved good-bye from his porch. "People liked it here
because of the wild, and because it's so quiet," Tom Smith
said. Back on the landing dock, a nutria slipped off a piling
under my feet. It was very quiet, except for the trickling of
the water.

———

Bar pilots meet ships at sea and guide them through the passes to
Pilottown, from which point river pilots take them into
New Orleans. On outgoing trips the reverse order is followed. It is
the ambition of nearly every boy in the surrounding territory to
become a pilot, an ambition difficult to fulfill, since there is a
monopoly on the profession held by certain families.
—*Louisiana: A Guide to the State*

EVEN the pilots no longer lived in Pilottown year-round. I
rode with one of them out to the ship caught on the sandbar
upriver. He kept his family in New Orleans and came down
to Pilottown to do two-week stints in the river pilots' rather
posh digs, which included satellite television and a twenty-
four-hour chow line of delicious food. Joe Ross's job, in this
case, was to advise the freighter's crew while it struggled to
get off the sandbar.

The stranded ship was the *Norman Pacific,* a Netherlands-
registered freighter on its way to Amsterdam with a load of
cattle feed. We rode to it on a launch that belonged to Dave
Smith, Tom's grandson, a part-time Pilottown resident whose
family lived ashore so that his children could get schooling.
The freighter was off-loading its cargo onto barges, and Dave
maneuvered his little boat up next to the outermost barge so
that Ross and I could leap across. Dave Smith—red of skin

and hair and temper—cursed the Corps of Engineers for the way it managed the river. I mentioned the land-loss studies that Gagliano and others were doing, and the problem of the sinking delta. "They don't need a study," said Smith. "Any damn fool who's been here knows what to do. They take another five, six years to do a study, and all the time it's going bad to worse. The corps built the lock system and fucked it up. Sinking, my ass. The land is washing away."

Here's how the river pilot system works: A pilot from the Bar Pilots Association comes aboard in the open water of the Gulf and guides a foreign ship through one of several "passes," deep dredged channels followed by the river through the last patches of delta land. The bar pilot steers the ship as far as Pilottown, but there his jurisdiction ends, and the boat must be turned over to a river pilot, who belongs to a separate association, for the trip up to New Orleans. On the way back out, the order is reversed.

The *Norman Pacific*'s captain, a bearded Scandinavian, described how his ship got caught on the bar as it drifted during a changeover from river pilot to bar pilot. At that point a fourth authority entered the picture: an insurance representative, who took command from the moment the boat went aground.

To get the boat off, the hull was partially filled with water, and then the grain was off-loaded into barges. The water would then be pumped out, and the ship would, it was hoped, float free. A small fortune was lost in such delays, but the captain, who had his wife traveling with him, leaned quietly against the back of the bridge and, unruffled, puffed his pipe. Only later, reading my notes, did I realize that his soft-bristle voice said many harsh things as we sat around on the bridge, watching the slow off-loading of grain. In fluid, accented English, he criticized everything from the river pilots (their system got his ship hung up) to American tugs (too

weak, too small) to American freighter crews (too many men),
and freighters (turn-of-the-century). He had a bad word for
me, too, for coming aboard his ship with no official purpose.

After a few hours on the disabled freighter, I monkeyed
my way back down the ship's side on laced tires, dropped
onto a barge, and finally jumped to a small powerboat that
had stopped briefly on its way upriver. The freckled, taciturn
boy at the helm—did he dream of being a river pilot?—
dropped me off at Venice, and I drove back toward New
Orleans, rubbing salty eyes in the dark.

EATING breakfast in Miljaks one morning, I learned that a
hurricane was heading toward the delta, with winds now at
seventy-five miles per hour and picking up rapidly. An emergency meeting had been called at the Empire Senior Citizens
Center, half a block away. Walking over, I was impressed
with how hot and glary and windless it can be when a hurricane is brewing offshore. Some gray clouds were mounding
to the south, but there was no other suggestion of trouble.
Yet I wrote in my notebook: "yellow, DANGEROUS air."

Germaine Curley ran the meeting. She sat at the head of a
rectangle formed by four long tables, around which were seated
lawmen, firemen, school officials, and other important people. She greeted me with her characteristic laugh. Then she
got down to business, quieting the crowd with her deep rum-
ble of a voice.

Timing was discussed. If there was to be an evacuation of
the delta, and there almost certainly was, then school buses
needed to be fueled, the ferry had to be scheduled, and evacuation shelters needed to be designated on higher ground, in
Belle Chasse and elsewhere, so people would have a place to
lay their bedding. The parish had discovered the obvious in
a recent hurricane evacuation: When only one road leads in

and out of the delta, quick exits are difficult. The unpopulated four-lane road I'd driven down on made more sense when one considers the logistics of a mass exodus, but that good sense was entirely negated by the places where the road narrowed back to only two lanes.

The difficulties ranged from the mundane to the momentous. The sheriff wasn't sure where he'd find a DO NOT ENTER sign to hang on the school; hurricane boards had to be put up over the windows of all public buildings with a single parish cherry picker; a timetable had to be established for letting out schoolchildren early; and how would they evacuate the old man—Archanna Christos—from Fort St. Philip? The island lacked a landing spot for a helicopter or a dock site for an ambulance boat.

For those who didn't have to cross the river, evacuation meant piling belongings into and on top of vehicles throughout Empire. I left the meeting and drove through the little towns where families were packing busily, and arrived at the Our Lady of Good Harbor School. An imposing sign arched over the driveway: DELTA HERITAGE ACADEMY. Children were streaming from a metal warehouselike building and were boarding buses. They yelled and waved at my camera, hopping up and down in their plaid skirts and white shirts. The early dismissal, and the evacuation that would fill the upcoming afternoon, had the kids in high spirits. Still, the sky was bland.

This was the first year Our Lady's doors had opened since it was bombed in 1963. The next generation of Curleys, Germaine's four grandchildren, is enrolled. The Delta Heritage sign remains and reminds that after the Catholic school was bombed, these grounds housed an all-white private school for those who refused to send their children to integrated public or Catholic schools. In 1984 Delta Heritage ran out of money.

The Catholic school reopened with 305 students in grades

K–8, and 10 students in the ninth grade. There are only 3 black children enrolled.

"They're waiting to see how the first year goes," said Nuala Byrne, the principal. She was a thin-lipped Irishwoman, small in stature. Wearing glasses, she seemed a little timid. Probably not. She came to the United States from Dublin in 1968, and had made her own way since.

I found myself lifting typewriters up onto file cabinets— -a flood precaution—as we talked. "Reopening the school is a very big event for the parents," she said, "more than I probably realize. I think we'll grow; yes, our enrollment will probably grow."

Then we rushed down the hall, making a last sweep of the classrooms for malingerers, and joined the exodus north from the delta.

———

In Louisiana the traveler must remember that old towns and old houses will always be found near a river, or bayou, as water was the chief means of transportation in the early days. Modern highways make traveling easier, but those who wish to visit older places must take the less frequented roads.
—*Louisiana: A Guide to the State*

CARS stacked high with precious furniture and goods inched patiently along the highway. The sky was darker now; the air was heavy and still. I inched along with them, and my temperature gauge seemed to rise another notch whenever I passed a steaming old station wagon on the shoulder.

Near Port Sulphur I pulled off and joined Germaine Curley and her staff in a parish district office, adjacent to the jail, where they had set up a command headquarters. On the other side of the levee, paralleling the poky line of evacuating cars, a bumper-to-bumper flow of tugs and barges and ships pushed

upriver to safer harbor. It seemed a dignified procession from
the shore, the royal court parading through a chaotic colony.
And overhead flew the gnatlike helicopters, ferrying men from
the offshore oil rigs.

Curley, barefoot now, padded around the office. There were
problems with the shelters and buses. "He won't use the old
plan," she said of another commissioner. "He wants to show
he's the boss. Well, he's one of two bosses—him and his
mother-in-law." The loud laugh. She stopped and put her
feet up on a big desk and, with other parish officials, listened
to weather reports, interrupted constantly by the telephone.
At the mention of a female adversary's name she muttered,
"One of these days I'm going to climb over this desk and *get*
that broad." The sheriff, after struggling to get a reluctant
old woman to come in off the roadside and rest in the jail,
sat down with us, stifling his first yawn of a long day. So it
went for twenty-four hours (I saved myself the cost of another
bed): We snacked from trays of food, watched television, told
stories, checked the traffic, and tracked Hurricane Elena on
the scorecardlike maps provided by the National Weather
Service.

Around midnight I hitched a ride down into the delta with
a couple of sheriff's deputies who were patrolling to discourage looting. They were on orders to come back as soon as the
wind blew too heavily. Also reconnoitering was a television
newsman from a New Orleans station. For his benefit, the
officers turned on their sirens to flush out the last holdouts;
he wanted an interview. "I thought for *sure* there'd be *some*
asshole still here," he said when no one emerged. His unlined
face had begun to collapse into pudginess. Even the wind
would not cooperate. It had stopped blowing, and he could
not get a shot of himself with the wind whipping his hair
("Live, from the heart of the hurricane . . .") Finally he shot
some footage of the sheriff's car spotlighting the grounds of

an oil company's headquarters. The deputies drove out into the empty lots by the offices for no reason except to accommodate the television crew.

We returned to the command center. And then Elena backed off. She turned her nose toward the Florida coast. Residents of the delta, many of whom had spent a night sleeping on the floors of high school gyms and armories, hurried back to their homes. The tottering piles of furniture inched back down the highway; the pickups of the rig workers returned to the parking lots in Venice.

Out at Fort St. Philip, the residents of Velaashby felt a little strange. While they were proud of themselves for forcing the storm away from the delta—yes, it was they who had done it—they realized they might have to take responsibility for whatever it did to the Florida coast.

———

Where few men live and where both sea and sky are filled with seagulls, terns, and pelicans, and where life goes on as it has done from time immemorial.
—*Louisiana: A Guide to the State*

IT was one of those skills that Archanna had taught them: how to make the clouds move where you want them to, how to break them apart, through meditation. At a gathering two nights later, Tasha and her mates worried the problem through. The hurricane had not gone away, it was hovering off the coast, and they wondered now whether they should wish the hurricane ashore or leave it in the Gulf, gathering strength.

Friends and supporters of the community, mostly from New Orleans, had come down to Velaashby for the weekend to celebrate the Feast of the Amram, or "The World Made Manifest." I had stopped by Smokey's place, remembering the fishing trip we'd planned, only to find him packing for a voyage inland. So I rode across the river to visit again.

This time the weakening Archanna lay silent in his second-story room, breathing pure oxygen. Veleja said they had no evacuation plans. The buildings here were built to withstand a hurricane, she said, and the ground was high enough to let the storm sweep across it, regardless of breaks in the levee. It was on this ground that the old man wanted to die.

I walked with Arthur, a black street preacher from New Orleans, over to a pond fed by marshes just outside the fort's northern wall. We passed the old man's ragged house, where he lay on his bed on the second floor, aswim in his beard and his thoughts. No visits, they said. Arthur, a tall, almost gaunt man, could not stop talking about his own spiritual journey. His was a fairly passive faith; he warned the others not to mess with moving storms, which manifest God's will. His words had the same pleasant inconclusiveness as Archanna's, a string of popcorn which he held up to marvel, spellbound by his own mind. But I didn't feel the generosity in him that I had in Archanna.

I had Archanna's face in my mind as we stripped to swim, and it was as I took my change and pocketknife from my pants that I realized what had seemed familiar about his face: He resembled the knife-wielding derelict who had stumbled in front of me on the street in New Orleans. The moment it occurred to me, I was angry at myself; it seemed facile and inappropriate, and it was not so much a brotherly resemblance as a more superficial collation of loose clothes, pallid skin, and the heavy manes of hair tossed to one side. I could not see either one now—one was probably dead, and the other was dying in the house nearby—so I transposed them easily in memory, and wondered if this had subliminally colored that first cynical impression of the little man on the bed. The hurricane had blown down a few of my defenses, underlining what a vulnerable and brave adventure Archanna had begun here, and I felt protective of him and his fragile Velaashby. I remembered the rapid turning of his ideas, and the eager way he ran through them. He had allowed me to feel superior then; he didn't care. So I like to think the connection I made between him and the man with the knife was just a kindling of sympathy: If I had failed to see the intellectual hunger of the old man, and his generosity, the first time, perhaps I needed to look more closely at the man I saw abused on the street.

Mullets broke the surface of the cool water in which Arthur and I swam, and diving cormorants fished nearby. A rookery of egrets squawked in a cypress at the end of the pond nearest the river. A woman named Betty joined us in the water; an older woman from New Orleans came and sat on the shore. Arthur talked all the time, in his happy, near-hysterical way, his chin jutting up from the water. At one point a big gar raised its ugly face between Betty and me, and she cringed and slipped back onto the dock, holding herself and grabbing for her towel. The shyness about nakedness surprised me. I stayed in the water after they'd left, standing on the prow of a sunken skiff, and watched the birds. They filled every level of an enormous cypress tree, and watching them was like looking into the windows of a large apartment building, all busy with life.

Throughout the afternoon more supporters of the community arrived from New Orleans, and that night, after a meal, a Houma Indian named Running Bear conducted a smoke ceremony. The company sat in a circle on the floor of the living room, smoked a pipe, and meditated while he chanted. Running Bear, solemn and shirtless and sweaty, sighed deeply when it was over.

Echoing sighs went around the circle, and then a participant said, "You were really getting up there. I could tell that was addressed to higher spirits, and then you came down to lower spirits, like us."

Running Bear thought about this a moment, then said, "Yes, I did four high, and then four low."

Arthur asked, "Four high what?"

The group was quiet for a moment, until a woman said, "I counted a lot of sevens and eights. In the chant."

Running Bear said, "Four of some and four of the other makes eight. Four and seven are magic numbers, they come up everywhere. Like the Seven Tribes of the Sioux."

Heads nodded all around.

Running Bear was the "minister of culture" of United Houma, a Louisiana tribe which was struggling to identify itself, after years of diffusion and mixing with other cultures. The Houmas were also chasing federal funding support available only to officially recognized tribes. There was great difficulty sorting out claims of Houma blood, said Running Bear, and even greater difficulty, it appeared to me, recovering the lost culture of the tribe.

Running Bear's problem reflected the larger difficulty here on the island: There was so little historical humus in which to root a community. Uriah had moved to New Orleans, and the ethereal Darda confessed to me now that she had spent part of the summer with her father in Houston, and would soon be moving away. They wanted a culture, yet they hadn't the right glue: the generational memories; the time-tested rituals; the blood ties to this delta country.

Facing the loss of Archanna, and the departure of many of the children they'd been raising, Veleja and Tasha, who were pretty much running things now, spoke bravely of a future. I wasn't sure. But I admired them for letting the kids go when they felt like going, and the clearly difficult struggle of Tasha to verbalize the ideas of Archanna—before they lost him!—was moving. I hoped they would survive here, among the bugs and behind the old ramparts, and keep struggling to create the "Light Center." The world does, indeed, need light and changing.

{Inhabitants of Chênière Caminada} returned to their homes when the {hurricane} wind fell. At nightfall, as they celebrated their deliverance with a dance, the wind suddenly veered and drove the waters of the Gulf in mountainous waves upon them.
In 15 minutes the water was four feet deep. The torrent carried everything in its path; boats were snatched from the grasp of men struggling desperately to save their families; children were torn from their mothers' arms; and houses, swept from their foundations, floated like egg shells upon the boiling waters.
—*Louisiana: A Guide to the State*

THE hurricane was coming back. It teased Florida and then swung west, picking up speed, and it headed straight for the delta. The cars assembled again at the Port Sulphur bottleneck, and Germaine Curley was padding around barefoot at her command center, barking orders. I spent a night in an evacuation center on higher ground in Belle Chasse, where families of all colors erected blanket camps in a big high school auditorium. Little huddles of grandparents, children, and family familiars formed, the smell of cold food and diapers enriched the air, and I found myself waiting in line for a pay phone to call home. There had been so much action, so much to do on my journey in Louisiana that my usual loneliness for family got pushed away, shoved ahead each day to the next; but here, with so many generations snuggled about, the longing returned. By the time I got to the phone it was after midnight. My wife answered sleepily (she had fallen asleep in front of the television, waiting for a report on the hurricane), and we talked for a while. She teasingly suggested I find a family of five—with no one in diapers—and curl up next to them. In the dim light and amidst the murmur of many small televisions, I laid my sleeping bag down near a family from Boothville and watched "Dallas," interrupted frequently by weather reports.

The next day I got Curley's permission to drive back to the end of the delta. When I stopped by Smokey's houseboat, he was hurriedly hooking up his boat trailer to his car. "Ain't that something," he said. "Damn thing can't decide where to go, so it's doing this to me." He drove off toward New Orleans.

I drove down to Venice, which was a madhouse. Helicopters were zipping back and forth to the rigs nonstop. I asked the dispatchers if I could hitch a ride out, and was refused. I went to several boat docks, where they were sending out crew boats to retrieve rig workers, and was refused again. In frustration, I took a walk along the riverside, where the levee had been shored up with finely crushed white shells. I stopped in at the bar where Smokey went some evenings to share his tuna dip.

WOMAN (to barkeep): Where's your mama, she packin'?
BARKEEP: No—just watchin' TV. Says she ain't leavin'.
WOMAN: They'll make her leave. They don't want no lootin'.
BARKEEP: She ain't gonna loot. She weighs two hundred and fifty pounds.
WOMAN: They'll make her leave. How 'bout you?
MAN: I'm goin' home and watch TV, see what happens. I already been out once, dammit.
BARKEEP: I'm stayin' long as I can. Shit, we're out of cigarettes. Ed, you run 'cross the street buy me a pack? No, wait, buy me a carton.

I went back to the docks, and a Chevron dispatcher, heated up by the cacophony of voices and radios in his cramped quarters, threatened violence if I set foot in his "employees only" office again. I walked disconsolately to a fueling station, and there Huey Buffinet, the Cajun pilot of one of the rig service boats, the *Thunderhawk,* waved me aboard. He didn't care about the rules if I didn't.

——

Within a few miles of the city the traveler enters a primitive country of shrimpers and fishermen, who live as simply as their grandfathers did. Here are communities of men and women who are descendants of Lafitte's smugglers and pirates, men in whose veins flows the blood of many nations
—Louisiana: A Guide to the State

WE motored out through the Southeast Passage, hoping to make quick work of the evacuation and get safely back to shore. But the radio squawked, and the *Thunderhawk* was ordered to hold off for a few hours. In open water about twenty feet deep we tied up to some pilings, a remnant of an earlier drilling operation. The crew boat bucked gently on the swells under a faintly whitewashed sky. The rig we were to evacuate was miles south, in deeper water. The sky kept getting darker, and there was nothing to do until the crew on the rig finished pulling up the drill string.

Kenny Willard, the deckhand on the *Thunderhawk,* went below and cooked four steaks. I anchored the plate between my arms on the careening table, and got it all down. They were watching me.

By the time we were cleared to approach, it was night. We motored out and tied up loosely to one of the rig's pilings. The brightly lit, multistoried rig platform stood two hundred feet above the water, a Xanadu minus the pleasure.

We drifted downwind and waited, rolling in steep seas that made the hemp shudder violently. The storm began to accelerate, and Buffinet radioed back to Venice that he couldn't wait any longer to take the men off the rig. Not long ago, Willard told me, a man had been swept off his boat during an evacuation like this and never found. Buffinet was on edge.

Crouching on the upper deck and watching Willard work the ropes below, I remembered another wild and sometimes beautiful place where men put themselves in jeopardy for a good wage. It was in Wyoming's Gros Ventre Mountains, where I spent a few winter days with a drilling crew on a rig called the Last Hope Federal. That, too, was like being at sea: the rolling swells of snow-covered mountains; the brightly lit tower; the man working above on the monkeyboard like a foretopman high in the rigging.

The whitecaps were breaking like tiny avalanches down the swells. On the uppermost platform, a crane lifted and dangled a raft suspended with netting over the edge of the rig; men clung to it like bees to a honeycomb. The boat bucked and pitched, and Willard danced nimbly on the open lower deck. Twenty feet above the boat, the raft stopped, as the crane operator waited for the right moment to drop it on the rocking deck. When he did, Willard jumped forward to steer the raft down, though it could easily have knocked him overboard. Several loads of rig workers followed; the first to arrive on the *Thunderhawk* stayed on the deck to help guide their mates down. The last two men—the crane operators— swung like Tarzans on long ropes from the pilings to the *Thunderhawk*.

The rig workers sat in the passenger quarters below as we headed out around the delta toward the Southwest Passage. Huey Buffinet hardly said a word on the way back; the tension that had taken him over when we backed up to the rig persisted, although the boat was moving smoothly through the buffeting winds. On the radio we listening to a strained exchange between a dispatcher in Venice and another crew boat captain who was refusing to go farther out for another rig crew. Buffinet shook his head.

One of the roughnecks came up from below and sat looking out the window at the whitecaps on the Gulf, evenly spaced like the design on a bedspread. His wife and kids lived in Mississippi, and his six-year-old son lay awake on nights like this. I asked him if he liked the camaraderie on the rig, and the good food. He shook his head. "It just tires me out," he said. "I used to want to be out here for thrills. Now I just think of how dangerous it is. No, I want out. I've had it with the life."

We closed the hatches and motored in darkness and silence back through South Pass and up the river.

When we reached Venice, at least one roughneck called to reassure a six-year-old, and then we all joined the long line of cars evacuating the delta, again. I would not call my own children until I was high and dry in New Orleans.

I drove a side road east of the highway, actually the old Louisiana 31, through communities that the writers' project guide called "picturesque" in the 1930s. I looked into the empty screen porches. Still going north, I passed through what was once the Orange Belt. Many races lived here, voodoo was practiced, and behind the shallow orchards the trappers found marshes rich with muskrat. No more. The weather has taken charge, and the river never was sympathetic. Peering into the dark heaviness of the empty houses, I forgot for a few minutes that it was the wind at my back which had emptied them.

Point of Departure

Kansas City

STANDING atop Kaw Point and facing west, a solitary Hereford and I stared through the rain at the gray streets and warehouses and train tracks in the floodplain of the Kansas and the Missouri rivers below. There, earlier in this century, thousands of cattle lowed in stockyards before meeting abrupt ends in Kansas City's meat-packing plants. Young people, like my grandfather, who grew up on the Missouri side of the river, found summer work in the plants; he learned how to cuss and work long hours elbow to elbow with the immigrant Slavs and the children of the "Exodusters," freed blacks from the South who'd migrated to this area after the Civil War. "I'd load hams on a cart, push the cart, put the hams in another place, and watch these women make sausages, you know." My grandfather described it to me. "Some of them had developed massive forearms, like men, from twisting

A place to stay for stockyard workers in Kansas City, Kansas.
Arthur Rothstein.

sausages all day long. It was a six-day week and ten or twelve
hours a day."

The Hereford that shared my view was a chartreuse color;
he did not look well. Perhaps it was acrophobia. Not only is
it a long drop from the bluff to the river, but the Hereford
Association of America had mounted him, all three thousand
pounds of bovine plastic, atop a thirty-foot spire next to its
headquarters. Without the consolation of his doomed breth-

ren across the river, his life as an anachronism was lonely as well as dizzying.

According to the Federal Writers' Project's Kansas guide, the stockyards housed an enormous concentration of beef on the hoof in the 1930s. Eleven packinghouses, including the "Big Four"—Cudahy, Armour, Swift, and Wilson—were located there. The meat-packing industry took root in the 1870s; Charles F. Adams, a descendant of presidents, built the first stockyards, and the packinghouses crowded in after him. From the beginning Kansas City had oriented itself westward, pulling in the products of the prairie and distributing finished goods to the settlers. The railroads throve on this exchange, and turned Kansas City into the trading hub that the earliest settlers of Kaw Point, the Wyandotte Indians, had predicted it would someday be.

The stockyards and meat-packing houses that once gave Kansas City its character and its characteristic smell were gone now, moved to less urban locations, where taxes, transportation, and room to grow made business easier, and the smell was not a matter of civic controversy. As a novice in Kansas City, wandering its windy, hilly streets for the first time, I expected to find in it some urban reflection of a depressed midwestern farm economy. What I found instead, as I drove through the busy downtown and around the glistening high rises of the new Crown Center, was a most prosperous city. It was not clear just what industry had replaced the stockyards and packinghouses, but it was obvious *something* had.

Although the meat-packing plants were gone, some of what my grandfather had described, the steep and winding narrow streets, for instance, had not much changed. The twists of the two rivers, and the bumpy hills, shape the city, divvying much of it into distinct neighborhoods and commercial dis-

tricts with steep and skewed streets; the city was once, in the
words of the Kansas guide, "a consolidation of villages," and
this is still somewhat true of its older parts. And the city is,
of course, shared by two states, divided by a line that first
follows the Missouri River, and then, at the junction with
the Kansas, shoots south in a straight line, through the old
stockyards and up onto the hills. The University of Kansas
has built its medical center right on the Kansas side of this
invisible border, and that was the area where I stopped to call
some friends as the night grew late.

Meaning to use the phone, I entered a small nightclub on
a quiet street; as I swung through the door, a woman charged
at me, tearing open her blouse to thrust bare breasts in my
face. She collapsed a few inches before impact, giggling gid-
dily, and her friends dragged her away like a wrestler being
pulled out of the ring. The bartender looked up at me with
lidded eyes and asked, in a slow, deadpan voice, "So, you're
not a cop or anything?"

The next day, with a few leads from my local friend, I
sallied forth in the rain to find knowledgeable people who
could put some new ideas in my head about the rural Midwest. I had only an uninspired notion to visit the literal
"heartland" of the United States; the geographic center of the
lower 48, which lay not too far west in Kansas. In the 1930s
this heartland was torn apart by drought and dust storms;
" 'black snow,' " the Federal Writers' Project Colorado guide
called it, "so dark they couldn't see to lace their shoes."
Bankrupt families hit the road for California, abandoning the
Jeffersonian dream of tilling their own pieces of land, thinking only of survival. From what I read in the newspapers, a
new wave of foreclosures and migration was occurring now.
The geographic center seemed an appropriate place to take a
firsthand look.

I plotted a day in Kansas City that would take me from the offices of lawyers and bankers to the old neighborhood where my grandfather grew up. The folks in the high rises could perhaps articulate answers to my questions about the Midwest—what it was, what it was becoming, what would be left of the little Sherwood Anderson towns and family farms.

The Kemper family is a powerful force in today's Midwest, and David Kemper is what every family of wealth dreams of—the son or grandson who is poised, bright, and uncomplicated enough to embrace the family heritage and preserve the war chest. I called the office where he helps run his family's large banking and real estate interests, called him from a pay phone in the Kansas City library with no introduction, and he said, "Sure, come right on up, we'll talk."

I walked dripping into one of the whiter offices in my experience—white carpet, white walls, white furniture—with room enough for a Ping-Pong table as well. Kemper's corner window, on the fourteenth floor of the Bank Compshares building, looked out over Kansas City's downtown, which was getting sucked southward by the Crown Center, which the Kemper family had a hand in. Kemper's light hair and youthful face, his white shirt and tie gave him the look of a prefect at a prep school. He sprawled loose-limbed in a white chair and seemed to be in an expansive mood.

I asked him to explain the "midwestern" personality to me, and Kemper rattled off a string of predictable adjectives: "Self-reliant, pragmatic, results-oriented, not overly analytical . . . you won't find much psychosis here. . . . I've always believed that where people are raised in a tougher physical environment, with tougher weather, it really gets them charged up." Then he apologized for how clichéd this sounded.

Kemper once wrote an article in which he playfully invited

New Yorkers to take $4.2 billion they were planning to spend
fancying up a few miles of freeway in the Westways project
on the West Side, and spend it instead to relocate thousands
of the New York commuters to the dirt-cheap farmlands around
Kansas City. This was not entirely a joke. Kemper cited the
positive business atmosphere, the simple midwestern moral-
ity, and the high productivity of midwestern workers, most
of whom, he would have you believe, are like him: indus-
trious, happy to be there, and mildly witty about the Midwest's prosaic reputation.

But Kemper didn't work on a farm. He shuffled money,
and as long as buildings were going up, it mattered little to
him that his city was no longer the supreme agricultural and
livestock center. He and I both liked demographics.

"The decline of the family farm has really been going on
since the 1920s, and now it's going to accelerate," he said.
"As those farmers suffer and there's less money in the economy, they can't support those towns. What I think is going
to happen is, you're going to have a few winner towns around
the Midwest that are big enough that people like to live there,
because they'll have a lot of amenities. They'll do very well,
and these other towns will consolidate. And some of the towns
will just dwindle away."

Nor did Kemper think the 1970s trend to country living—when urban-to-rural migration outpaced rural-to-urban
migration for the first time since the Great Depression—would
be anything more than a fad. He mentioned Russia in the
1890s, when intellectuals decided they would go out and live
with the peasantry. "They went out for about three years,
and then said, 'My God, I'm not going to live in the swamps!' "
He laughed.

Kemper was a likable fellow, with the sort of flexible mind
that could find something amusing and hopeful in the most
convulsive change. He fitted the times nicely; Kansas City is

enjoying an aggressive, confident era, with just a touch of Epicureanism.

It may not have been so different in my grandfather's time here, not long after the century turned, though Kansas City was young and perhaps more raw then. My grandfather's circumstances were quite unlike Kemper's, of course, but the city itself was bustling and eager, and his family appears to have thriven, at least for a while, along with the city. Investors were arriving from the East, and new neighborhoods were opening; William Rockhill Nelson, founder of the *Kansas City Star,* had successfully campaigned to clean up and beautify the frontier town.

My grandfather had lived not far from the downtown area where Kemper now had his office. I drove down Admiral Boulevard and then Independence Avenue to Brooklyn, where I turned right and parked the Mustang. Walking down Brooklyn toward Seventh Street, where the Griffins lived, I entered a neighborhood that was not quite a slum, just leaning that way. My grandfather and his sister and their parents knew it during a grander era. The block they lived on was an easy walk from Central High School, where Allen Griffin was a popular kid and had "romance after romance," according to his sister.

There was a period, around 1910, when the Griffins had a cook, a maid, and a laundress. All this, my great-aunt told me, they owed to a propitious union of oysters and bread. My great-grandfather William Griffin was a plumber, the son of failed Lincolnshire farmers who had come to Canada in the 1880s, when his father's drinking lost them their land. My great-grandmother was part Alsatian and part Polish Jew, with an interesting past that she revealed only selectively. She arrived in this country with little more than an iron will to prosper.

She considered herself the money-maker of the family, and

disdained the heavy tools and dirty fingernails of her husband's trade. One of her entrepreneurial ventures was selling
bread around the neighborhood. One day she had the idea to
stuff oysters in the bread, creating an "oyster loaf." At Mar-
ledge's Oyster Bar, long gone today, this creation caught on,
and pretty soon the Griffins had a sizable all-night bakery
. . . and the maid, cook, and laundress. During the oyster
loaf prosperity, before the First World War, my great-grandmother provided her son with a piano teacher, toy soldiers,
and the sturdy certainty of the rewards that hard work, patri-
otism, and class pretensions would provide.

But the Griffin prosperity was short-lived. The success of
the oyster loaf attracted notice, and a big corporate competitor put the squeeze on them. Francesca Griffin fought and
lost; then she departed for California rather than allow her
neighbors to see her in lesser circumstances.

That would have been a lesson for my grandfather, too:
that in America you could, after failure or disappointment,
move away from your old home and make yourself over in a
new place, starting fresh, even paring away the less useful
parts of your personal history. That, at least, is what I think
I see when I look at the life my grandfather made for himself
after the family left Kansas City.

As I walked down Brooklyn, I passed on my right a three-
story cream-colored apartment building with a deep porch
and ornate gingerbread woodwork that could have been a
century old. The place had been gutted by fire, vandalized,
and boarded up. On the front porch someone had drawn the
outline of a person, titled it "Lester," and decorated it with
small-caliber bullet holes. My camera, slung over my shoulder, had a pretty high street value, and I began to wish I'd
left it in the car.

On the opposite side of the street, two sets of steps led up a small grassy slope to . . . nothing. A man who was sawing wood blocks to shore up the stoop on a nearby duplex came over to explain. He wore a worn tank top undershirt pulled down over his bulgy gut. His gray hair was a wild swirl. "My brother owned it," he said, pointing with a saw at the houseless stairs. "They burned it down. The ones that lived in it. They let any-fuckin'-body live in your place now, and you got no control over it; it's like they own it."

I told him I had come to Kansas City from Wyoming. "Still got mustangs out there?" I smiled; he had not noticed the car. "Got too many, right? They ought to just feed 'em something, so they wouldn't have any more . . . they can do that, you know.

"Like people—food and sex is all they want. So that's how you take care of it. These Africans, the Ethiopians? You know, anybody can fuck. A dog can." He dismissed the starving world with a wave of his arm and turned away from me. As he walked back to the duplex, he gestured to the bombed-out apartment house. "I thought you was here from the city. When they gonna rebuild that fucking dump?"

Half a block away was the street where my grandfather lived. Surprisingly, Seventh Street where it dead-ended at Brooklyn was still composed of red brick cobble, unusual in a city where the roads today are asphalt and blacktop. Perhaps pavement was unnecessary, because Seventh Street appeared to be closed to vehicles. Whole blocks on the west side of Brooklyn were enclosed with chain-link fence, and where once there must have been houses, now there was green open space and some large institutional buildings.

Across the street from the fence, I introduced myself to a man who was sitting on the porch of his parents' home with a friend. He was Lee Drummond, and behind his house, there was a gully thick with trees. The friend lounged with one leg

up on the parapet, finishing a toke, but Lee, a barrel-chested
man with curly, oiled hair and lidded eyes, came down to
talk.

O'G: Can you tell me, what's the building over there?
LD: They got the nurses livin' in there, that's right. Work at
the hospital, live there. Fence keeps 'em safe, I guess. You
live here?
O'G: My grandfather, he lived on that street.
LD: That's right—not you, cuz it's been . . . I was born here
in 1949, and the houses been gone there long as I can
remember. You takin' pictures?
O'G: Not really. My grandfather went to Central High, before
the First World War.
LD: I went to Central, too. What's his name?
O'G: Griffin. But a long time ago. How is it living here?
How's the neighborhood?
LD (looking at his friend, chuckling): I like it. My folks came
here in 1940. It's okay, right, man?
   The friend nods, unsmiling.
O'G: Is it all black?
LD: No, white, too, it's *mixed.* Mixed.
O'G: A good place to live?
LD: We get along okay. So, what you doing here?
O'G: I'm a writer. I wanted to see where my grandfather was
born.
LD (pause, then big smile): I get it. You doing a 'Roots'
thing, right? [Pause.] You want some of this?

   I walked slowly back up the street, past the empty block
of Seventh Street, which led, I learned later, to the KC College of Osteopathic Medicine and the Conley Maternity Hospital. It seemed likely that a young Allen Griffin had once
placed one foot in front of another just as I was doing, walk-

ing this route to high school. I could picture him, because I had watched him walking so often as an old man, good stride, head back, arms swinging.

When he was done here in Kansas City, he headed west, and now I turned the Mustang in that direction, too.

Destination

Smith Center

*On the continental map, Kansas is in the exact center of the
United States, a parallelogram with one corner nibbled off by the
Missouri River. The State on this map looks flat and uninteresting
topographically, for within its boundaries are no lakes, no
mountains, no really navigable rivers. It seems to be a rectangle of
prairie grass with no more need for a guide book than is met by its
highway junction signs.*
—William Allen White, Introduction to
Kansas: A Guide to the Sunflower State

AFTER studying my maps and guides, I was ready to accept
William Allen White's ironic evaluation of the state he made
famous: Kansas seemed to have not much in the way of dis-
tinctive landmarks to attract the traveler, only the somewhat
amorphous distinction of its centrality. There is no pot of
gold or Fountain of Youth to mark the exact geographic cen-

ter of the United States, no shrine to the wellspring of national character. The honor of centrality must be qualified, too, by the distinction that Kansas is the geographic center of the conterminous United States, the lower 48, while the prize for geographic center of North America goes to North Dakota. It isn't even quite accurate to describe the point of all this as the geographic center. It is the *geodetic* center, which is a geographic calculation covering such vast distances that adjustments must be made for the earth's shape and curvature.

But travelers of my sort are always ready to aim ourselves at a weightless objective and take flight, because flight itself is the stimulant. I talked to my wife the night before I left Kansas City, and she asked, "Where have you decided to go?"

"Smith Center, Kansas," I answered.

"What for?" she asked, with her usual directness.

"It's the center of the United States," I answered.

"Well," she said, rather too slowly.

"It's the *geodetic* center of the United States," I said, more impressively.

"Mmmmm. Is there anything actually there?"

"The center. The fountainhead. The heart of the heart of the heartland."

"So, is there a stick in the ground? Or what?"

When you're hundreds of miles apart, one of you chasing fanciful visions and the other refereeing the cereal wars, you sometimes find your respective views somewhat at variance. I heard the upstairs phone click as a small hand picked it up, and then television sounds and childish shouts of triumph and defeat, and over it all the heavy breathing of a young listener. We Are Not Alone. . . .

My wife said, "Well, take some pictures." Which meant: You see what I'm putting up with?

So I played another card; the writers' project Kansas guide
had an intriguing item about Smith County. " 'Home on the
Range," composed in 1873, was the first widely popular song
of genuine Kansas origin,' " I read. "The cabin where that
was written is right there in Smith County, too."

"Right exactly on the center?"

"Now, come on."

"If there's a curio stand or something, pick up something
for the children, okay? You didn't bring them anything last
time."

My wife surrendered her receiver to another heavy breather,
and my daughters and I sang a verse:

> Oh give me a home,
> Where the buffalo roam,
> And the deer and the antelope play. . . .

I VIEWED this journey as a trip to the Midwest heartland, but
actually there is some uncertainty and misunderstanding about
just where and what the Midwest is. Most of us respond primarily to the first syllable of the term: The Midwest is the
country's midsection, the middle somewhere between the
Appalachians and the Rockies. Others define the Midwest by
accent or agriculture: pigs and corn, a flat twangy way of
talking. I stopped in Lawrence, Kansas, and visited a geographer named James R. Shortridge to see if he could set me
straight.

Like most of us, Shortridge at one time accepted, unex-
amined, the notion of the Midwest as a settled agricultural
buffer vaguely "midway" between the civilized, urban East
and the wild and woolly West. Shortridge, a Missourian
himself, attended Dartmouth as an undergraduate, and there
"people started *accusing* me of being from the Midwest." That

1930s gas station. *Myers.*

got Shortridge interested. His fellow students probably didn't know exactly what they meant by "being from the Midwest," but the term had a derisive whiff of bovinity and hayseed. Shortridge retaliated intellectually, delving into historical records to determine what "Midwest" really meant and when the term first came into use.

"Midwest" failed to turn up in nineteenth-century books about Ohio. But there was one 1890s author who called Tennessee the "Midwest." Then, as Shortridge burrowed through Kansas literature, he found the term used there in the 1880s, when Kansas was still a western frontier area with settlers pressing in. Something was amiss, he decided.

Then he understood: The "Mid"-west was the middle of what was called the "West" in the 1880s, on a north-south axis: There was the southwest (west Texas, Oklahoma, etc.) and the Northwest (the Dakotas, Ohio, etc.), and there was the Midwest. "It was a way to differentiate the West—you had the pioneering states of the Northwest, the distinct Indian and southern culture in the Southwest, and these more settled states in the middle," said Shortridge. I was less sure that western Kansas qualifies as Midwest, but then, if you used the term as it originated, the Midwest today would be somewhere near San Francisco Bay.

Shortridge, a red-bearded university professor, has a dry, ironic laugh that reminded me of the laughter I'd heard in Kansas City. He called himself a "cultural geographer," a wonderfully open discipline whose practitioners pick up some clue in the landscape and then zoom off into whatever area of study it implies. I'm applying for membership.

———

> *Wheat is the alpha and omega of {central Kansas}. Remarks*
> *about the weather are not mere tokens of conversation for drought or*
> *prolonged rain may be the difference between a lean and fat purse.*
> *In June wheat becomes "The Wheat" of anxious inquiry. Under*
> *the brassy sun the yellowish stalks droop and turn golden.*
> *Blue-overalled men go into the fields and a burnished stream of*
> *grain pours into Salina. Often the storage bins are filled to*
> *overflowing so that the grain is piled on the ground like sand.*
> —Kansas: A Guide to the Sunflower State

MY route to Smith Center took me due west from Lawrence to Salina, where I would link up with the Smoky Hill River and follow it north into Smith County. If the signs are to be believed, most Kansas towns are sending their favorite sons into outer space. Salina, "Home of Astronaut Steve Hawley," is distinguished by its unwillingness, in 1862, to become a terminus for rowdy Texas cattle drives, according to the Kansas guide; it became instead a milling center for central Kansas's wheat producers.

I drove this way to drop in on Wes Jackson's Land Institute, which is trying, with a little money and a lot of young volunteers, to study and solve some of the problems that are depleting the soil and the economy in Kansas and other plains states. My interest was more in the depleting of culture, but the two are in some respects the same thing, as Jackson has emphasized in his writing.

I got lost on the way to the Land Institute, which lies inconspicuously in a hilly area near the Smoky Hill River, distinguished only by a couple of towering jet age wind generators. Rain was falling, and the fields around the institute were muddy; wood sidewalks connected the buildings. In the garden next to the main building, greens were lush and strawberries were ripening and peas were ready to pick, though it was only May, a time when winter still held sway in Wyoming. Odd little outbuildings—an adobe building, a yurtlike structure, an outhouse designated "World Headquarters"—expressed the various history of what participants here call "The Land." The place is not a showcase of New Age farming so much as it is a cluster of ongoing experiments, with the reassuring flaws of a working farm. I was to hear about worms attacking the fruit trees and construction of the new barn stalling midway to completion.

Wes Jackson has the credentials, if not the budget, for serious research, and the institute has concentrated on studying ways to preserve the fragile plains soil by planting perennial crops that mimic native plants. The trick is to provide a harvest as well. Jackson has written extensively about the industrial style of farming that "mines" and depletes underground water, solves pest and nutrient problems with chemical additives, and gobbles up "family" farms that can't compete and prairie grasslands that shouldn't have to.

The Land Institute is tied into what is sometimes called the "New Age network," a motley underground of groups that view themselves as oaring against the American current; the group I had met on the island down in the Plaquemines Delta considered itself New Age. New Age aficionados have some heroes in common, among them poet Gary Snyder and writer Wendell Berry, but their beliefs and intellectual rigor vary widely.

Jackson, a sturdy, dour middle-aged man, welcomed me and then made it clear he was too busy to sit down and talk—busier, I thought with amusement, than the powerful bankers I had visited in Kansas City. My guide instead was Carol LaLiberte, a gangly dark-haired intern at the institute. We slogged up through the herb garden and over the hill, and she fended off some questions about herself, sticking to the subject of agricultural innovation. She showed me a plot she was managing, where Maximilian sunflowers had been planted the year before; this year, different species were being planted, to see if the sunflowers' ability to suppress weeds would continue in the soil when other crops were planted. The Land's star perennial this year was Illinois bundleflower; in the past, wild senna. Clearly, there have been setbacks, but Jackson has said all along that his research will take "up to a hundred years." He has a farmer's time frame.

The community in which Jackson and his followers worked, explained Carol, was larger than Salina. It was a worldwide community of like-minded people, who corresponded and met at annual gatherings. Carol talked with inspiration of reeducating today's farmers, and described morning "warm-up" meetings in which institute members discuss issues, read poetry, and talk about "responsible" relationships with the Good Earth, giving themselves a little more brain mulch as they go about their outdoor chores.

By this time—we were looking at a slope of native grasses, some of that rare Kansas commodity that had never been tilled—I had become more curious about Carol's background. Slightly hunched forward, in the shy way of tall young women, she talked about finding a place where she could settle and nurture the land and a family, but her references began in the present and went forward, never back. When I asked her where she was from, she laughed with New Age irony and dodged the question. She grew up in the Northeast, I finally determined, and went to college in Maine.

You run into it everywhere—a compulsion, sometimes unwitting, to disown the landscapes we grew up with, and start anew. It may have something to do with the crowded, throwaway world where money is made; many people dream of leaving it all behind, and sometimes you find them covetously searching the handsomer rural areas of the country. That's pretty much what I did, so I find it natural enough. But it seems not to be enough for many people simply to inhabit a new and, they think, better place; there is the desire, too, to graft a new root system, and accomplish in a few years the kind of rapport with landscape and its history that it once took generations to establish.

That may not be so easy, though. A young man I met in Wyoming tried for years to extract local lore from old-timers around the Teton Valley, where he had moved from the East; he knew there was a treasure trove of history there, and he sincerely wanted to know the country better through their stories. To his dismay, the old folks were reticent. When I had occasion to talk to one of the old-timers myself, for a newspaper story about a new road, I mentioned my friend's frustration. The old fellow said, "Well, he hasn't told me where *he's* from." That was all.

━━━

I remember:
how the grass under the mulberry trees
hid the soft blue berries
that splattered our brown feet.
Mulberry sweetness purpled our teeth,
stained our fingers and faces.

Summer long we ranged the road
between the swift parenthesis
of dawn and dusk:
herding hungry cattle.

—*Direction.* vol. 1, no. 3 (1938), featuring
"American Stuff," by workers of the
Federal Writers' Project

NORTH of Salina, the interstate petered out, and I drove on smaller roads through smaller towns. Rural Kansas is as good a place as you'll find for a mind-vacuuming drive: ahead, the long, flat roll of the horizon, accessible and inviting as a gentle beach, with tall silos like faraway lighthouses; above, thunderheads by day and a sea of stars at night. I turned off onto narrow, straight country roads, flanked by planted and fallow fields, windbreaks of layered olives, evergreens, and willows, and, occasionally, an empty, leaning clapboard house. A billboard announced: SAME GUNS THAT ASSASSINATED FOUR PRESIDENTS!

Late on a Sunday afternoon I drove into the town of Smith Center, Kansas, and found a motel. Church would have been out by that hour, so I went where I thought there was a chance of finding people: the fairgrounds and softball fields.

There was a prospect livestock show, a competition for animals not fully mature, going on in a small, open arena at the fairgrounds, so I sat in the bleachers and watched.

Wind—that fierce, dry plains wind that will take a patch of eroded ground and expand it into a desert—kicked dust in our faces as the round-bellied judge, holding a microphone, paced around in the brown dirt, examining the cattle.

"You've got a steer here who isn't far along on fat cover— you've got some catching up to do. . . . Smooth, long muscles here . . . this steer's picking up some grease. . . . Good length of stride, more on top is desirable. . . ."

Young adolescents, boys and girls of widely various sizes, led their steers around the ring, each from time to time reaching under the animal with a long-handled prod to rub its belly, a technique that greenhorns view with curiosity, but which calms the animal and keeps it from drooping. The steers were only a step ahead of their masters in the race to adulthood, and one could sense in several shy teenage faces a feeling that they as much as the animals were being scrutinized for fat cover and such. The judge restricted his comments to the relative merits of the four-legged beasts, but those of us in the bleachers were free to size up the more extreme variations among the young humans, from a slouching six-footer with a vague mustache to a tomboy with a six-year-old's body and a Band-Aid across her nose. The most positive contribution of animal husbandry at the 4-H level may be that kids get to see, in the livestock, how things pretty much even out once the hormones finish their work.

"He's got a lot of butt on him," said the judge of a husky Simmental, and I was unsure whether that was a compliment. "A lot of masculinity, stylish and straight." He said that while looking at the front end of the animal, and masculinity was clearly a desirable thing, even in a steer. I watched the smallest boy in the ring struggle to lead, rather than be

led by, his Black Angus, a determined beast that didn't like
turning corners to his right.

"A little coarse up front, you want to smooth him up and
extend that neck out," said the judge to a confident-looking
girl with breasts and a big Stetson. She took another critical
look at her animal and spit.

The boy with the Black Angus was leaning his full weight
against the steer's neck, trying to turn him back to my side
of the ring, where the others had lined up. Finally he got his
animal in order, and the judge came to him. "He's pushing
a little more grease than I like to see at this prospect stage,"
he said, and gave the boy a red ribbon.

Afterward I approached the boy's father, Steve Hofer, and
he expressed disappointment with the red ribbon. But he
invited me to come out to the Hofers' feedlot later that week
to talk about life at the center of America.

That evening I jogged around town looking for a softball
game, without luck. I fell into bed in a room that by now
seemed quite familiar: the musty smell of the rug and the
stiff, drab curtains; the spot-hiding brown-and-green pattern
of the bedspread; the TV movies about gotta-dance teenagers
or visitors from outer space. Perhaps I had not traveled all
that far to get to Kansas.

Motels—an innovation of the 1930s, when America's
romance with the road was firmly established—have a way of
cooling off a traveler. The phone, the yellow plastic chair,
the throwaway cups wrapped in plastic, the flicker of the tube
conspire to banish the sunbaked confusion of hours on the
highway. It's just one more thing that every region in America now has in common; perhaps I was worrying too much
about how I would gain access to these shy midwestern lives.
The evening news was, after all, the same here as everywhere
else in America.

Drovers taking a break in the Kansas City stockyards.
Arthur Rothstein.

*{The homesteader} is, often enough, the salt of the earth. The
courage and fortitude he has shown are amazing. He sprang from
a race of adventurers—young men and women who saw visions and
dreamed dreams. For a time he held Nature in subjection but in
turn was compelled to bow to Nature. He has gone. His place must
be filled by a new race who follow another star.*
—Guy H. Rader, *Direction,* vol. 1, no. 3 (1938),
featuring "American Stuff"

THE Hofers lived southwest of Smith Center in a modern
house with a two-car garage. It was a far cry from those old
shingled houses with tottering chimneys and empty-eyed
window frames that sit out on the treeless prairies. An artist
might paint one of those; you get the urge, driving by, to

pull over and sit on the porch with a book by Willa Cather.
Newer houses out here are more horizontal than vertical. I'd
like to think this was a sensible response to the howling winds,
equivalent to the dugouts that early settlers built here, low
to the ground and burrowed into the occasional chalk ledges
or hills. But it may just be a lucky match between popular
taste and environment, since the ranch house style is cloned
from Frank Lloyd Wright's Southwest and Far West crea-
tions.

The Hofers' house was built in 1971, when Steve, returning from college and the Army, married Ruth, a local Lutheran
girl, and bought eighty acres. He bought the land from family; his relatives had been in this area for over a century. In
front of the house grew bushy pines.

Steve and Ruth Hofer's place stands within view of the
four small silos where Hofer & Son, Inc., mixes feed for fat-
tening cattle, beside a creek lined with shrubs and tall elms.
Behind the house there is a satellite dish, and while Steve
and I talked, his son Michael, nine, master of the red-ribbon
Angus, watched television in the other room. He would pop
in and out to tell us the more exciting details of a car wreck,
or to ask me if I was interested in prairie dogs or coyotes.
Shooting them, that is.

Steve Hofer had brown hair and the lined neck of an outdoor man, a smile that revealed large white teeth, and an
interest in history. He and Ruth, whose skin is so pale you
fear for her walking fifteen yards to the car in direct sun, gave
an impression of easygoing wholesomeness. But they had the
humorous tic that I was beginning to view as a regional trait,
and no fear of discussing subjects that weren't particularly
wholesome.

Originally the Hofers were innkeepers in Southeastern
Switzerland. Steve's grandfather's grandfather, Johannes, came
to the United States in 1873, about the time a red bandanna

was mounted on a seven-foot tree limb to mark the location of Smith Center. The first Hofer in America briefly ran a hotel in Wisconsin, then came west to homestead in Kansas. This would have been a time of great excitement. Kansas had been a state (admitted after prolonged struggle as a nonslavery state, in 1861) for less than a decade, and Indians were still raiding settlers and getting raided in return by the military. The Homestead Act of 1862 provided 160 acres for twenty-six to thirty-four dollars and a promise to live on the land for five years, and European immigrants were being hustled off the boats and out to Kansas by railroad agents.

Steve's grandfather Richard Hofer started the farmer-feeder operation, whereby cattle are bought, fattened up, and sold to slaughterhouses. In the 1980s the business mirrored Smith County's precarious, side road existence: The Hofers survived by picking up the odd lots of steers, all sizes and shapes and colors, that the enormous feedlots in Texas and Missouri didn't want. They had suffered like everybody else when land prices collapsed in the late seventies. A bank in which they invested went under, and Hofer was worried now that he might have to lay off his hired hand.

Hofer and I drove north through his property and across the path of a recent tornado. First we came to the silos and cattle pens, crowded with lowing feeders ticketed for a truck ride to the slaughterhouse in a few days; next we passed a creek bed, where low, gnarly trees gave off a cool breath of creek air; beyond, the land rose slightly and a tree-shaded dirt road broke off to an empty farmhouse. Then came the hog pens, where slash piles of tin and and wood on both sides of the road were all that remained of sheds ravaged by the wind. We were on a slight rise; the field to the east stretched away flat and empty, relieved only by a failed windbreak of scraggly trees, leaning toward each other for consolation.

When he was young, Steve told me, the farmhouse on the

treelined road was occupied, and in the empty field stood a
one-room schoolhouse. It had been consolidated, when he
was in grammar school, with the school in Gaylord, about
twelve miles away. So, eventually, were the schools in the
nearby town of Cedar, once a candidate for county seat and
now a ghost town. Cedar, which was well situated and well
settled in the 1870s along the Solomon River, lost out,
according to the Kansas guide, because L. T. Reese and a
dozen other homesteaders up in the Smith Center area faked
a long list of "bona fide" settlers on a petition to the governor
for the county seat. "We had a terrible time thinking up six
hundred names," Reese said later.

Only a year before my visit, the Gaylord school had been
cut back to grammar school and junior high. The kids are
now bussed up to Smith Center for high school. Schools are
a "leading indicator," to use the demographers' jargon: While
the bankers still smile cheerfully and say things are fine, while
the store and the restaurant hang on bravely, a school will
shut down, and the future is writ clear.

The one-room school fit the idyllic stereotype, with a big
open field behind it and the creek only a fourth-grade sprint
away. In the thirties there would have been a different home-
steading family on nearly every quarter section, with plenty
of children to fill a schoolhouse every few miles. Things are
different these days: You have to farm much more than 160
acres to support a family. The result is fewer people, consolidated schools and long bus rides, and towns that are drying
out like husks in September.

South of the Hofers' home, alongside the Solomon River,
shoots of oats were sprouting unevenly from rows running up
and down steep hills. It's the kind of planting that costs a
farm topsoil and produces a scraggly crop at best. Hofer,
snorting in derision, said the land had been bought four or
five years ago by a city fellow who needed a tax write-off. The

owner hired people to cultivate and harvest his land; the land is unloved. Just beyond was a healthier, more densely planted field, owned by a local. But it was up for sale; the owner was bankrupt.

Steve and Ruth were in better shape than most of their neighbors, because they hadn't bought as much land and machinery during the spendthrift days of the 1970s, when farmers, encouraged by foreign markets and politicians and bankers, went on an unprecedented buying spree. And even the farmers in trouble here are philosophical about the ups and downs of the economy. They're apt to be much more impassioned about things like . . . well, things like the roller rink and the drive-in.

Steve Hofer sat in his living room, wearing a V-neck T-shirt, rubbing his neck, and looking tired around the eyes. There was Little League baseball still to come that evening, and decorations for a junior high dance. Ruth Hofer was trying to control David, their fourth, and unexpected, child, who was one year old and doing a wobbly-legged dance atop the coffee table. The sun was going down, spreading a red cloak on the horizon outside the west window.

Steve said, "The boys who like to fish and hunt, they fish and hunt, it's fine for them. I worry about my daughter, because she's about fourteen, and I don't know what she's going to do—well, on Saturday night. When I was that age, we still had drive-in movies. We had a roller rink. I remember that there were lights with tin cans and stars cut in tinfoil. And another thing was: Vietnam was on, and we still had a draft, so when the boys finished high school, you either went to college or went to the service. Now, with no draft, and they don't have the money to go to college, there's nothing to do, but they can go up to Duffy's and drink legally. We had two girls at the high school get pregnant this year, to guys who were out of school.

"I can't help but hope that one of my sons will take this business over. It probably can't support more than one family now. But what happens when my son goes to Kansas State? Most likely he's going to meet a girl from Kansas City. She isn't going to know a cow from a bull. And he's going to want to come home and go in with his dad the way I did with my dad, and my dad did with his dad. And she's going to come out here and look around—no McDonald's, not even a movie theater, the closest movie in Smith Center, twenty miles away, only open on weekends, and the movies are old. A nice place to visit, she says, but she wouldn't want to live here."

———

*In 1934 William Goodwin and his wife, of Tempe, Arizona,
filed suit . . . against radio networks and motion-picture
producers . . . claiming that they had written and copyrighted
"Home on the Range" in 1905 under the title "My Arizona Home."
The defendants instructed their attorney, Samuel Moanfeldt, to
find out who really wrote it. . . . Moanfeldt traveled through
Arizona, New Mexico, California, Nevada, Utah, Idaho, and
Oregon before . . . he came in 1936 to Smith Center and was
directed to the home of Clarence (Cal) Harlan, then 87 years
old. . . . "Pa," said Mrs. Harlan, "get down your guitar and let's
see if we can't sing it for the gentleman." Accompanying themselves
on guitar and banjo the old couple sang the song as they had
first sung it 63 years before.*
—Kansas: A Guide to the Sunflower State

NORTH of Smith Center there is a little cabin on Beaver Creek where Dr. Brewster Higley wrote "Home on the Range." The cabin belonged now to Pete Rust, a large man in overalls who was working in his yard when I drove up. Rust was puttering around the front of a sturdy white frame house, but that turned out not to be Higley's. The original "Home on the Range" was a small, sagging log-and-plaster structure that sat off to one side among the trees.

Rust, a round-bellied man with some missing teeth, talked a little about a farmer's favorite subject: cropland. He said that in the 1970s, when land values skyrocketed and agriculture boomed in Smith County, people were buying land for $1,000 an acre (back in the homesteading days, the railroads offered land at about $1.50 an acre). Rust sold about seven hundred acres himself, though he won't name the price he got.

"I feel sorry for the ones that bought it," he said. "You can't sell it now, for much of anything." We talked about wild turkeys and tornadoes, both of which have recently had a resurgence in Smith County. The turkeys have come back in direct proportion to the exodus of people, who have left because they can't pay for the land they bought back in the seventies, or can't entice the next generation to return to the hard work and isolation of the farm.

As for the tornadoes, people tell you different things. Kansans downplay the storms, but outsiders who have read *Giants in the Earth* and other epics of the Midwest arrive on the prairies with their collars turned up and a wary eye on the horizon. Rust insisted, as Hofer had, that tornadoes were a rarity in Smith County.

Rust may have enjoyed talking tornadoes more than the subject of Higley, which must grow tiresome as one more tourist drives up humming the famous tune. When Rust first moved to this place, Higley's old cabin was a dilapidated chicken shack over by the gully. Now it is on all the maps, and there are brief printed biographies of Higley by local historians at the cabin itself.

Higley was living in La Porte, Indiana, and practicing medicine when, one day in 1871, he closed his practice, dropped his children off with relatives in Illinois, and contin-

ued on west. He left behind his fourth wife, and took along
the bottle he had come to rely on. In Kansas he reformed
himself, if we can believe his sanguine biographers, and built
a successful medical practice, as well as his home on Beaver
Creek. In 1875 he took Wife No. 5, Sarah Clemens. The
doctor was reputedly a good surgeon, but he was better known
as a singer and fiddler.

He built his cabin on Beaver Creek in the summer of 1872,
luring with a keg of beer an enthusiastic crew to lift the logs
in place. That fall, he wrote the words to "My Western Home."
It took awhile, but eventually the doctor was encouraged to
show his lyrics to Dan Kelly, of the local Harlan Brothers
Orchestra, and Kelly put them to music. In April 1873,
during a dance at the home of Judge and Mrs. John Harlan,
the song, sung by nine-year-old Virgie Harlan, had its debut:

> A home, a home
> Where the deer and the antelope play.
> Where seldom is heard
> A discouraging word
> And the sky is not cloudy all day.

No one is sure how the song was disseminated around the
country. In the years that followed, it was shared by cattle
drovers, miners, and other itinerants and modified to fit each
new setting. I came across supposedly indigenous versions in
several different states' guides. From the copyright fracas that
ensued in the 1930s, one might gather that the song had
sprung simultaneously into the minds of folks all over the
country. By that time it was President Franklin D. Roosevelt's favorite song, and Admiral Richard E. Byrd reported
that he sang "Home on the Range" to penguins during six
lonely months at the South Pole.

On the day of my visit Higley's shake-roofed shack was

A failed Kansas bank. *Arthur Rothstein.*

crammed with more paraphernalia—rifles, a coffee grinder, a plow, chairs, a stove, and even the doctor's tax receipts— than could possibly have fitted, along with the doctor and his growing family, into a home/chicken coop that measures only about fourteen by sixteen feet. It was not easy to imagine these cheerful lyrics flowing from the pen of a man in such cramped quarters. He must have played his fiddle very loudly or downed a lot of hooch to keep from muttering at

least one discouraging word. Perhaps he spent a lot of time
out on the range, though, you may note, "range" was not
mentioned in the original lyric.

DON'T talk to the bankers. People in Smith County told me
that.

In part, it's because some feel the bankers suckered them
into the current agricultural crisis, offering them generous
loans in the 1970s for expansion based on land values that
couldn't hold up. The $1,000-per-acre prices that Rust talked
about have fallen to as low as $150 to $200 for pasture or
$500 to $600 for good cropland. That's a stiff dose of reality,
but bankers are still accused of painting a falsely optimistic
picture.

I ignored the warnings and talked to two, thinking it would
be interesting to see whether bankers sink into their high-
backed chairs when the going gets tough. One was Bob
Bethorst, of Smith Center, an old-fashioned business-out-of-
a-pickup banker who puts out a newsletter, "Chips from the
Cowpath," with such chestnuts as: "Animals are such agreeable friends—they ask no questions and pass no criticisms."
Bethorst explained the cyclical nature of lending in a farm
community: loans in the spring for milo, corn, soybeans, and
feed crops, to be paid back in the fall; more dollars advanced
in the fall to get the winter wheat in, repaid in the spring;
rolling credit for feeder pigs or stocker cattle. A farmer today
is on intimate terms with his banker. But Bethorst down-
played the Farm Belt's problems, and wished the media and
the coffee shop philosophers would stop emphasizing the
negative. He was like a small-town newspaper editor who
discovers there are fewer problems if fewer problems get written up in the paper.

————

*{Kansan Carry Nation} smashed saloons with zeal and won for
herself a permanent place in history, although her actual
accomplishments were little more than a ripple on the pool of the
State's "Wetness." The problem of liquor is still vexing. In 1937
the State legislature legalized the manufacture and sale of beer of
3.2 per cent alcoholic content. Sterner liquors, although legally
banned, are frankly in evidence in many communities.*
—Kansas: A Guide to the Sunflower State

SOMETIMES in Smith Center I got an invitation to dinner;
some nights, tired of spending evenings with my notebooks
and a television, I took myself out. One night I went out to
the notorious Duffy's, the only hard-liquor club in town—
members only—at the invitation of the owner, who had seen
me around and approached me in the supermarket. All the
tables were empty; I drank some whiskey sitting abreast of
the bar with five or six local men. None showed any interest
in a stranger; they sagged tiredly against the bar and looked
ahead even while they talked to each other about construction
jobs. I finished my drink and went back to the television and
notebooks.

Another afternoon I found myself at the northern end of
the county and elected to cross the border into Nebraska for
an evening meal at a fairly prosperous inn with a horseshoe
bar in the rear of the restaurant. It was Sunday, and the afternoon buffet crowd was just breaking up. A little girl in a
pink dress with a spout of hair ponytailed on top harassed the
white-haired man at the cash register. She kept asking him
questions from a question-and-answer game.

"Okay, where is the Henry Ford Museum? Who played,
uh, William Hol . . . ding's brother in *Sar-bee-nuh?*"

"Dearborn; and that's *Sabrina*. I don't know who the brother was." To a customer: "Good meal?"

The customer nodded. He was tall and weathered, with a cantaloupe belly jutting out; his wife was powdered and round, and clutched a turquoise purse at her waist. The man sensed my stare—or perhaps he sensed his wife's discomfort under my stare—and gave me a curt glance.

"Grandpa!" said the girl. "Which of the Hawaiian Islands has active volcanoes?"

"Hawaii," answered the man who had just paid his bill.

"Did you give me Kansas dollars?" the man at the cash register said sternly after his departing customer. "We don't take foreign currency, Jim." Everyone who heard smiled and looked down, as if they had heard it often enough before, as if you didn't laugh out loud in public. Feeling anomalous, I wondered if my presence had put a damper on things.

"*Grandpa!*" shouted the girl. "What were the last three U.S. states to join the Union?"

"Alaska," he answered, ringing up another tab, "Hawaii . . . Good food?"

Another couple, cut from the same body mold as the first, but different in the face, nodded. The man took a toothpick and put on a hat as they moved toward the door.

"*Three,* Grandpa," said the girl.

"What, Kansas?" responded the man. Again, I saw some private smiles around the dining room. But I hesitated to smile myself, with the man at the cash register now looking at me; a solitary stranger on a Sunday evening was strange indeed here.

Both at the Nebraska inn and at Duffy's I found myself examining my mission in Smith Center. The locals couldn't figure out why I was there, and it wasn't easy to explain. When I encountered this sort of practiced indifference, my curiosity faltered and I began to feel a little spooky. Take away the mantle of my journalistic mission, and what was left was a stranger with no history who wandered into town and wanted to join a softball game or answer a child's Trivial Pursuit question. I've picked up hitchhikers like that in Wyoming. They start off talking softball, and in a few minutes they're telling you about their abduction by extraterrestrials.

So it was back to the motel room. It was too late to call Wyoming, so I lay down and turned on the tube. On television I watched a movie about a newspaperman who moved from the big city to a small town in the West, and there became suspicious of mysterious drug experiments involving livestock. Soon he was dead, and it was left to his buddy, a maverick big-city cop, to figure out what our nefarious government scientists were up to in their spooky desert laboratories. And there in the lab, doing nasty things to cattle, I recognized a friend from Wyoming, a young rancher from a town named Cora, John Perry Barlow.

Startled, I sat up, shaking. Historian Daniel Boorstin has written of the "particularly American menace of unreality." A recognizable real person had suddenly materialized in the paranoid prairie movie I'd been watching; the real had begun to meet the unreal halfway. I decided I'd better lay off the stuff. One American drug—the road—was enough.

———

We shall raise up a new generation here,
We shall turn all the soil and freshen it,
We shall build all the houses over, clean and with large windows,
We shall heal every man of failure or success,
We shall take every child to show him your birds and rivers,
And to learn the sound of the wind in the tall cottonwood.

—"A Legend Passing," *American Stuff, An Anthology of Prose*
and Verse by members of the Federal Writers' Project (1937)

EARLY on a couple of people had mentioned Joe Befort, a wheat farmer living east of Smith Center, as someone who could give me an earful about hard times on the farm. The first time I called him and asked if I could drop by, he said, "But I don't know who you are," in an uninflected, clamped voice. The conversation wilted like drought-stricken wheat.

Persistence, though, seemed to pay off in Kansas; I tried Befort again, and the second time he agreed to see me. Not without a little more prolongation, though. I arrived at his farm, south of Lebanon and east of Smith Center, and he greeted me standoffishly. He was a tall, serious-faced man, built solidly and without taper; he wore dark-rimmed glasses, prominent against his pale, unaging face, and the ubiquitous cap with an equipment dealer's insignia. He walked a little bow-legged, with the last joints of his fingers in his pants pockets. Befort made no attempt to charm, but a spark of flamboyance shone when he gave a stylish two-finger salute to acquaintances as he passed in his truck.

We were going to talk about the financial bind of the midwestern farmer, and Befort's bind in particular. But I was left standing alone that first day in an enormous equipment barn, petting the Befort family's basset hound while Joe chatted aimlessly with a neighbor in blue-striped coveralls who happened to drop by. I watched his grease-streaked son Brian monkey his way around a huge John Deere Turbo 7700 combine, and after a while I said I'd be going. Befort didn't crack a smile; he just invited me back another time.

The next time I visited, on a day of fresh alfalfa smells, we got in his truck and drove south to look at some hay he had promised to bale for a neighbor. The hay was on marginal cropland, hilly and irregular; the hay we stooped to finger on the rise was dry, but in the low curve where the hillside drained it was still wet, with a sweet, beery smell, not ready for baling.

We stopped at another field to look at Brian Befort's barley, and the elder Befort showed me how to feel for the barley's head above a joint in the stalk, how to squeeze out the seed and check its quality. You could see the pleasure he took in working the stalk between his thumb and forefinger. At still another field we herded some feeder cattle back into a corral, with me running on foot and Befort heading them off with his pickup. In an afternoon he had shown me the geography of his day-to-day life.

Then we drove back toward Befort's house, a gray rectangle with a spruce windbreak, an orderly vegetable garden, some cattle and hog pens, and the big equipment barn, where Brian was still working.

The feeder cattle are one of several efforts Befort has made in recent years to diversify and outflank his financial problems, which are immense. The banks have helped him with these ventures. Of the four-year hog business, he said, "All I've gotten out of that is exercise," and that seems to be true of everything he's tried. Much of his land and equipment belong more to the bank than to him. And yet the banks keep him going, advancing him money for his experiments.

That may be one reason why farmers here talk bleakly about a terminal economic crisis, while the bankers and others deny the severity of the problem, pointing to the relatively few bankruptcies and forced auctions. Determinedly optimistic, and doomed if they're wrong, bankers don't count the Joe Beforts as failures. But Joe confessed that he hasn't made a payment on land or equipment in two years. In fact, he gets special loans for hogs and feeders, pledging not to apply whatever profits the feeders produce against his other delinquent loans, so that he can use the income to support his family. "I'm not sure I'd want everyone on the top level to know what's going on down here," he said. "If they knew how bad it is, they might try to fix it, and make it worse."

I'd say the bankers are right to carry Joe Befort; you have to choose your risks on character and live or die with them. Befort is a stoic, with shoulders broad enough to carry a lot of worries. He's also honest. "I'm not able to make my land payments, and I'm just biding my time," he said. "As things go, we're not putting any young people back on the land. Not when someone like me gets beat around every year, and I've got twenty-five years' experience."

Brian Befort, one of those young people, still lived at home. Brian began dragging big combines around the country to "custom" harvest while he was still in high school, and when I visited, he owned two big combines worth six figures. He'd been fixing up the John Deere for two months, and he would have to leave soon for Kingfisher, Oklahoma, the first stop on an odyssey that follows maturing crops north. A custom harvester can take in crops for a farmer whose own equipment would take four times as long to do the job.

Custom harvesting is a respectable sideline for farmers. Brian's grandfather, seventy-four, had done it all his life, and his younger brother, fourteen, was about to buy his first combine. It was a rough, itinerant trade, though, a little like working carny shows. If rain should hit Kingfisher when a dozen harvesting crews are in town, "They get a little excited, waiting around," said Brian. "Well, you get kicked out of a lot of hotel rooms."

Brian was one of the last students to attend Lebanon High School. There were only two in his class. His father was on the school board that decided the year before to merge the district with Smith Center. It was the death knell of Lebanon as a community, and Befort was considered disloyal and worse for going along with the decision to close down Lebanon's school. And now the younger Befort boys were away from home more, usually on long bus rides to school and sports events.

When Befort's father bought his farm in 1947, wheat was selling at $3.40 a bushel. In those days you didn't jack up your soil with fertilizer and douse it with pesticides; fuel was less expensive, and you didn't have such monstrous equipment to finance either. Some forty years later wheat was selling for $3.10 a bushel, and you had to pay for all those extras.

Volume is now the accepted way to make farming pay, but that has its costs, too.

The drop in land prices and the desperate financial straits of many farmers in Smith County and elsewhere were recent, and may prove merely cyclical; but the slow decline of the population is long-term and irreversible. From 1978 to 1982 the number of farms in Smith County dropped from 804 to 761. Family farms were down from 710 to 658. That's not good, and it doesn't tell the whole story.

The problem is, it had been going on a long time, just as David Kemper said. Back when the second generation of Hofers were buying up a quarter section at a time in Smith County, the farm population in Kansas was 838,000, according to the U.S. Census Bureau. That dropped to 709,000, in the upheaval of the Great Depression, and by 1969 it was down to 263,000. In 1969 there were about half as many farms as there were in 1900.

The acreage farmed hasn't, incidentally, dropped; in 1969 there were 49.4 million Kansas acres farmed, compared with 41.7 million at the century's turn. People from urban or suburban areas tend to think that our open space nationwide is quickly running out, that farmland is being paved over, but they haven't visited Kansas lately. Farms are simply bigger, more than twice as big as fifty years ago.

This makes a difference politically, too. In 1920 politicians had to pay attention to farmers. They made up a solid block, nearly 30 percent of the population, and they were more diligent voters than city folk. These days fewer than 3 percent of Americans farm, and many who do are weekend or hobby farmers who hold other jobs.

Joe Befort didn't go on the road to custom harvest anymore. He stayed at home and tried to figure a way out of his problems. His undemonstrative manner masked an inquisitive, adventurous mind. He was trying no-till planting, an old idea for saving topsoil and trouble that has been pushed in recent years—belatedly, some would say—by the local agricultural extension agents. And Befort was planting amaranth.

Befort pushed back his cap and leaned on the kitchen counter while he talked about amaranth, and he seemed to forget the precarious tilt of his life. He brought out snapshots of his crops over the last two years: There he was standing among the eight-foot plants, like a proud grandfather among tall youngsters. Amaranths have wavy, narrow leaves on a single long stalk, and small clustered flowers. Befort thought amaranth might be the perfect crop for this in-between country, which gets less rain and has less topsoil than rich lands to the east, but which is not as flat and easily mechanized as farms to the west. He had planted sixty-five acres in amaranth, but only one-third had been harvestable—another failure, but the kind that farmers who are in it for the long haul can live with, and learn from.

Befort pulled out brochures proclaiming the glories of the plant. He sells what he produces to a health food store in Texas.

Montezuma, the Aztec chief, used to demand tribute from his vassals in bushels of amaranth seed, which is said to have as much protein as soybeans. It's used more and more in bread and granola, and the leaves, when young, are edible, and richer in minerals than chard or spinach. Milton crowned the angels with amaranth in *Paradise Lost*.

————

*. . . the work is difficult, fatiguing, and lonely. Most of the times
the cowhand is isolated from family life, dances and movies. His
meals, habits and life are simple and seldom thrilling. Of course,
round-ups and rodeos are exciting, but very few hands get to be
rodeo performers. Like every industry, there is a tendency for the
work to be routine. But the boys who loves the out-of-doors and
simple pleasures will enjoy living on the plains by day and sleeping
under the stars at night.*

—"History of Grazing," unpublished

THE Hofers were loading cattle the morning I went over to
say good-bye. Steve, perhaps feeling a little jealous of my
time with the Beforts, wanted me to get to know his colorful
crew: his father; Curt, his hired hand; Frenchy, the driver;
and old Shorty, particularly.

Shorty stood outside the rear fence, brandishing an electric
wand but staying out of the livelier hubbub in the corrals,
where the others slapped and yelled until the mixed bunch of
cattle stumbled up the ramp into the truck's "jailhouse."
Shorty's red-rimmed eyes and the broken blood vessels in his
face hinted at a hard life, and his movements were stiff and
precarious. He was round above and below the neck, and had
one yellow tooth front and center. He wore Key overalls ("the
aristocrat of overalls"). A generation ago there were many
more like him. They lived in small cabins and took low-
paying work as it came, with no aspiration but to go on an
occasional bender, tell a tale, and live in this country. We
were equally embarrassed at being thrust together.

SHORTY (looking over cattle): These ain't going to get anybody very rich.
O'G: So I gather. Steve pays fifty-three dollars and fifty cents
a hundredweight and sells them for fifty-seven dollars.

SHORTY (slowly, without interest): Zat so?

O'G: These guys keep telling me stories you've told them.

SHORTY: Who does?

O'G: Like about your mules?

SHORTY: Mules?

O'G: About cutting hay with mules, on a hillside so steep the mules are walking on each other's backs?

SHORTY (prodding cattle): I don't have any mules.

Things went a little better with Curt, the Hofers' young hired hand. I rode with him as he mixed feed for the remaining steers, using a tractor with a fancy stereo system to dig some fermenting silage from a big mound of it. Then we mixed corn and milo and supplement from two shoulder-to-shoulder silos, and rumbled over to the troughs alongside the pens. Curt is young Michael Hofer's idol; he introduced the boy to the splendor of shooting coyotes and prairie dogs.

Curt is married, and he and his wife have had some difficulties in childbirth, which makes the distance to good medical care—another symptom of declining population—a cause of concern for him. But he loves to hunt and trap, and the wildlife is increasing hereabouts. He doesn't mind the low wages. He thinks that Smith County is near paradise, and the fewer people there are, the better. He dreams of getting land of his own someday—a quarter section to start, which he could work while still taking a wage from bigger operators like Steve Hofer. He's not afraid of the way markets and land values have fluctuated.

"I wouldn't want to live in a city like Salina," he said as we poked along to the pens and dropped another load. "I tried that. I want to be able to piss off the porch."

——

Hard surfaced roadbed over half the route, remainder graveled.
Open all year except during severe snowstorms.
Usual accommodations.
—Kansas: A Guide to the Sunflower State

IT was after six o'clock. I got a full tank of gas, turned on the radio and spun the dial until I heard Bobby Bare's voice, and then headed west on U.S. 36, past the old drive-in movie theater, converted now to a used equipment lot where Latin American buyers come to buy up foreclosed tractors; past the Pizza Hut and the other shiny fast-food factories, set down flimsily wherever the ground is cheap and the traffic sufficient, without regard to the town's old habits of commerce; past the raked roadsters of a couple of those high school dropouts, parked indecisively by the intersection where you can either zoom off down the highway or turn into the quiet, shady streets of Smith Center.

I had spent my last days simply watching and listening and standing by as people worked; few of them wanted to linger over my questions about the past and future. I was tired of asking them, and ready now for some more highway time: the smooth curve of the steering wheel; the static landscape set in motion; the mastery and escape.

Literature and history have marked rivers as the favored conveyance of the American imagination, from Lewis and Clark to Huck and Jim. But in the last half century our rivers of escape have been roads—first the packed dust of backcountry two-tracks, then the sturdy rural blacktop, and finally, beginning in the 1950s, the smooth, manicured interstates. The interstates have not been kind to Smith County; travelers who once would have visited this country on their way west

from St. Joseph, Missouri, would be likely now to take Interstate 80 through Nebraska or Interstate 70 through Salina.
The shadow of a cloud passed me on the road. I watched
it move ahead, the trail of a little gray puffball too busy to
linger over the paralyzed green floor of farms. I depressed the
accelerator, slowly pulling up on the shadow, which encom-
passed only about fifty yards of the road. Then, in concert we
sped along, at sixty-eight miles an hour. I felt light, as if I
could roll forever.

———

*Land and water economy must be adjusted to "the State's scant and
unreliable water supply," Professor Harlan M. Barrows, of the
Water Committee of the National Resources committee, has pointed
out. "No more is possible. Harmonious adjustment to the ways of
nature in the Plains must take the place of attempts to 'conquer'
her. To hope that she may change her ways is futile."*
—Kansas: A Guide to the Sunflower State

DRIVING across Kansas toward Colorado, you ride a gentle
westward incline through country flat and cultivated. The
green of the plains once diminished as you moved west,
draining out of the landscape as you drove into the long rain
shadow of the Rocky Mountains. From the rich cornfields of
eastern Kansas you moved through the hilly in-between country
of Smith County, and then onto the flat, dry plains. When
the homesteaders tried to plant this country, the paucity of
rain and the intrusion of their plows untied topsoil already
damaged by open-range grazing, and set it blowing east. The
severe drought of 1933 brought with it towering dust storms.
In a few years the homesteaders who had arrived and claimed
their own quarter sections with such high hopes of emanci-
pation were gone, emptying the sod houses and the clapboard

frame houses, some of which were still standing, stark and empty, as I passed half a century later.

A chunk of tumbleweed rolled in front of the car, and I swerved, barely avoiding it. My eyes had not been on the road; I was looking at a photograph on the seat next to me. It was taken in the 1930s, and it showed a towering gray cloud dwarfing the main street of a small town. The cars parked along the street were Chevrolets and Packards of that era, and a few human figures moved in a blurred rush across the camera's view, faces turned toward the cloud.

A kind of black humor prevailed: A stranger stopped by a plains homestead and marveled at a cloud on the eastern horizon, according to the writers' project Colorado guide. "Think it'll rain?" he inquired. "Hope so," said the farmer, "not so much for my sake as the children's. I've seen rain." Some who lived through those times have said that a farmer out past the Missouri didn't lose a penny when the stock market crashed; it was the drought that withered their dreams. Again, from the Colorado guide: "Part of my farm blew off into Kansas yesterday, so I guess I'll have to pay taxes there, too." It was worse than that. "Gently sifted with a nice precision, the finest parts of our Plains soil fell upon boat decks and waves of the Atlantic far at sea," wrote Russell Lord in 1938. The soil went east; bankrupt farmers generally went west.

But the thousands who gave up their attempts to "conquer" this arid land would be astonished to see it now. The highway was an absolutely straight two-lane road, allowing my attention to drift to the rich green of the surrounding fields. Pivot irrigation systems, long, spidery pipes circling the fields automatically on tall wheels, pump water from wells sunk deep in the Ogallala aquifer. The irrigation has turned western Kansas into a breadbasket. Smith Center will miss out on this boon, just as it has been left out of transportation corridors and other such benefits, because the Smoky Hill country is too rugged and uneven, and requires a more personal touch. Some would say that in the long run this shortcoming may be a blessing for Smith Center: Critics like Wes Jackson have warned that the costly "mining" of the Oglala aquifer, an enormous underground reservoir beneath eastern Colorado, Nebraska, and western Kansas, will eventually exhaust it. In any case, the extensive cultivation it makes possible has not repopulated the region. The scale is enormous, and the method mechanical, and the haunting old houses still lean empty into the wind.

I LEFT Kansas through its northwest corner, passing through little towns like St. Francis ("Friendly people live here") and Bird City ("Lindbergh's Playground"). Bored, I was tempted to pull off to search for Colonel Lindbergh's jungle gym in Bird City, but the Federal Writers' Project guide to Kansas explained that Lindbergh never frolicked there; he merely flew over the town after his transatlantic flight and dropped a note of tribute to his old aeronautics teacher, Banty Rogers, who owned a house in Bird City. Banty didn't happen to be home that day.

Little by little, I had climbed from an elevation of 744 feet at Kansas City to 3,291 feet above sea level at St. Francis. The topography was irregular again, and with the pivot irrigators gone it had resumed a less green coloration. The wind picked up, and there were legions of tumbleweed crossing the highway as I passed into Colorado. I was forced off the road when a furious ball of the stuff—"wind witch," as the Kansas guide calls it, or Russian thistle, its proper name— got caught in the grille and began slapping up against the windshield.

Tumbleweed seed arrived in this country in the 1870s in a sack of flax seeds brought by Russian immigrants to South

A farmer's son on a dune of drifting soil near Liberal, Kansas.
Arthur Rothstein.

Dakota. It was unpopular here among early settlers, who saw
tumbleweed, which casts its seeds prolifically, competing with
the grains they wanted to grow. The plant also spread prairie
fires, picking up sparks in one burning field and pinwheeling
into another, hence the nickname wind witch.

The Russian thistle could withstand drought, and it was among the first plants to return to the plains after the dust bowl years; unpopular though it was with farmers, tumbleweed held what topsoil was left and provided food for prairie animals. Tumbleweed gets woody as it matures, and eventually the bushes, which can grow to three feet across, break off and start to travel, dropping as many as twenty thousand seeds each as they go. One of the reasons roadbeds here are better off raised a little above the landscape is that tumbleweeds on a sunken road have been known to gather in a deep cut and link up to form a blockade as thick as a roll of barbed wire.

By nightfall I was in Fort Morgan, an eastern Colorado town of cottonwoods and wide streets where ranchers' pickups sat incongruously next to Subarus with Windsurfers lashed on top. I went for a run in a warm wind that carried cruising, lacquered pickups—the teenage kind—along the drag in a cozy green field smell; then, too heated up to sleep, I crossed the street frequently from my motel to the Sonic Drive-in ("America's best drive-ins") for lemonade (*not* America's best lemonade). There was no lingering dust bowl melancholy about the girls at the window; they were flirty and happy when the middle-aged manager wasn't watching, in the grip, like me, of small-town restlessness. I was headed for California, in the direction my grandfather had traveled before me, in the footsteps of all migrants who had given up on the plains but had not given up hope entirely. Their new dreamscape was California. Seedpods from elm trees blew in light waves across the pavement, making a fine rattling sound, like the rustle of long skirts.

Point of Departure

Knott's Berry Farm

AT SOME point, as I traveled into Southern California from
the east, the fabricated landscapes began to take over. The
first hint that this was happening came at Lake Havasu, on
the Arizona-California border, where the London Bridge has
joined many other retirees in an improbable settlement next
to the impounded waters of the Colorado River. There is a
long stretch of unredeemed desert between the bridge and
the elaborate fabrication of Disneyland and its ilk in the Los
Angeles Basin, but Lake Havasu is still, quite literally, the
wellspring. Back in 1939, just as the writers' project guide
to Los Angeles was being assembled, the Colorado River
Aqueduct began carrying water along a 392-mile route of
tunnels, pumping plants, and canals from the Colorado to
the arid Los Angeles Basin. Coupled with power from the
giant Boulder Dam (now Hoover Dam), which began send-

A gas station and tourist cabins in Shannon County, Missouri.
John Vachon.

ing electricity west in 1936, this was the dynamo that made
Los Angeles and its fantasies possible.

The natural landscape began literally to fade for me as I
completed an early-morning run across the Mojave Desert,
arriving at the town of Victorville with the Mustang steaming under a hot sun. I stopped at the Roy Rogers Museum,
housed in an ersatz fort on the edge of the desert, while the
Mustang rested its aching radiator in the parking lot. It was
still early—night being the sensible time to drive an old car
across the Mojave—and I found myself alone in the air-conditioned gallery . . . alone, that is, if you don't count Roy

Rogers's bowling trophies, his guns, his stuffed horse, and his stuffed dog.

"Roy jests that Dale Evans has the same plan for him," said a newspaper clipping. Mounted next to Dale's sunny smile, the quote is Hollywood macabre, but I was less affected by the idea that Rogers would end up stuffed and mounted than that he would end up stuffed and mounted *here,* among the glass cases and within the cinder-block walls that shut out the bleak desert light. Rogers was not born a cowboy, but rather a midwesterner, who raised a prize 4-H hog in Duck Run, Ohio. He moved about, the way many of us move about, and after his stellar career in Hollywood he ended up on a ranch in this parched place, with the endless memorabilia of his made-up screen life under glass. Does he sometimes feel precarious, here between the Mojave barrens and the wilderness of Los Angeles, when he turns off the light and falls toward sleep, so far from Duck Run?

The car cooled, and I motored between the San Gabriel and San Bernardino mountains and into the hazy basin, broad and deep and opening toward the west, brimming with homes and highways and a few remnant orchards. The change from the burnt, arid countenance of the desert was fairly sudden; now there were the low-slung houses, the wheezing and whizzing traffic, the bushes and lawns jammed in like packing materials. Yet I felt much as I had in the desert; the forces around me were as overpowering as the desert sun.

I skirted the city, cutting south on the Orange Freeway to Anaheim. And there, just as I had escaped the desert for Roy Rogers's air-conditioned dreamworld, I ducked out of Los Angeles and into Knott's Berry Farm.

Knott's Berry Farm was the original, the first of the amusement parks, built when the writers' project guides were being published. Now there is no place in California where you will not find Disneylands and Summerlands and Santa Claus Villages, on top of one another like unmatched shoes in a closet. They come good and bad, mostly bad, and their aim—well, the aim is to make money, of course, but the visions they promote are fantastically at odds with the world around them: The best of them are intense dreams of community, but of a perfect, more unchanging past or future than we've known or will ever know.

Like many California enterprises, Knott's Berry Farm started with a fruit stand. Cordella Knott began serving pies and chicken dinners during the depression years, and her husband, Walter, with time and money on his hands as the business grew, fashioned a counterfeit ghost town beside the restaurant in 1940.

I parked and walked under an overpass into a carefully planned maze of souvenir shops, restaurants, clothing stores, film kiosks, and more restaurants. I entered in a small crowd, and felt something like the limbering exhalation of players coming off the field after a tough game; we were separated from our cars and entering an ambulatory world where there was no need, no way, to hurl ourselves around at seventy miles per hour in a tin can. One effect of this released tension was to make people hungry the minute they left the parking lot. So all sorts of edibles enticed us on the way toward the amusements, or away from them.

I entered a kid's world without my own children, which made me a little lonely and self-conscious. But I marched busily with the crowd, in a counterclockwise direction toward Camp Snoopy and Montezuma's Revenge, one of those swooping roller coasters that turn their riders upside down. There were a surprising number of solitary men here, though most of them were retirement age.

After suffering through the "Revenge," I searched in vain for the rest of "Fiesta Village," of which "Revenge" was supposedly a part. Amusement parks tend to re-create real places with the teeth extracted; Disneyland's Main Street USA becomes 1910 without the grimy Industrial Revolution. What, then, would Knott's Berry Farm make of a Mexican village, and how many brown faces would I see there, given that L.A. is largely Hispanic? Fiesta Village is "extraordinarily beautiful and almost peaceful," according to Los Angeles architectural critic Charles Moore. But I was disappointed: Fiesta Village was getting a face-lift, and for the moment it was mostly fenced off with plywood. Looking through the cracks, I saw construction squalor, perhaps more closely approximating a poor Mexican town than the "Happy Sombrero," "Fiesta Plaza," and the other "exciting rides" to come. The Hispanics I ran into elsewhere in the park, and there were quite a few, many of them speaking Spanish, showed no special interest in Fiesta Village, and one family that I talked to—from Irvine, though the mother spoke only Spanish—said they had come for the Sky Jump, and didn't know there was a Fiesta Village.

The light was fading as I followed them into the Sky Jump, where I was locked into a chest-high metal cage and yanked up a few hundred feet on a cable to the top of a sky tower, fighting back an old mountaineering urge simply to jump out of the thing and be done with it. At the top you could see the urban honeycomb and its yellow film extending for miles; it was like looking over the wall of a fortress at the goriest of battlefields. Then I was dropped, a parachute opened, and I skidded down the guiding wires to the bottom.

In and out of exhibits I wandered—a diving dog at the Pacific Pavilion, singing and dancing tots at the Good Time Theater—until I arrived at Knott's ghost town, one of the oldest sections of the park. It is not so much a ghost town as a town of the turn-of-the-century West, with a lived-in look. The streets were quite uncrowded; there were no harum-scarum rides here. In the dark—it was after 8:00 P.M.—the lighting was modest, and deep shadows gave the imagination a little more to do. The town was artificial enough to be admired for its artifice and sincere enough to open your heart to romantic illusion. At the "Boot Hill Diggin's," I walked through a log entryway that formed a proscenium framing a stark and dramatic landscape of deserts and mountains. Vegetation, old mine shacks, and mine structures concealed, for just a moment, the borders of the mural, which was painted on the back of a building. I crossed a little bridge, and there was a crude sign that said: WITH FEW TOOLS AND WITHOUT GOVERNMENT AID THESE HARDY PEOPLE SUBDUED OUR GREAT WESTERN WILDERNESS. Author's message, erroneous but heartfelt . . . Walter Knott erected much of the ghost town himself, by hand.

Primitive but neat stores, all within short walking distance of each other; wide streets without much commotion; and big shade trees. Of course, few western towns a century ago had shade trees, and half the time the wide streets of yore were mud wallows or dust bowls. But Knott's Berry Farm is not history. It's a child's world where food, pleasure, and entertainment are always within reach. It's also a reminder that a large number of us respond to the same idealized vision of community, something on a smaller, more agreeable scale. The vision is filled out with a few simulated antiquities and some decorative craftsmen at work producing wares by hand. Where once people took vacations to get away from the stuffy little towns where life seemed cramped and limited, now they take their children to places like this for a glimpse of that glorious town life of yesteryear.

The managers of Knott's seem now to be turning their attention elsewhere, to thrill rides, and when I walked through the frontier town, many of the storefronts were closed and in shadow. This was much as it would be in a real town, though;

I noticed, too, that there were many more adults than children in this section.

I boarded a slow-moving train pulled by a real steam engine at Calico Square. Two women and a boy of about six were sitting behind me.

WOMAN 1: There's going to be some robbers coming on, but don't be scared because they're not real.

BOY: You mean *robots?*

WOMAN 2: Oh, Lord. She don't mean that.

WOMAN 1: I mean, not real *robbers.* Real people, but they ain't gonna rob us, really.

WOMAN 2: She don't want you to wet your pants.

BOY: Get *off* it.

WOMAN 2: Oh, isn't this the one we see dinosaurs on, or is that Disneyland?

WOMAN 1: You tell me. I've been to five amusement parks in four days. They're starting to run together.

A robber enters, with a bandanna over his face, waves his guns, and shouts to a cohort to collect valuables.

BOY (loud voice): He ain't real!

WOMAN 2: Oh, can't you shut him up?

BOY (to robber): Get *out!*

WOMAN 1: Aren't you going to have so many things to tell your friends at school!

Destination

Los Angeles

—

U.S. 101, connecting modern communities with the assistance of modern road-building techniques, deviates from the {El Camino Real} that developed in more primitive days. Today several missions—notably San Gabriel and San Fernando—are several miles from US 101. The unofficial revival of US 101 with the old name, a comparatively recent development, was partly the result of a desire to perpetuate the Spanish name, and partly a commercial device to attract visitors.

—Los Angeles: A Guide to the City and Its Environs

I TRAVELED north on Interstate 5, roughly following the route of El Camino Real, motoring shoulder to shoulder with a '59 Plymouth, metallic blue in a former life, whose perspiring brown driver saluted me with a Coke can as we thundered up the interstate toward the Promised Land. He was ebullient and apparently confident that he could make it all the way

238

from wherever he'd begun to wherever he was going without taking a left turn. The jagged edge of his bashed-in front wheel well on the driver's side would perform surgery on his balding tire if the tire moved so much as an inch that way. The sight of my Mustang, with its dents, torn upholstery, and peeling paint, seemed to awake in him a hearty camaraderie, and he kept toasting, insistently, reaching farther out his window, until I, fearing for our lives, returned his salute with the nearest thing at hand, a can of thirty-weight oil.

We were equals in the kingdom of the automobile, a city so honeycombed with pavement that a two-hundred-dollar Plymouth or a beat-up Mustang opened all the world's possibilities. Liberation, of a festering and anarchic kind. The Plymouth held as many as ten passengers. Smaller folk in the back seat had pyramided soft drink cans in a kind of shrine behind the plastic that was taped across the rear window cavity.

I was thinking historically, or trying to, reminding myself that I was motoring roughly along the route of El Camino Real, the old footpath that linked the Catholic missions along the California coast in the eighteenth century. The logic of the mission system was a series of small, orderly agricultural settlements each separated by a day's walking distance. When the Spanish governor Felipe de Neve heard from the missionaries in the 1780s that there was an "excellent" site for a community along a small, treelined river north of San Gabriel, he laid out a plan for a pueblo: four square leagues, cultivated fields surrounding a plaza. Without irony, the writers' project guide to Los Angeles notes that this was "one of the few cities on earth which has been deliberately planned in advance."

The thin ranks of padres who made their way north in the 1780s wouldn't survive thirty seconds if they steered their burros into today's bewildering rush of traffic. The logic of the old missions' spacing is gone, but the route persists; it has been overlain first by railroad lines and then by the elevated freeways. I found that consistency stabilizing and in my imagination I tried to picture the padres' landscape, wiping away the circus of signs and mongrel buildings that stretched as far as I could see.

The invisible thread of El Camino Real kept me moving in a single direction, and I needed that. L.A. offered too many choices, and that sweatiness on the back of my legs was my response. My travels with the writers' project guides had mostly been away from cities, toward the remote hollows and peninsulas where I hoped old cultures might survive. Here the man-made landscape was so low and dense that in the sunbaked rush of things I was losing my way.

The Spanish missionaries walked beneath clear skies and looked west to a sparkling sea. At the missions they taught Indians to plant in rows and gave them the Gospel and various devastating diseases. The layout of the mission and pueblo was neatly ordered to focus on the small central plaza, with seven-acre fields arrayed around; each settler had his own house and land, though there was a wide gulf between the mud-walled huts of the pueblo and the enormous land grants of the ranchos. It was a decipherable and purposeful community, much easier to sort out than the chaos that overlays it now.

Like a dutiful padre, I traveled north through the sprawling municipalities with citrus names—Orange, Lemon Heights, Garden Grove—where orchards have been supplanted by subdivisions and community margins blend together. I was searching for the heart of an urban wilderness that some say has no center. If I kept in step with the padres, I would emerge in a few weeks from the northern side of the wilderness and move toward more familiar ground.

The passengers in the Plymouth probably would not go as

far; they would likely join relatives and friends in eastern L.A. neighborhoods that have become virtual foreign colonies. But who knows? Perhaps you can go all the way to Alaska without turning left, and perhaps they would.

The top of the Mustang was down, and the air, fruity and stinging, rushed by me. Flat-roofed eateries and warehouses and assembly plants of cinder block and stucco pressed the freeway on all sides. The wide, busy streets and billboards and thrusting signs replicated forever off toward the smog-smudged horizons; the tropical palms rose up from little nests of crumpled fast-food wrappers and kept their indifferent watches above. Mindlessly, I counted gas stations and restaurants and motels as I peered over the Santa Ana Freeway's landscaping. Their numbers were astounding, and each one represented thousands of people who must gas and eat and sleep in this gasping, bleached-out setting. I sank heavily into my seat. It was becoming a steamy day; the radio announced a smog alert.

The Mustang did not share my botheration. It purred happily, without a hiccup of backfire. Where it had slunk in embarrassment through the small towns of the Midwest, it now seemed to throw back its head and run, the shreds of its canvas roof strung out behind us like the mane of a gamboling colt. Southern California is the spiritual home of Mustang convertibles.

———

The Los Angeles of the future is likely to evolve along highways. Already there is a vast network of superb roads. In other rapid transit facilities, however, Los Angeles is outranked by many a smaller town. Cumbersome, old-fashioned trolleys still rattle through the streets. The interurban service is incredibly slow and antiquated. . . .
—Los Angeles: A Guide to the City and Its Environs

I MAINTAINED good speed through the downtown area and into the maze where the Santa Ana, Harbor, Hollywood, and Pasadena freeways intersect. This is a spaghetti pile of ramps and pillars that works awesomely well for four hundred thousand drivers a day, and the ivy creeping up the supports lends an air of antiquity. The Mustang, in its element, roared into the four-deck interchange and came out on the Pasadena, the most senior of freeways.

In the late 1930s the powerful Automobile Club of Southern California proposed an elaborate, eight-hundred-million-dollar system of elevated roadways, but the writers' project guide's authors did not fully foresee the day when the new, short freeway segments in Hollywood and Pasadena would expand like chopped worms into a seven-hundred-mile system, and the word "freeway" would become synonymous with Los Angeles.

The Pasadena, under construction as early as 1934, vies with the German *Autobahn* for the title of World's First Freeway. It was called the Arroyo Seco at first, in honor of a steep watershed, seasonally dry, that drains from the San Gabriel Mountains to the Los Angeles River roughly along the route the freeway now follows. It may say something about the cultural geography of Los Angeles that residents, who can tell you where nearly anything is in relation to a freeway exit, are often vague about the location of the Arroyo Seco, if they know it at all.

As an early experiment in the design of high-speed, limited-access motorways, the Pasadena Freeway enshrined many mistakes, and there is little space available around the roadway today for corrections. If you're a confident driver, you'll find the mistakes interesting, and they may give you some idea of the speed and size of cars—and the driving style—of the 1920s. (Why 1920s, when this freeway was completed only in the 1940s? Because planners, I was later told by professional planners, move in such a sluggish governmental current that they are generally implementing plans designed to resolve problems encountered twenty years before.) Tight pinwheel on-ramps conclude with the briefest runways for cars to attain freeway speed and merge; parts of the freeway are submerged rather than elevated, flanked by narrow shoulders and high walls, with vegetation spilling over the top; abrupt stops confront you on short off-ramps. Cars were slower and more fragile then, and the fresh delight of mechanized motion did not require great speed.

A plane was buzzing overhead. It was a little Cessna, and its path seemed exactly to mimic mine, as if there were a tether three thousand feet straight up from my bumper. With the Mustang's top down, I felt a little weightless, enough that I could imagine myself looking down, on a fresh morning like this, at the green ant colony of the L.A. Basin, insulated by atmosphere from its crowds and fumes.

The rap on Los Angeles is its amoebic sprawl. Almost from the beginning, Angelenos set out to build a utopia of uncrowded, low-profile neighborhoods, with gardens for all and horizons uncluttered by high rises, and the ocean and parks within easy reach. Dare we call it an urban nightmare when your old car and five dollars for gas will have you at the beach in half an hour, or wandering through MacArthur Park in less?

———

The PLAZA . . . is a circular plot shaded by rubber trees, palms,
and bamboo, and surrounded by a low saw-toothed brick wall
with recessed seats. The unbroken rows of wooden benches are
continually crowded with loiterers, who doze in the shade or
listen to the harangues of economic saviors and religious zealots

*who hold forth from low concrete platforms that in the 1870's
were watering troughs.*
—Los Angeles: A Guide to the City and Its Environs

I DOUBLED back on the freeway and got stuck in a traffic jam, an increasingly common occurrence in L.A. now that the downtown is becoming a tight patch of high rises. I inched off the Pasadena onto the Hollywood Freeway south, got off on Los Angeles Street, and parked in front of Union Station, which had just been erected when the writers' project guide

The Mexican quarter in downtown Los Angeles, now the site of
Union Station. *Dorothea Lange.*

came out. It was so new then that the writers weren't quite sure what to make of it; the only adjective they conjured up was "huge," and they noted that the southern patio, full of pepper, olive, and palm trees, was "intended to represent" good California garden design, as if they doubted the task had been accomplished. Maybe the beauty of the structure, with a clock tower reminiscent of a church bell tower, its fine woodwork and ceramic mosaics, was less obvious then, when the huge terminal was crowded with people, and dozens of passenger trains came and went daily. It's virtually empty now.

I sat at a table in the high-ceilinged waiting room, streaked with cool light from arched, paned windows. The station was built in the popular Spanish Colonial Revival style, with walls thick as a mission's and rancho-style courtyards, but there are also Art Deco elements and detail work molded in slick curves like the old trains and Airstream trailers—this was known as "Streamline Moderne." Thronelike wooden chairs, most of them empty, put today's flimsy airport lounges to shame.

Part of the Mexican quarter and the joss houses and opium dens of old Chinatown were torn down to make room for the station in 1939. A new Chinatown went up a few blocks to the north, putting just a little distance between the Orient and the Hispanic central plaza, which stands opposite Union Station. Little Tokyo is a short walk east, and right next to that is the primarily black Skid Row; to the southwest are a dozen tall government buildings, erected approximately on the site where yet another race, the Yang-Na Indians, lived long before the pueblo was founded here in 1781. Just beyond these offices are fancy new high rises with names like Crocker Center and Bonaventure Hotel. "Downtown" has been in the same place for centuries. And they say Los Angeles has no center!

After a cup of coffee, I crossed Alameda Street and walked

on Olvera Street, which is closed to car traffic. An ancient
sandstone watering trough marks the north end, and the street,
which leads to the plaza, is lined with insubstantial little
cafés and shops selling curios and Mexican food. In the morning, awnings were being lifted and grills were just starting
to crackle.

The plaza, bushes and brick and huge fig trees, was quiet,
too. It was hard to imagine, in the warm, peaceful morning,
that in the nineteenth century booze joints, gambling, and
prostitution dives were all around. Nor was there a trace of
the orators—anarchists, Commies, cranks of all kinds—who
filled the air with spittle in the 1930s. Two teenage boys
with *papagayos* decorating their shorts sat on one side, clutching skateboards, plotting an itinerary. Across from them, a
bag lady sat on a tiled bench and ran her fingers compulsively
through stringy gray hair. Voyaging between them, I made
my way to the government buildings.

———

*Though its tendency to spread and sprawl has been more or less
unrestricted, the city has strangely enough denied itself the right to
soar. Since 1906 a municipal ordinance has limited buildings to
13 stories and 150 feet in height . . . it was felt that it would be
a mistake to erect tall buildings that would create traffic congestion
and turn the streets into dark, narrow canyons—conditions
which people from the East were trying to escape.*
   —*Los Angeles: A Guide to the City and Its Environs*

"THE height limitation was done away with in the late 1950s.
The amazing thing was that it lasted that long," Jere McKnight
said with a chuckle. McKnight is a smooth, narrow-faced
man in the Los Angeles County Department of Planning. He
comes from eastern Kentucky, but his attitude toward Los
Angeles is intimate and affectionate, and in his spare time he

guides visitors on walking tours of historic sites in the city. He wears striped shirts and combs his gray hair to camouflage a shortage of it on top.

McKnight's office is in one of several tall but tired-looking government buildings at the city's center, a short walk from the plaza over a sunken section of the Hollywood Freeway. On the southern side of this cluster of municipal, county, and federal buildings is a huddle of skyscrapers built since the ceiling was lifted. If you refuse to accept the old plaza as a bona fide, manifest "center" for Los Angeles, perhaps you'll take the skyscrapers, which are bunched tightly here. As this financial district fills in, Los Angeles is well on the way to having a downtown like everybody else's—congested and deeply shadowed.

The county building is what you'd expect in these days of hostility to government: scratched up, with clanky brown elevators and long hallways of no systematic organization. McKnight's office is at the end of one such hall.

"The height limitation was a genuine attempt to make L.A. different, to make it low-rise, and also to prevent earthquake danger," he said. "From 1880 to 1960 we filled out the L.A. Basin, all the flatland. We carpeted it with single-family housing and low-rise shopping malls, right to the mountains. It was higher density than back East in the suburbs, but lower than in the center of other cities."

In the 1960s apartment and condominium construction intensified in the L.A. Basin. The density is still low—940 people per square mile, compared with 5,640 in San Francisco—but now the increasing density is taxing the diffuse transportation system of buses and private cars. Planners are urgently implementing an unpopular freeway "diamond lane" reserved for public transport, and demanding a massive dose of federal and state funds to build a metrorail system serving the Wilshire Corridor, Hollywood, and Van Nuys.

It isn't just new condos and apartments; there's "a much bigger problem of overcrowding" in older housing, said McKnight, especially in central and East Los Angeles, where immigrants, legal and illegal, are arriving in droves. According to a Rand Corporation study in 1984, Los Angeles showed a net loss of 250,000 native-born Americans moving away between 1970 and 1980, and 675,000 moved out of the county—but the city showed a net population gain of 150,000, thanks to immigrants, and the demographers admit that their counts of illegal immigrants were probably low.

A few floors away from McKnight, George Marr runs the county's Population Research Section, a bookish little enclave with the desks hidden among tall shelves full of dusty documents. Marr, white-haired, round-bodied, and nearing retirement age, went from supervising a staff of seven people to running a one-man office in 1979, and now has inched back up to two or three staff positions.

"No one has a good handle on the illegals, or"—he smiled gently—"the undocumenteds, depending on your political views." The Census Bureau *thinks* it counted 40 percent of them in 1980. Marr, whose department is no longer equipped to make official population estimates, says "conservatively" there are half a million illegals in L.A. Building permits, school data, and the ICE (industrial commercial employment) surveys provide some information, but not enough.

No new data to guide decision making in Los Angeles are likely to come from Marr's understaffed department. He talked of his hope that new political leadership will "strike the clarion bell" and begin taking care of serious problems in the schools, in housing, in sewage disposal. He was sincere, but there was little force to his proclamations; he was a survivor who muddled along, and he might have been surprised to find that some activists view his office with contempt, and him as a Pétain, in the enemy's employ.

He produced what newsletters and demographic studies he could find, and our interview wound down with some bromides. "The area still has a lot of potential," said Marr, softly but earnestly. "We have to serve what we have and not cut off the opportunities for growth." He cleared his throat, excused himself, and left the room.

———

Prices for {movie} stories are of course based on the demand for them: agents frequently send copies of an original story to all major studios simultaneously, hoping the bidding will hike up the price. Nevertheless, it is not unusual for a relatively unknown author to be paid as little as $500 for a story which will be used as a vehicle for an "A" picture packed with stars and feature players.

—*Los Angeles: A Guide to the City and Its Environs*

THE only other worker in Marr's office was a long-haired fellow with pale freckles, wearing an untucked cotton shirt. He sat with his sockless tennis shoes up on a small desk to my left, a magazine on his knees, and after Marr left, I listened to him turn the pages. Finally he shut the magazine and sighed loudly, leaning back. He rolled his head in my direction.

"You a writer?" he asked, looking at me sideways. I supposed I was. "I'm a writer," he said, simply.

I wondered about his accent. It was open-voweled and clipped; he had to be from the South. His head hung back over the back of the chair, and his mouth was open a little.

"I just sold a script," he said, "to Geffen." He kept looking at me sideways, as if he expected to catch me chuckling.

"Congratulations," I said. "What are you doing here?"

"I mean *just*," he said. "I'm a part-time here. George hired me out of one of these agencies, cheap. I'll stay till I get the advance."

He lifted his feet down and put a long arm's elbow on the desk and leaned toward me. His jeans were worn and bleached. "It's a cop story," he said.

"Your first?"

"I've been trying to break in for six years," he said. "I knew I could do it. But I had to write a cop story. After you've been here for a while, you get this feel for what they want. I couldn't tick you off a list of things—one, two, three— but if you told me a script idea, I could tell you if it was or wasn't. I wrote a cop story. I didn't even have an *agent* for four years."

He had come to Los Angeles from Arkansas. He would get a $10,000 advance, $15,000 for a rewrite, and $250,000 if the movie gets made. Trailing the padres through the poorer parts of L.A., I had planned to stay on the east side, away from the world of Hollywood, which has plenty of chroniclers. But here sat a rags-to-riches story right out of *Singin' in the Rain*. I couldn't help laughing.

He looked at me for a moment, and then he laughed, too. He put his feet back up on the desk and opened the magazine. We exchanged names and addresses. As I left the room, he had his face in front of the magazine, but I saw his eyes darting around the room, excitedly, thinking of the possibilities.

———

The most impressive aspect of Los Angeles art history . . . has been the lively flow of experimentation, both in technique and materials, which has reached its highest level during the past five years. Local artists have shown a creative interest in the new forms emanating from New York and Paris. . . .
—*Los Angeles: A Guide to the City and Its Environs*

DOWN on the sidewalk as I walked from the county building along Temple Street, my shirt and coat were soaked with perspiration. I crossed to First Street, and walked along beside a city park full of homeless people. The weather was not humid, but the temperature was uncomfortable nevertheless, so when a tall blond man in a grimy striped sport coat approached me for change, I was surprised to see a fingerless glove on his hand. Asked why he wore gloves on a hot day, he said, "So they won't be . . . misplaced." He smiled with satisfaction at his own carefully chosen word. His face was as brown as a shoe, and his teeth were white.

The grass banks on the southern end of the park sloped upward to a plateau, and there the homeless had formed a kind of hobo camp, with bedding in one section and food in another, and their worldly goods out to air on the grass and bushes. Both sexes and many races were represented. The people looked, even on this dry day, as if they had been rained on a short while ago; their clothes sagged, and they squinted as they moved stiffly about. The panhandling around the park was discreet and, it seemed, organized, so that passersby did not face a gauntlet if they walked the sidewalk on the park side of the street. A number of the park denizens sat on the edge of the camp and passed their time smoking and watching with what seemed like professional interest the technique of the two or three panhandlers working the sidewalk below.

At least a thousand people downtown were camping in the streets, and another ten thousand wandered in and out of shelters and cheap hotels, according to reports in the local media. Many of the homeless were mentally ill. Some were immigrants, who quickly caught on to this life, according to a secretary in U.S. Representative Edward Roybal's office, which is located in a federal building near the park. The secretary described how a strong, eager-to-work young man from south of the border will enter Southern California to search for work in the fields, fail, and spend a few nights with the homeless downtown. In a short time he will appear in Roybal's office, she said, complaining of various ills and demanding benefits. The homeless life is infectious, and there are many tragic stories.

While I was in L.A., Mayor Tom Bradley announced that the shanty towns amidst the government buildings would be torn up, and the squatters removed. Where would they go? When I called up homeless shelter services, they were reluctant to give me information, or addresses of shelters, unless I could prove my own need.

I made my way down to Central Avenue, and asked a stranger for directions to what they call the "Temporary Contemporary"—the home of one of the best contemporary art museums in the country. It turned out that the rough brick wall we were standing by was the back side of the Temporary, a city warehouse which was remodeled to house modern art collections while a fancy new museum was under construction up on nearby Bunker Hill. The new Museum of Contemporary Art is now open, but the "Temporary" proved itself such a good exhibit space that it has been kept open.

Circling the south end of the building, I found myself walking through another colony of homeless. A bench at a bus stop was draped with a dozen men of all ages and colors; the bus roared by without stopping, and nobody reacted. Dozens of shabby characters squatted or lay in doorways set back from the sidewalk, and some slept on the pavement.

I rounded the corner of the building into a street which dead-ended at the museum entrance. The street was jammed with parked cars. There were people in them, and on top of them: A black man wearing a foul-smelling pea coat stretched out in the back of a small pickup; a woman with scabs on her face shared a cigarette with two grimy-fisted men in the front seat of a compact car without a hood over its rusting engine; they were muttering and sleeping and aching and staring coldly back at me. Portable latrines were lined up along the sidewalk. It did not seem a dangerous place, not in the late afternoon—more like a refugee camp on the outskirts of a war zone. Time pooled and lingered like stagnant water.

The cool air in the museum revived me somewhat. And though I am not a great fan of modern art, what I saw here was moving. The exhibit was called "Individuals: A Selected History of Contemporary . . ." Never mind. The blurby brochure talked about "20th century irony" and "anti-illusionistic" stuff, and that didn't mean much to me either.

Most of what was exhibited could have been assembled from the street outside, but in this setting, and if you ignored the brochure, it did not seem coy. Chris Burden's excavations that exposed the foundations of the building along one inside wall; Robert Rauschenberg's collages of newspaper clips, stained wood, and faded wallpaper, a softball, a bent fork; Lucas Samaras's dense boxes of pins and rope; Claus Oldenburg's soft, garish sculptures of pie and women's shoes. A ripening of the world outside, even if you refused the easy irony.

The city has given the Temporary Contemporary a dollar-a-year lease for the rest of the century. It's a worthy investment. I stood before a painting by Anselm Kiefer called "Departure from Egypt" that was all grays and browns and blacks—a huge canvas that envelops your peripheral vision. I was weary, even a little feverish, and forgetting now and then just where I was. I stood there a long time, and at one point dreamt I was outside in the dark, tumbling mass of mislaid lives, congealed by darkness into a many-eyed creature that moved from one large vision to another flaring on the brick walls of the alley, black and gray and brown. Either

we all would wake up together, or none of us would wake up
at all.

IT was late indeed when I got back to my Mustang. Steep
hills crowded into the downtown from the north and forced
streets to jog west or east, and I followed Sunset Boulevard
west. This part of the storied boulevard has never been glo-
rified; it climbs above the downtown interaction of freeways
and then levels out in a notch between Angeleno Heights and
Elysian Park. I would have liked a cozy neighborhood motel,
a place where I could lounge and forget my tasks and let the
spirits heal my back and head. Almost anything would do
that didn't cost too much. I wanted a television set, a table

One of the early drive-ins in Hollywood, California. *Russell Lee.*

to write on, and a flat bed, but whenever I saw a vacancy sign, I would hesitate and circle, like a mouse approaching a trap, imparting an awful significance to that "vacancy."

This was not the twisty little Sunset Boulevard with the famous billboards and overpriced restaurants. This was a sadder stretch where the glamour tapers off and the stores have wrought-iron lattices over their windows and SALE scrawled on butcher paper in three languages.

In the end I didn't make a choice. I simply wore down, and finally pulled into a nondescript motor lodge that I had rejected before, figuring it was preferable to die in a bed than in a car.

I swung the door open on a small waiting room and peered through a scratched window of hard plastic at a hunched Oriental man. His entire family, three or four generations, seemed to be crammed into the little closet-size room behind the plastic, watching a television. There was a small scooped-out opening at the base of the plastic where you could exchange money, keys, and other useful things. The man's skin was like melted tallow, and the black hair atop his head was thinning. He barked at the three generations, and they stared at him wide-eyed. The veins in his neck bulged whenever he talked, loud or soft, and I decided, inexpertly as ever, that he was speaking Korean.

He faced around toward me, still talking, and stopped abruptly, his mouth in a little circle. Then his eyes refocused above my shoulder, and he began talking and gesturing again.

I turned around and found myself face-to-face with three Hispanics, who had been blocked off by the door when I'd swung it open. They stared fiercely at the man behind the plastic. Evidently I had stepped into the middle of a conversation. One of the Hispanics held a fistful of ragged currency, chest high. The second man tottered behind him; his eyes appeared to have rolled up under heavy lids, and he wore a porkpie hat, very dirty. A woman with hair black as oil to her waist, carrying two old suitcases, stood to the rear. I got out of the way.

There ensued a conversation I could not possibly transcribe. I understood only an occasional word in the torrent of Spanish that flew at the glass like gale surf. The Korean bent forward so that his mouth was near the little passage below the plastic, and made angry sounds like an eruption of catarrh. The Hispanic waved his fistful of dollars and stamped his foot. The Korean, his veins frightfully abulge, pounded his side of the partition and furiously motioned the Hispanics toward the door. The Hispanic pointed to the woman and yelled something dramatic, and she began to cry. The Korean shaped the fingers of his right hand into a pistol and pointed it at the trio. Behind my back, I found the knob of the door and quietly turned it.

Suddenly the disputatious parties were silent. The Hispanic then pushed all but two of his dollars under the plastic window, and the Korean, with a big smile, pushed a key back, and waved a jerky little wave at the threesome. The Hispanics departed. The woman lugged the two suitcases.

I stepped up to the window. The little man smiled and showed large gray teeth. One of his eyes wandered to the left. He raised his eyebrows inquiringly.

O'G: I want a room, for just one night. How much is that?
HOST: Yes. Rom?"
O'G: Yes, but how much?
HOST (smiling broadly): Yes. Much, much?

I pointed to the keys on the wall behind him. He pulled one down and looked at it curiously, then held it toward me, on the other side of the plastic, and raised his eyebrows.
O'G: Yes. A room.

He held out his other hand, palm up.

O'G: But how much is it?
HOST: A *rom?*
O'G: How many dollars? You know what I mean?
HOST (spreading his hands): *Much* rom?
O'G: Pounds? Pesos? Yen? How damn much?
HOST: Dom? No? Yes!
O'G: All right. How much will you take for the whole motel?
HOST: Much dom!
O'G: Goddammit!
HOST: Yes!

And so the deal was consummated. With a big smile, he pushed the key into the opening under the window, without releasing it. I pulled out a credit card and thrust it under, and the key was mine. The room cost thirty-eight dollars. The bed had a crater in the middle, and strange stains marked the bedspread. The lock on the door looked as if it had once been shot off, and jangled loosely. The television picked up four murky channels, an impossibly small number in Los Angeles. The light was dim, but that matched the way I felt. I did not much like the person with the wet forehead who glared back at me from the mirror.

———

{The newcomer} encounters new and exotic types of people: movie actors and sombreroed Mexicans, kimonoed Japanese and turbaned Hindus. He develops an urge to try things that are novel and exciting, from Chinese herb doctors to Indian medicine men, from social credit to nudism, from a wine-colored stucco dwelling to a restaurant shaped like a hat. . . . He feels a certain strangeness in this place he now calls his home, a strangeness that is at once exhilarating and disturbing, and that he had not known in his native place "back East."
—*Los Angeles: A Guide to the City and Its Environs*

MY back had stiffened up and wouldn't tolerate the angle of a car seat, so I resigned myself to sojourning on Lower Sunset. I found it threadbare but attractive. Steep hills ascended on either side from the busy street, where there are narrow shops and bars. Small stucco bungalows edged up these hills in vertical groupings linked by steep steps and a common wall that enclosed open courtyards. Trees often grew within these enclosures, the shrubbery was fairly lush, though there was never lawn or close ground cover; the sandstone colors of the ground and the bungalows put one in mind of carless Mediterranean towns. The design was friendly and suited the terrain, but the neighborhood was a rough one; the bungalows were overcrowded and crumbling, and the walls were scarred with gang graffiti.

Sunset tops a steep rise next to Angeleno Heights and then drops down toward Echo Lake. As you walk down this slope, the sidewalks slowly begin to fill, and the glances between pedestrians become less wary. By the time you reach the Pioneer supermarket, just a couple of blocks east of the lake, the landscape has flattened, the little stores are crowding together more, and there is a lot of bustle. This is by no means a "safe" neighborhood, but the local merchants have banded together to clean out some of the open drug dealing that used to go on, and you can enjoy a smorgasbord of language and dress. An immigration lawyer told me that as a general rule the Orientals buy the stores in these run-down neighborhoods, and the Hispanics go to work for them. A Hispanic woman suggested to me that Orientals felt too much at risk running businesses in black neighborhoods, and the Hispanics often got into business there. People in the immigration business can take you on an interesting tour; they know exactly which blocks contain Salvadorans, which Hmong, which Nicaraguans.

The morning scene at the Pioneer was as busy as a Moroc-
can bazaar on a spangly, sunlit morning, with every shade of
skin and fabric. An earnest white woman in a tank top and
jeans collected signatures for an anti-Contra petition. Long
lines of people waited to use the pay telephones. A chubby
man in an ersatz uniform sought donations for the Angeles
Mission for the Homeless. People who must have been living
without water service were filling up jugs at fresh water vending
machines.

I walked over to Echo Lake, passing small houses with
wash hung on the fences and kids hanging out the windows.
With a footpath around it, the lake looked negotiable for
circumnavigation with my stiff back; it is about fifteen acres,
with a sloping lawn on the south bank and an island of enormous palm trees at the east end. Two men in high-heeled
shoes, one smoking a cigarette, kicked a soccer ball in the
picnic area. Three shirtless brown boys shoved each other
playfully as they ran back and forth on the cement path that
capped the lake's outlet.

The lake used to irrigate surrounding farms and supply
water power for a woolen mill. In the 1890s L.A.'s first oil
field was discovered just to the south. Now the lake has paddle boats and a fountain, and bungalows both shabby and
fine crowd the hills roundabout.

Big lotuses were in bloom on the little island, so I started
toward the footbridge to get a closer look. I passed the
grate filtering the water as it exits, adagio, from the lake.
Newspapers, clothes, wrappings, palm fronds, and the
smell of a subway had accumulated there. A small brown
hand was reaching up through the gray offal. My chest
tightened, and I started to back away. Then I looked
closer. It was a doll's arm, sticking out of the end of a
Pepsi can.

*The establishment of {Aimee Semple McPherson's} Angelus
Temple and its subsequent growth, coupled with the theatrical
nature of her services, furnished Los Angeles with its greatest
demonstration of the spectacular in religion. . . .*
—Los Angeles: A Guide to the City and Its Environs

THE Oriental lotuses in the lake are said to have been planted
there by Aimee Semple McPherson, whose Angelus Temple
is still the most imposing presence along its eastern shore.
The temple sits across Park Street, its low dome wrapped in
first a colonnade and then a curved wall of offices with windows that look like the rifle apertures in a pillbox. The overall effect is of a grounded flying saucer of the Bauhaus
school.

As I walked toward the temple, a young Filipino couple
emerged, freshly married, from a south entrance. In the small
bookstore three young acolytes chirped at each other about
various church meetings and activities as they set out new
materials and manned the cash register. I picked up pamphlets about McPherson's Church of the Foursquare Gospel
and bought a few printed sermons.

The sermons, which I read on a bench by the lake, proved
sincere but orthodox Pentecostal stuff, highlighted by an
interesting symposium Aimee McPherson described herself
having with God on the subject of what to wear for a sermon
in Rhode Island. She was, by reports, much more fun in the
flesh. At the five-thousand-seat amphitheater of her temple
she would chase horned devils around the stage with a pitch-
fork, dress up as George Washington crossing the Delaware,
and drive a motorcycle onto the stage. She maintained a fifty-
three-hundred-piece glass communion set, four choirs, and
an orchestra.

McPherson prefigured the rags-to-riches stories of today's television evangelists—she also had one of the first radio stations in L.A.—and like today's televangelists, she seemed at times to find the cross of her own celebrity too much to bear. In 1926 she disappeared from Santa Monica Beach, and after an elaborate offshore search, in which one man drowned, ransom notes were received by her mother. Thousands participated in prayer vigils until, eight months later, she staggered into Douglas, Arizona, with a dramatic tale of kidnapping and escape. Her fans lapped it up, but the press remained curious. Before long, reports surfaced that the evangelist had been seen shopping in Carmel, where she allegedly holed up in a cabin with a man who installed wiring at the temple. This controversy is understandably omitted from church literature.

A spokeswoman for the church told me that attendance at the temple dropped off after McPherson's death in 1944, but that it has been on the rise for the last fifteen years. There are now three separate congregations—white, Hispanic, and Korean—served at the Echo Lake temple, with as many as 1,300 participants at the Spanish Sunday service. The woman took a ten-year-old church pamphlet describing the church's "worldwide ministry" and with a pen updated the figures in it. The 3,436 "national pastors and evangelists" became 13,733; and 3,003 "churches and meeting places" grew to 12,911; and the thirty countries where the ministry works became fifty-seven. Not bad for ten years.

So how's the neighborhood? I asked. Rough, but improving, she said. They don't find bodies in Echo Lake as often as they used to, but she still wouldn't go out walking at night.

Every Tuesday and Wednesday from 10:00 A.M. to 2:00 P.M., the church gives out food and clothing. Over a thousand people a month come to the commissary, just as they

came during the Depression, according to the writers' project
guide. Now, as then, there are no questions asked, no pros-
elytizing, no red tape.

———

*Completion of the Santa Fe Railroad to Los Angeles late in 1885
brought matters to a head. The Southern Pacific was at last faced
with a competitor, and the two roads started a rate war almost
immediately. It has been said they colluded in luring a new
population—and hence a new market—to the West. In any event,
they reduced fares to the point of absurdity, until, on one day
in the spring of 1886, a ticket from Kansas City to Los Angeles
cost only $1.*
—Los Angeles: A Guide to the City and Its Environs

THE first suburb in Los Angeles was Angeleno Heights, sitting just above Echo Lake. It was subdivided during the land
boom in 1886, offering lots for commuters who could reach
the center of Los Angeles quickly by cable car. The neighborhood has been rejuvenated in recent years and in 1984 was
designated an "Historic Preservation Overlay Zone" by the
city. The Victorian houses along Carroll and Kellam avenues
have mostly been, or are being, restored. Parked in the drive-
ways of these stately Queen Annes were BMWs and Mercedeses;
right around the corner, a group of shirtless Hispanic teenagers tinkered with an old Chevy in front of a graffiti-scarred
apartment house, while a radio roared.

In the 1880s new arrivals, lured by the cheap fares and
propaganda like Charles Nordhoff's *California for Health,
Pleasure and Residence,* poured into the state, and carnivallike
real estate promotions were the style. There were parades and
free hot dogs, circus elephants and colorful kiosks on the
beach, where you could wade out into the water and inspect
your "lot."

Angeleno Heights was sold without the elephants; the developers aimed for upper-middle-class buyers. There were tennis courts and a delicious view west. But when the boom went bust in 1888, only a few Victorians had been erected here. Over the years the hill gradually filled in with bungalows and multiunit dwellings, isolating the turreted beauties in just a few blocks. The recent movement for restoration has brought a few Victorian transplants here from other parts of town.

If Angeleno Heights had gone the way of other Victorian neighborhoods—had been demolished, that is, to make way for denser, low-cost housing—we would see its homes only in the Keystone Kops comedies, some of which were filmed here. But a group of Carroll Avenue residents banded together to fight for neighborhood preservation in the 1970s, and it has succeeded.

Tom Morales, who lives on the corner of Carroll and East Edgeware, was seven years old when his parents, immigrants from Spain, bought a Carroll Avenue home from Aaron P. Philips, a hardware store owner, in the 1940s. It's a beautiful house today, with gabled roof and leaded glass, described by architect Charles Moore: ". . . a lacy white Queen Anne monument with a touch of Eastlake agitation." Indeed.

Morales, a roundish, bald man, was a touch agitated, too, sitting in his high-ceilinged living room surrounded by antique rocking chairs, a mahogany table, a gaudy Victorian candy bowl, and a red kerosene lamp. He started the preservation movement here with a series of newspaper articles on the old houses in the 1970s. "I wanted to create a sense of identity and pride for the whole neighborhood," he said. "But people get suspicious. They think, 'What are they going to take away from us?' Then I went berserk."

And his neighbors eventually saw the light. There are now twenty-six historic monuments in the neighborhood. Included are not only the Victorians, with turrets and wraparound porches and fine detail work, but also squat, wing-roofed houses built around the turn of the century in the uniquely Californian bungalow style.

"Most people think of this as a modern city, a changing city where you take out buildings and put in parking lots," said Morales. With no irony in his voice he credited the freeway with saving the old houses here while they were perishing in places like nearby Lincoln Heights. The Hollywood Freeway cut the hill off from the oil derricks and the trashier development along busy Temple Street—"the hell hole of Calcutta," according to Morales. In Los Angeles, freeways are the main geographical demarcations, like rivers or mountains elsewhere. People stay on one side or the other; you notice when you drive in Los Angeles that the pedestrian walkways above the freeways are virtually empty most of the time.

Morales and his home have a prosperous, long-settled look, but he expressed pride in the flows of immigrants that have poured into the heights. There were the original midwesterners; there were Armenians during the war with the Turks, Jews from New York around the turn of the century, and Latino immigrants throughout. There was even an avant-garde period in the 1920s, when some of the movie studios were located near Echo Lake. The latest arrivals, just around the corner in their hopped-up cars and run-down bungalows, would seem to pose some threat to a home like Morales'. "People will criticize the aliens," said Morales, "but they're good people. . . . I blame the landlords for the conditions."

FROM Carroll Avenue I turned onto East Edgeware Road, which wraps around the knob of the heights to join its West Edgeware counterpart. It was about 5:30 P.M., and older-model

Little Tokyo in downtown Los Angeles. *Russell Lee.*

cars were stopping, apparently to drop people off from work. A tawny boy threw a ball against a garage door while his friend watched. A fellow with a leather cap in a raked Buick was smoking a joint by himself. A couple of giggling Hispanic kids bombarded me with flower petals from their sagging porch as I walked by. A stooped Chinese woman with a shopping bag was accompanied by a young girl with school books pressed against her chest. A little man in a tuxedo painted on the Western Exterminator truck raised a sledgehammer to whack a bug.

Edgeware curved around the contour of the hill, and hanging on the edge of a steep drop stood the Internationale Store, run by Lupe Peralta and her husband. Three men loitered on the sidewalk in front, alternately sitting on the sidewalk and standing, talking and drinking from a paper bag. During subsequent visits to Angeleno Heights, there were always men hanging about here, sometimes as many as a dozen.

The store was no bigger than a one-car garage, and poorly lit. The shelves held mostly canned goods. It resembled the neighborhood store I visited in Barre, Vermont.

"I don't make much money, but I do okay," said Peralta, an elderly woman. "People know I'm here, and they do business." When she took over the store a decade ago, the neighborhood was mostly Hispanic; now it was becoming more Oriental. Only one person made a purchase while we talked, and even with the radio playing in the background, it seemed very quiet inside the store. The radio reported a search in East L.A. for the killers of a kidnapped four-week-old baby.

When I emerged from the store, a short man with a gimpy leg was sweeping the sidewalk. J.R. was Hispanic; his two friends were white. "I try to keep these guys from drinking too much. Cops come, we pour out the beer. But they're out of work, you see." J.R., who is on disability, has not been abstaining himself. He sweeps toward the gutter; then he sweeps back toward the store.

He leaned against his broom and looked up and down the street. One of J.R.'s eyes wandered to the side; he had wavy black hair. He had lived in an apartment in Angeleno Heights for thirty-two years. Most of his friends moved away as property values on top of the hill rose, but a few still live along the rough alley down the steep steps behind the store. There parties tumble into the street, and gangs are active. But the territorial lines seem to be drawn just a half block farther up the hill. While Lupe Peralta said her store had been broken into a few times, J.R. insisted that the more serious gangs— which control, variously, Eighteenth Street, Temple, and Echo Park—don't bother the folks on top of the hill.

"I have a friend in one of the gangs over there came to visit me here," said J.R. "He saw this little store, he couldn't believe it. 'If that was in my neighborhood,' he said, 'we'd hit it every day.' 'So, you rob stores?' I say. 'No,' he says, 'I mean the gangs, they'd hit it.' 'Don't get any ideas,' I say." J.R. sweeps just to help out.

He began pointing out some of the houses down the block— one of the city's finest artists lives there, a rich Chinese bought that one four years ago—but was interrupted by a cry from one of the two men sitting on the sidewalk. The fellow had found a discarded grocery bag with unused food stamps in it. J.R. set aside his broom and went over to celebrate with beer and cigarettes.

——

Wind and water eroded the rock until much of California,
including what is now the Los Angeles area, was a low plain.
Geologists depict the southern California of the early Tertiary
period as a jungle-covered lowland bordered by a broad, shallow,
island-spotted sea. . . .
—*Los Angeles: A Guide to the City and Its Environs*

A FEW days later I was looking down at J.R.'s domain from about two thousand feet. The friend of a friend had invited me to see the city from the air, and my back felt good enough to fold myself into a Grumman TR2, a single-engine plane that seats two and flies about 150 miles per hour. We took off from the Santa Monica Airport and skimmed out over the ocean. The right wing dipped, and we banked above Malibu and rose up over the Santa Monica Mountains. From the air the low-slung homes of Los Angeles look like mosaic tiles, the roads like binding cement, and the swimming pools in the foothills are flakes of turquoise. Only mountains and skyscrapers stand out in relief, and we followed the string of new high rises extending along Wilshire Boulevard toward the downtown. The downtown itself looks like a fragile little asparagus patch, just waiting for an earthquake. We veered around it to the north, and there was Echo Lake, shaped like a ballet slipper.

The ground cover of houses and buildings and roads was as densely packed as jungle canopy, broken occasionally by the dark channel of a freeway. Indeed, we followed the freeways just the way pilots in the bush follow rivers—east along the Santa Monica, south above the Santa Ana.

And what a handsome plot of land Los Angeles seems, seen from up above! Especially on a day like that, when the wind has blown off the yellow epidermis of smog. The steep canyon of Sunset Boulevard, the ribbons of freeway funneling toward Cahuenga Pass, the high rises along Wilshire like an exposed ridge of granite amidst softer weathering stone, the river of cars pouring down to the ocean at Long Beach, and the bright blue ocean itself holding the margin snug.

I was able to enjoy the view because I wasn't, except for a few brief moments, behind the controls. To fly around Los Angeles, you have to rise and drop like the pneumatic jets in a carnival ride. Zones radiating from the L.A. International Airport require that you be below the path of landing jets in one section—over Echo Lake, for instance—and above in another. Without a trained eye, you often don't see the other small planes, which disappear against the busy background of the city below. When we were right over the middle of the city, flying illegally low by the skyscrapers and making our turn to follow the Long Beach Freeway south, a big 747 came in off the ocean, banking around to approach the runway, and slowed to such a crawl that it appeared virtually motionless in the sky. My pilot laughed. "He's afraid of us."

I didn't laugh. I was afraid of us, too. Planes suddenly seemed to be all around us, and as we dipped low toward the tops of the tall downtown buildings, helicopters added to the confusion, coming and going from landing pads on the roofs.

The weather, not to be outdone, complicated things further. We were buzzing the harbor in Long Beach when we noticed a bank of a dark clouds advancing on Santa Monica. It was time to get out of the volatile altitude, and we veered north and called in to the flight controller. She sent us east again along Wilshire Boulevard to line up behind five other small planes hurriedly trying to escape the darkening air. A poky Cessna forced us to circle back—blind in the clouds— and start our approach again.

My pilot snapped at the air traffic controller, but he was not overly concerned. At one point he handed me the controls, briefly. He appeared to enjoy the maneuver in which he dove sharply to get under the cloud cover. We talked through the headsets as we throttled down and bounced on the runway, and the static thickened his Polish accent. He smiled at the relief on my face. "This one . . . was not so bad flight," I think he said. I put him in touch with a friendly lawyer who handled immigration problems.

———

Over the spirits of the starving migrants the desolation they had
seen lay heavy—until they remembered that they were going to
California. That horizon was a bright one, for they were sure that
in the State which supplies nearly half the Nation's fresh fruit and

a third of its truck crops there would be a place for them
among the pickers.
—*California: A Guide to the Golden State*

I TOOK a regular stroll around Echo Lake at twilight, when the shore is at its busiest and the fountain is spouting, and I looked at the passing faces of runners, strollers, and folks lolling on the grass, and wondered what sense of this place they carried in their heads. At the boathouse, the bright light from the pinball machines shone forth as an attendant closed the doors. On the lakefront behind, a middle-aged man in overalls with a weatherworn face taught a young boy how to bait a hook.

Three great interlocking cogwheels whir around Los Angeles: the outer edges of Asian, Hispanic, and North American cultures. You can feel it here at Echo Lake: the intensity of the Filipino jogger; the swagger of four Latinos making an exchange in the park; the sensuality of an interracial couple necking behind the boathouse. Statistics gathered by the United Way or the Rand Corporation tell you the ups and downs of the races competing for space in L.A., and the changing complexion of the City Council is the dilatory political indicator, but here in the public parks the same message comes across viscerally, and you walk with your ears perked and your nostrils flared.

The small children were mostly gone by this hour, and teenagers lolled in the swings at the park. They wrestled and flirted, and their eyes flickered at me as I walked the edge of the lake; preening confidence and fear vacillated behind the makeup. A sadder pair, a black man in a shiny worn suit and a younger man of mixed blood, were stretched out on the sloping lawn, handling something they shouldn't have been. My passing didn't frighten them, and I was careful not to look too hard. Among the lily pads in the lake's corner, I could see Richard's Wild Irish Rose wine, a 7-Eleven Big Gulp cup, a Budweiser can, a dead mallard.

A sycamore tree stood at the north end of the lake; next to it lay a shopping cart, dead of multiple injuries after a collision with the sycamore's trunk. Gang graffiti of some untranslatable significance had been gouged in the tree's bark. A prosperous-looking white couple walking their beagle apologized when his leash caught my leg as we passed. The cogs jam up against each other and grind—slum-crowded apartments next to dolled-up Victorians; Hispanic gangs collecting protection money from Chinese merchants; hosannas from the Angelus Temple drowning the mutterings of dope dealers exchanging prices across the street. I've been taught that humankind once ventured outward from some single lake bottom and, as eons passed, found its way into such widely separate corners that color and body features and language diverged broadly; here, there was something thrilling as this remingling took place, glorious but also charged with fear. That fear was what heated the air, and the heat made us all more liquid, so that we slid by each other as we circled the lake.

At the north end sat an iron-jawed man with a crew cut and a Mediterranean complexion. He had been there every night that I walked that way, and I'd stopped hailing him because he never reacted. This last time, as I climbed over the bushes behind the retaining wall on Bellevue Avenue, he turned his head and nodded. I heard the fwomp, fwomp of a basketball hitting the floor, emanating from the Echo Lake Park recreation center. I looked in the window and saw a full-court game under way, played to the cheers of a ghetto blaster. My back felt better. I found my way inside, picked up a ball lying against the wall, and, when the game ran down to the far end, I joined a couple of others shooting around at the open basket.

————

The Business of Pleasure
—Los Angeles: A Guide to the City and Its Environs

ENTRY into East Los Angeles society at a certain level is not all that different from entry into the life of a West Virginia coal town or a Florida health spa. The muggy smells of the high-ceilinged gym are the same in most places. There are baskets at either end, and baskets on each side, and the high yellowy incandescent lights are shielded by wire grates; the varnish has been worn off the floor under the main baskets. You lace your shoes up slowly, checking out the game and the dead spaces where players are sitting or practicing. You go to a side basket and take shots at one while the team is at the other end of the court; you rebound for other shooters there until one waves your pass off. An insouciant dribble takes you to the top of the key, and you lob a lazy jumper— swish, you hope. Take best shots only—twenty-footers, left-handed hooks, in my case. Always, an eye on the center-court game. In this case, that game rushes end to end.

When a game breaks up, you move in fast to the main basket, and stick to your best shots. A few guys drop out, and you're playing. Hardly a word, except a muttered name here and there.

My teammates included a middle-aged Hispanic fellow and a black kid of maybe seventeen and two other fellows who didn't want to run much, and tended to camp out under the basket while we played defense at the other end. The five lined up against us included a tall, acned young man with a military haircut and four Hispanics, two of them friends who played mostly with each other and ignored their teammates. One of the two was a busy dribbler with a headband that made his hair stand straight up in front, a three-inch wall;

the other was a fire hydrant, about five feet four inches and 250 pounds, smelling strongly as if he had just come in from a picnic in the park where onions and hamburger were plentiful.

The black kid was our go-go player. He liked to take the ball up high, back behind the free throw line, and, when his defender closed in on him, spin around and drive one dribble to the hoop. His grail was the sight of his own hand gracefully twisting the ball as it released by the rim; his superb concentration erased all distractions, including his teammates. I could imagine his coming to the gym alone, playing all day, then wandering home slowly to a crowded apartment.

Our Hispanic partner had his own concerns: He did not like being jostled. He gave the impression he was pulling back a bit to preserve himself, the style of a responsible family man playing hooky. He wore a nice set of matching yellow sweat clothes. He cruised about twenty feet from the basket, and when a carom came his way, he would dribble out and take a flat-footed thirty-footer. The other two on our team yelled for the ball at half court so they could run a few fast breaks; otherwise, they didn't bother us.

It quickly became more or less a game of three-on-three. The two amigos on the other team played catch as if they'd been doing it for ages, and perhaps they had. The Wide Body planted himself under the basket, and the Dribbler circled his friend like a child skipping around a maypole, laughing and chattering, throwing the ball in, rotating and taking his friend's return pass. They remembered now and then to pass to their third man, the military-looking kid, who could score. When a shot went up, the big man spread his arms to create an empty space the size of a Dumpster around him, while opponents slipped and sloshed in his sweat. If the military kid shot and missed, the big fellow laid it back in. The white kid did his job stoically, sometimes talking to himself, never to his teammates, drops of sweat on the spikes of his flattop hair. His scabbed fingers indicated a summer construction job; next fall, I imagined, he would be watching television ads during a football game and decide to go into the service. Score: 12–3, theirs.

The game had settled into this pattern when, after a particularly enervating run of lay-ins by the large fellow, the black kid looked at me for the first time. He had a flat nose and a soft coffee-colored face, and when our eyes met, his quickly clouded with irritation; his brows clenched, and the muscles worked in his cheek, and he averted his face. I suppose he was there every day, playing a hard but hopeless style of game; his muscular body was small, too small for the college and pro dreams that sustain so many inner-city kids through high school. Sweaty Sunday showdowns in a crowded gym were a kind of revenge, and he was rarely bested by the merry, trifling Hispanic enemy, or the workaday white players. But how he panicked at the thought of losing! Only that thought could compel him to give up the ball, accept me as another minority, and agree fleetingly with his eyes to make common cause. It was a limited contract; after that first look, his eyes never met mine again. But we began playing together.

Since the Wide Body was immobile, our opponents found switches difficult, and we began working some give-and-gos. My black conspirator was startled at first when he got the ball back after passing it, and running off my pick. Our Hispanic teammate was tired, but he saw we were going to try, and he obligingly moved his shot in a few feet and began helping with rebounds. Score: 16–11.

Short jumpers were falling for me. The white guy on the other team was mad at his mates, who joked in Spanish and didn't seem to care much about our comeback, but his back was turned to them when he grimaced, so only I could see.

When he made his good moves toward the basket, his large teammate failed to pull out of the way, and he had to swerve and put up bad hooks. Score: 19–20.

Now the black kid stutter-stepped at the top of the lane, started a drive, and, cut off by the white guy, passed to me in the left corner. The Dribbler stepped out on me, and I drove around him, only to find the Wide Body waddling over to help his friend. Whoosh—a pass to the black kid, who had slid behind the basket, right behind the Wide Body, and there he is with an easy lay-up, but his face hardened, his secret was about to be revealed: no left hand. The shot hit the rim and rolled off, angry teeth bit his lower lip, and he soared for his own rebound. He wouldn't take it up again and look awkward; he whipped it out to me, top of the key, and sulked off to the left corner.

And I felt strong, knowing this was the last point. I faked right, though I rarely drive that way, and lowered my right shoulder to drive left by the flattop. He spun around but didn't get his foot out, and white guy had beaten white guy. I jumped as high as I could, watching my hand and the rim.

Then I smelled him, before I saw him. When I looked down, because I was coming down, I saw the broad, upturned grin and pocked cheeks of Wide Body. His shoulder was under my rib cage, a big shiny tire of a shoulder decorated with a tank top strap, and I was dropping on him, and then off him, my hips swinging down and my feet groping for floor. I threw my arm around his neck, intent on dragging him down as a cushion, but he didn't even bend, just smiled at his friend, amused by our embrace; then my fingers slid on his sweat, and I fell off, landing on my heels and then my butt.

Something twinged in my back. Wide Body stood right where he'd stood the whole game, putting his tank top strap back in place, smiling. I decided not to get up right away.

The ball rolled away, right by the black kid, who struck a defiant pose and ignored it. The Dribbler picked it up and shot it, swish, and then jogged over to where I lay. Speaking in English for the first time, he asked if I was all right. Then he put the ball under his arm, and he and the Large One wandered off together, laughing, to rejoin a picnic in the park. The flattop came over with an empty, constricted face and offered me a hand. I spotted the black kid, moving off the court without a word, his eyes on the ground, walking with a prideful, jutting stride that was just to buck himself up, not for anybody else.

I looked slowly around the gym at ankle level. Lots of Hispanics, chattering, playing hard. A few whites, working out in a businesslike way, avoiding too much contact. One black, walking off alone and bruised.

Point of Departure

Glendale

IN 1912, when my grandfather was eighteen, his parents suf-fered economic setbacks in Kansas City, and they moved to Southern California. They were part of the great resettling movement that brought Americans—often immigrants or second-generation citizens of lower economic class—to Cali-fornia in waves, starting with the gold rush in the 1840s, another leap in the 1880s, and a third great jump during the Depression.

In many ways, William and Francesca Griffin were typical middle-class Americans of their day: They were of European immigrant stock, and they kept moving west in search of advancement. They shifted about in Los Angeles, living in Redlands and Santa Monica, before settling in Glendale, a little boomtown at the eastern end of the San Fernando Val-ley. A primary goal of the Griffins was to see that Allen, my grandfather, was afforded a college education, even if it meant

Walking to Los Angeles. *Dorothea Lange.*

that my grandmother had to work for a time as a domestic. Her son touched down briefly in his nineteenth year to "toughen up" in a Los Angeles lumberyard owned by his uncle John Griffin. He was given the lowliest jobs at the lumberyard, and he'd come home at night with his hands red and swollen with splinters. His mother would take those hands, sensitive hands for which she had secured piano lessons years before, and laboriously pick the splinters from his palms. As my great-aunt Margaret Webb told me, and she remembered it all astonishingly well, it was Francesca, and not Allen, who would cry.

Glendale was born along one of the railroad lines that pumped humanity into the L.A. Basin in the nineteenth century, and to a visitor today it is indistinguishable from the other foothill communities standing shoulder to shoulder along the San Gabriel foothills—Monrovia, Burbank, West Covina. The writers' project guide to Los Angeles described its "frame bungalows and white or pastel-tinted stucco houses with gaily colored roofs," the "flourishing" of its open-shop industries, and the Verdugo Hills, "purple in the distance." The mountains looked brown and undistinguished now as I drove north out of Los Angeles, and the name Verdugo would mean little to Glendale's current residents. In 1794 Corporal José María Verdugo was given one of the largest Spanish land grants in California, thirty thousand acres, and the festive rancho he built survived Mexican and American rule, but not the partitions and debts of subsequent Verdugo generations. The Verdugo name draws blank stares from many of today's residents; they know little about the first Glendale land boom of the 1880s, when the Southern Pacific came through, or even the orchards that once produced prunes and peaches, then gave way to the manufacture of everything from mattresses to light posts. All these events happened before the Los Angeles guide was written in the late 1930s; in 1931

half the population of Los Angeles had been living somewhere else five years before. My grandfather's parents would
have been old-timers in Glendale.

I looked for 131 East Garfield, another address that Margaret, now nearly ninety, remembered exactly. The street
was shaded and quiet, with parallel rows of bungalows nosing
it like hobby boats in a small marina. Their sloping roofs,
deep porches, and neat front lawns were interrupted occasionally by the protruding bow of an apartment building. I
stood on the sidewalk across the street from where 131 should
have been, but was not. In one direction was the rush of
traffic on Brand Avenue, now a major arterial street, and in
the other a mix of houses and small apartment buildings. An
older couple was walking a Yorkshire terrier, and a block
away four young Hispanics were swarming over the engine of
a 1969 Chevy. Across the street, two men on the porch of a
cream-colored house looked at me inquiringly, and I
approached them.

They were Mitchell Williams and Fedor Koratschenko.
Williams was a leather-skinned, stooped septuagenarian in
crisp handyman's clothes, wearing his wristwatch on the outside of his shirt sleeve. Ever since an accident with a chain
saw, he told me, the wrist aches when the metal watchband
is against the skin. Koratschenko, on whose porch they were
sitting, had the bowling-pin build of one of those plastic
punch bag figures that bounce back upright whenever a kid
hits them. Like the top of the punch bags, his head was
round and smooth-shaven, and he chain-smoked.

Koratschenko had served in the Russian Army and was
wounded and captured by the Germans in World War II. He
came to the United States after the war with only one leg,
and suffered then the only two weeks of unemployment he
had known in his life. Most of his years had been spent working as an orthopedist with amputees like himself. He was

now on the verge of retirement, at which time the two men
and Koratschenko's wife planned to climb aboard the camper
parked next to the house and travel around the country. Williams bought his first house on Garfield in 1946; his Russian
friend moved here from downtown Los Angeles in the 1950s.
Though they remembered the neighborhood of thirty years
ago fondly, they sounded eager to absent themselves from the
neighborhood of today.

Koratschenko invited me to stay for a cup of coffee. Williams mentioned that the last member of the Verdugo family
to live in Glendale had kept a house on Garfield until just a
few years ago; then he sold his home to an apartment devel-
oper.

Koratschenko gestured at the men working on the Chev-
rolet. "And that's what comes with the apartments. Last month
the police came. Dozens of Mexicans on the street at night
with dope and big radios. They busted them all out."

Williams seemed a little embarrassed by the venom in his
friend's voice. "Lots of foreigners," he said.

They pointed at various homes and buildings that had been
bought by immigrants. A Chinese man had bought the mor-
tuary on the corner two blocks away and turned it into a car
dealership. A Yugoslav lady had sold her house to an Oriental
man who arrived with a shopping bag holding two hundred
thousand dollars in cash. Williams laughed, "She didn't know
what to do. She had to order an armored car to get it to the
bank." The two men spoke scornfully of the poorer Hispanics
who had moved in, crowding into small apartments and
spending their time on the street.

"It used to be nice here when I came," said Koratschenko.
"But you see, now, all this trash moved in."

And what, I wondered, was Williams in 1926, when he
arrived in Southern California? He headed west from Chicago
that year with $36 in his pocket, talking his way into jobs

and meals as he traveled. He bought a house on Garfield in 1946 for $9,500. In the 1980s he sold that house for $150,000.

"Glendale was, what, fifty thousand people in 1960," said Koratschenko. "It's a hundred and fifty thousand. Foreigners!"

"But you came from Russia," I said. "People have always moved around, moved here and there. *You're* a foreigner."

Koratschenko was not fazed; he put his big forearms on the table and leaned forward. "I was foreign but I excused myself. I came over here, took an American's job. I breathe American air, eat American food. Some others come over here and live twenty years and they're not satisfied here. I tell them: 'You sons of bitches, pack your suitcase and go.'"

"Yeah," said Williams, shaking his head and smiling, "yeah, he does."

Destination

Monterey

As late as 1924, dwellers in these lovely coast mountains were reported never to have seen "anything . . . except something which can be packed on horses and mules." The story is told of two youths, 17 and 19, who were asked how they amused themselves. The younger volunteered, very shyly, that a year before they had been up to Pfeiffers, on the Big Sur River, seen a dance and a lot of people. The older one guessed that, maybe, next year, they might get to make the trip again.
—A *Guide to the* Monterey *Peninsula*

THROUGHOUT my travels I had been training my eye to spot clues to the local culture by cataloging the landscape, natural and man-made; but as I drove up the Big Sur coast, the note-book lay closed on the Mustang's passenger seat. It would have been too self-conscious an act, to impose the clinical vocabulary of lichens and basalts on the narrow beaches and sheer cliffs, to count the pillars supporting a highway viaduct or map precisely the gradations of cumulus in the atmosphere. That would be an oddly reductive vision of a place I knew through the skin, knew well enough to ignore its details.

My mind was mostly occupied by memory, foraging back in that peculiar privacy that an automobile provides. The rhythm of the road set the pace for my thoughts, and it was a faster beat than my pen could have sustained. So I did not mark down the odometer reading at the place where the redwoods broke off and the grazed meadows began, nor did I turn the pages of the writers' project guide to compare what I saw with the descriptions of fifty years ago. I tried to focus on my grandfather, because the Monterey Peninsula was his country, and if I could place him in his setting, perhaps it would illuminate why one man chose to live where he did.

Surprisingly, Big Sur was much the same as I remembered it, with no Lego-like condominiums stair-stepping down the steep hills. That a state could both tolerate the mad sprawl of Los Angeles and forcefully protect such extraordinary real estate as this says something for its diverse view of itself. In one sense, the Sur appeared to have become even less cluttered: The roadside was clear of the young hippies who camped on the beaches and in the canyons twenty years before, when I last lived in the area. I was one of those Big Sur vagabonds for a brief interval, but my strongest memories of Big Sur were still earlier. The thumb that gripped my coffee cup as I sat at Big Sur Inn had a faint indentation on the top. As a boy, stripping a branch for a makeshift pole to dip for crawdads in a stream that hung in one of the green clefts above the sea, I had pulled the knife toward me, sliced the thumb, and bathed myself in blood. When I looked at the faces drinking coffee around me—faintly familiar, prosperous, and wrinkling relatives of those I'd met on the road in the 1960s—

I felt my precedence keenly. How many years had they been here? Well, I had been here earlier. It was the most isolating sort of nostalgia.

I spent a few nights at a friend's house near Pfeiffer Beach; much of the time I soaked in an outdoor tub, stars and ocean and soft voices from the house up the hill, soaking and softening my memories. I imagined I was shoring myself up for the trip north into Monterey and my grandfather's haunts, but I kept hunkering down in the gray water and putting it off. My arms felt extraordinarily heavy; my voice, when I spoke, was a low croak. The past is a different community, and I was stymied by the strangeness of my memories.

Days went by as I soaked and conjured images that had retained some power over me in the years since I'd left Monterey, but I failed to find Allen Griffin among them. I remembered junior college students in pea coats drifting about the shabby clubs and piers of Cannery Row; the dew-damp paths that snaked through the gullies of Jack's Peak; the cigarette glows and our cracked-voiced conspiracies just outside the cone of a streetlight on Monterey Circle. My grandfather was on the other side of Carmel Hill, the small, forested hump that separated Monterey, Seaside, and Pacific Grove from Carmel and Pebble Beach. He lived in Pebble Beach in an enormous Spanish colonial-style house, with courtyards on either side and sheep in the meadow down the hill. He sat by a small fireplace in a green leather chair, looking at me above a crookneck reading lamp. His glasses were down on his nose, and his eyes were watery above the ruddy skin of his flat cheeks; below his mustache, his mouth seemed to hang open, the corners slightly drooped. I froze at the sight of him; I had forgotten a tie *again*!

The hill between Monterey and Pebble Beach was like a wall between our lives, and I grew up knowing almost nothing about Allen Griffin. My friends and I in Monterey were always in motion. We built a two-story fort on an empty lot, stored cigarettes and little stolen flasks there, and hurled tennis shoes at each other through the apertures between rooms; the balance of bravery and stupidity in us was tested daily. I played pinball for hours at Red's downtown, and was mildly dependent on a friend who could enter a cigar store on lower Alvarado and emerge with a couple of nudist magazines under his coat. We would take a wheel off one wobbly bike and hook its frame to another; then with four legs pumping we'd race down Martin Street and ignore the stop sign, daring the drivers on Pacific to mow us down. But the motion stopped when I pedaled over the hill to Pebble Beach. Then I would walk past the unchanging ancient Chinese scrolls and modernist canvases on the walls and the plants that seemed not to grow and the ceramic canister with a topknot of walking sticks, and the perspiration would chill under my shirt. There seemed to be no place for me there, and no easy understanding of the man whom I came to visit. I'd search the rooms in the farthest wings of that big house, find the old books there, and wait to be called. He would lend me a tie, and I would sit silently through the meal.

But twenty years had gone by. My parents were both dead, and the various Monterey homes we had lived in had long ago been rearranged to suit others' needs. Only my grandfather's home remained as it was. It was really the only place I could think of where I could turn on myself the questions I had asked in Louisiana, Vermont, and all around the country: Where in all this motion is the place we come back to, the community that both succors and makes demands of us, the place against which we measure our growth and our happiness? Where is the place we call home?

I did not want my own answers, because I was still, in a

sense, wandering; I wanted the answers of a man who had made a choice. But I had never asked him directly; surely it would have been one of those confused, ethereal questions that Allen Griffin would have waved off.

He settled in Monterey by choice, and in some ways he had much in common with the Mexican illegal who lived in Los Angeles by choice. They shared an aspiration to betterment, the confidence to test themselves, and a certain willingness to conceal their backgrounds, when it seemed the practical thing to do. My grandfather became wealthy, but he did not begin that way, and the Mexican immigrant might feel a real affinity with the young Allen Griffin. The key difference between them would not be economic; it would be the way they viewed their family and their past. The Mexican was likely to remember his home in Mexico, to continue, in a sense, to live there, sending money and returning when he could; for my grandfather, the earliest landscapes were transient, and it was the last place where the memory rooted.

He arrived in Monterey in the 1920s, a decorated soldier married to the daughter of a congressman, rather presumptuously searching the state for a newspaper to buy. He claimed later that Monterey had no special allure; he simply couldn't afford a newspaper anywhere else. He gave as a reason for settling on the peninsula: "Stupidity. They wanted me in Monterey, for no better reason than the fact that they wanted to get rid of the old newspaper. That's all."

The old man who remembered was sometimes contemptuous and dismissive of the people he dealt with in those early days. He was always a snob about people. But sometimes the younger man spoke through, gleefully describing the raid on a speakeasy where he, a green newspaper editor, found himself used as an unarmed decoy at the front of the police squad; or the way, in the desperate early days, he'd get his father-in-law, who published a San Jose morning newspaper, to ship down used type to fill the inside pages of the fledgling Monterey broadsheet in the afternoon.

One afternoon a man named Don Donor dropped by the home where I was staying in Big Sur. He was a small man in his eighties—my grandfather's age—with a halo of wild gray hair and a scarf hanging around his neck, and we talked a little about Allen Griffin. "Your grandfather? Ah, I made him nervous. Because I don't give a shit."

Wherever my family has lived over the years, there has been on a wall in the house a charcoal drawing by Donor of another Big Sur resident, a poet; its rushed, swirling lines had reminded me for years of Donor himself—a man with a loud laugh who danced around a Big Sur campground with a wine bottle in his hand when I was a child. Now he spread some garlic paste on a cracker and jabbed me with it, then put his face a few inches from mine. "The secret of a long life." He nodded and spun away, shouting over his shoulder that I should come visit him.

The trip to Donor's house in the Carmel Highlands drew me closer into town. I walked up rock steps through a handsome, unkempt garden and past a Ping-Pong table. I could smell the bouillabaisse, but before Donor let me eat, he read a letter from James Joyce to his wife in which the writer recalled a privileged view he'd once had of his spouse relieving herself. Hearing the Irishman's words spoken with a Russian / Yiddish accent, punctuated by Donor's wild, waving arms, made me laugh. When he had finished reading, Donor declared: "Isn't that beautiful? Such love! Now, eat, and then I'll beat you at Ping-Pong."

The writer Henry Miller taught Donor to play Ping-Pong. He hunched into a ready position that lowered his nose almost to the edge of the table, then lunged at a couple of hits and missed badly. I was careful at first to serve gently. He bounced around, concentrating on his game, but talking about other things. I asked him how he felt about his own neighborhood, which had become frightfully expensive, like most all the real estate on the peninsula. He began hitting the ball harder and said, "I wish I could be Samson and pull it all down. I would even give up all my hair."

He beat me, 15–12.

JUST across Highway 1 from Don Donor's home is Point Lobos, a preserve of extraordinary tide pools, and the southernmost home of the Monterey cypress. The park has been protected by the state since the 1930s, and my grandfather was among those who campaigned for its preservation.

On a bluff above a narrow inlet just south of Whaler's Cove I saw a sea otter, on his back, meandering away from the shore. A great blue heron rested on a large chunk of wood marooned in a kelp bed. A cormorant dived farther out. A few bewhiskered boulders around the cove turned out to be harbor seals. Looking east, I could see what was called Jap Bay and curving north beyond it some private sand and then Carmel Beach. Finally there were the green golfing shoulders of Pebble Beach protruding. The town of Carmel approached the beach with low-slung bungalows, their facades forming an undulating line like the stratified rock and sand along a riverbank. No giant hotels fronted the beach; no six-lane freeways ran alongside it; no oil rigs floated offshore.

The Monterey Peninsula had somehow exempted itself from the cluttered commercial landscape of the last half century. Growth had been controlled.

There was a pay phone by the Point Lobos park entry booth, and I fumbled with the phone book there. I looked for the names of friends from Walter Colton Junior High School, up on the hill in Monterey. Searching out old friends is a booby-

A refreshment stand by a West Coast highway.
Dorothea Lange.

trapped business; there were only a couple that I might have
dared to go visit. But they were not there. None of them. It
seemed impossible that the troop of boys and girls I knew
back then had departed en masse. Some, I expected, had gone
into the service, others had probably given up their names in
marriage, and a few would have gone elsewhere for more education. But many of my friends had been more likely only to
finish high school and look around for the nearest job. Where
were they all?

Well, they were not in the phone book. I started up the

Mustang—there was an ominous bearing rattle—and started
down the road toward Monterey.

———

So dependent is Monterey upon the sardine for its livelihood
that the industry's seasonal fluctuations now affect the local
economy with the precision of a seismograph recording earthquake
tremors. Merchants solemnly claim that they observe "a falling off
of trade even during the full moon periods and in rough weather
when the boats do not go out."
—Guide to the Monterey Peninsula

BECAUSE there is a new freeway system that bends around
Jack's Peak and slides east past Monterey, I had to backtrack
from Seaside toward the downtown. The road from Carmel
used to come straight into the heart of Monterey, and stop
abruptly at a streetlight. Today's traffic would back up all
the way over the hill under that arrangement. I drove back
into town on Fremont Street, by the El Estero Car Wash,
where I sometimes hung around, and into the heart of town.
The heart—Alvarado Street—is all cleaned up now. There
are restaurants with menus written in French, a convention
center, the whole works. Gone are the divey bars and pool
halls where soldiers would sometimes buy a small bottle of
hooch for a couple of strutting youngsters.

We'd take the stuff and drink it and quickly get sick, and
all I derived from it was a reflexive twinge in my stomach
whenever I went near the part of town. All spruced up, it
seems less inhabited now. Traffic is trickier, but smoother,
with one-way streets and multilane ramps going off to Pacific
Grove and Fisherman's Wharf. I turned up past the new
Doubletree Inn, which finished off Alvarado. The Doubletree makes a halfhearted attempt to blend with the historic
old adobes, and manages only to demean them. Obscure behind

the hotel would be the Pacific Building, a nineteenth-century saloon and hotel that had a bull-and-bear fighting pit. The old Custom house—wraparound balcony, tile roof, my grandfather's ten-thousand-dollar VA benefit—was somewhere back there, too.

I turned up Calle Principal, feeling that old Lower Alvarado queasiness, and headed back a few blocks to the Old Capitol Club.

The club was off limits to me as a boy and a young man. I was either too young or, later on, too ill kempt. It was one of my grandfather's haunts—a men's club, with stuffed chairs, antique rugs, snug little rooms where one could drink and chat, and a patio luncheon where Monterey's powerful men met daily.

I lunched there now at the invitation of Ted Durein, a kind man of pink complexion and rounded features who had worked for decades at the Monterey newspaper. We had a drink first in a small room off the entrance hallway, sitting in red leather chairs beneath framed prints of red-jacketed huntsmen riding to hounds. Two gray-suited men entered the room, exchanged greetings and sat off to one side, and the air dilated with discretion.

Durein had worked for the Monterey newspaper for forty-six years, first for Allen Griffin, and then, when my grandfather sold the newspaper in the 1960s, for the new owners. His memories of the early days were proud and amusing, but when others joined us and indulged in some mild bashing of the newspaper's present-day leadership, he abstained.

According to Durein, the event that had the biggest impact on Monterey during the last half century was the closing of the canneries in the 1940s. "Monterey was the third-largest fishing port in the U.S.A.," said Durein. "Then they built these big reduction ships and started doing it three miles offshore." Some blame the high-volume ships for the disappearance of the sardines, but no one really knows why that happened.

The annual sardine catch in the 1930s was about 215,000 tons; the writers' project guide to Monterey reports, in a droll moment, that if the sardines caught were laid end to end, we could put a sardine on the moon. The catch dropped in the 1940s to almost nothing. The whistles that called the workers to the big canneries—a different pitch for each cannery— ceased blowing.

We helped ourselves at the buffet to prime rib and carried our plates to the patio, shaded by trees and high walls. The club is one of many remaining Spanish colonial homes from Monterey's early days. Most of these casas feature long balconies and enclosed gardens like this one. Men who knew my parents and grandfather stopped to say hello. All here looked prosperous, and most seemed eager to greet a new, or perhaps I was an old, face. We exchanged news hurriedly, pretending to remember the names of children and second wives . . . or perhaps they really did remember all that, and it was only I who had forgotten. They had after all been living here for the twenty years I had been gone, and eating for twenty years in this club, where a glance at a particular chair might remind one daily how a man sat and the peculiar way he sipped a martini.

I sat across from Ken Ehrman, a gentle-voiced lawyer who was close to my grandfather and my mother. We ate slowly, and every now and then I would attempt to explain what interested me about Monterey Then and Now. This evoked some chuckles and a few glib anecdotes from our tablemates, but Ehrman, a compact man in a prim dark suit, kept thinking. Finally he said, "There used to be people you could go to when you needed something done." We sat on wrought-iron chairs and drank wine. I couldn't be sure whether by "something" he meant the removal of a building inspector or a loan to start a business or the installation of new playground equipment at El Estero Park. "If one of these men said yes, you could do it. Now it's much more fragmented. The neighborhoods have become powerful. And there are minority groups, specialty groups, gay groups, all of them organized. In the old days, it was just Griffin, Morse, Ferrante."

Griffin was my grandfather. His friend Sam F. B. Morse controlled Del Monte Properties, which developed the golf courses, resort hotel, and residential properties of Pebble Beach, as well as other properties all over the peninsula. Ferrante was the most colorful of the three: Peter, or Pietro, Ferrante, an immigrant Sicilian who invented a sardine net and became a political leader in Monterey's large Italian community, was a powerfully built man with a shock of white hair.

"Another reason you don't have just a few people running things anymore is that we're so mobile now," said Ehrman. He smiled; his eyes had the squinty wrinkles of minute examination. "People come and go, but you don't find many children staying here," he said. "That's always been a complaint: The children have to go because there's nothing for them to do. Unless they're lawyers or doctors."

My grandfather had begun coming to this club as a fairly young man, in his thirties; so had my father; so had these men with whom I ate lunch. On this Monday it appeared I was the only diner under fifty.

Ted Durein told a story about the way my grandfather let his lieutenants run the newspaper. "You know, the Colonel was gone most of the time anyway. I mean, he was always back in the Army or off traveling, it seems like. I can only remember one time he tried to interfere." That was when a prominent local military man committed suicide, and Griffin suggested the story be kept quiet. Durein printed a seventy-two-point front-page headline on the death, and they never discussed it again. While Durein laughed at the story and rubbed his eyes, Ken Ehrman had quietly left the patio, walking away with an economical, slightly hunched gait.

———

Perhaps it was Old Monterey's very neglect that preserves it against oblivion.
—A Guide to the Monterey Peninsula

RETURNING to the scenes of childhood is a tricky business; the past becomes vivid and immediate, but the present looks you over blankly. Invigorated by my reception at the Old Capitol Club, I turned the corner up Polk Street with a bounce in my step. A few blocks away stood the newspaper office, an unimposing gray-and-white suitcase of a building. There I planned to rummage in the old files of the newspaper "morgue" and read the things my grandfather wrote when he was my age and just beginning to put his stamp on things.

Entering the *Herald,* I waved off the receptionist with a smile and walked back to the office of the newspaper's publisher, a tall, white-haired man whom I had met the year before at a California Press Association banquet honoring my grandfather. His secretary told me he was in a meeting. But as she was speaking, he walked into the office from the newsroom.

O'G: Hi, good to see you again.
PUBLISHER: Yes, yes, how are you . . . [tilting his head] now, is it—
O'G: I met you at the press convention last year. Colonel Griffin's grandson—
PUB.: Of course. How are you?
O'G: Fine. I wanted to spend some time in the morgue, digging up some things he wrote—
PUB. (a moment of confusion): Well, actually, we have a rule.

Only the staff can use the morgue. That's the rule.

O'G (giving him a chance to correct himself, smiling): I won't need a whole lot of time. There's just a couple of years particularly—

PUB.: I'm sorry. It's a rule we have at all our newspapers. No exceptions.

O'G (chuckling): Surely this wouldn't—

PUB. (moving along, a wave to the secretary): It's so good to see you again. How is your grandmother?

Dead, actually. But he was gone before I could answer. My grandmother died in the 1950s, and he was undoubtedly referring to my grandfather's second wife, a hardy, elegant woman who survived him and still lived in the big house in Pebble Beach.

So I left the *Herald* and walked across the street to the Friendly Plaza, a block of shrubs and flowers that was once, in the days when Monterey was still the Mexican capital, the city's center. Where was the center now? Was there a solitary marker on the grounds of one of the shopping malls that had grown up between Monterey and Carmel, like the solitary, vandalized marker I had visited at the country's geodetic center near Smith Center, Kansas?

I fell asleep for a while under a huge walnut tree, and when I woke, I walked back down the street to the library. Holding a couple of reels of worn microfilm of the 1930s *Herald,* sufficiently humbled, I waited my turn on the microfilm machine.

THERE was nothing stupid about starting a newspaper in a spot where the competition was weak, a place that would soon be discovered by Americans in search of domestic Edens, a community dominated in the 1920s by "weak men with nothing special about them." Allen Griffin tried to strike a crusading pose, setting out to rid the area of "blind pigs" (this was during Prohibition) and corruption in government. He also got himself a cut of a lucrative real estate deal in the Carmel Valley, and by the 1930s the paper was thriving, and so was he. This gave him a strong voice in the debate over Monterey's future: Would it be the fishing industry—with its associated cannery smells and blue-collar workers— or the developing tourist industry, or both?

The sardines unexpectedly assumed a big role in that decision, by disappearing in the 1940s. But even before the fishing industry collapsed, my grandfather had vigorously endorsed the tourism option. He made the preservation of historic buildings another crusade, pledging his World War I veterans' benefits toward the city's purchase of the Old Customhouse, which was threatened with becoming a Greek restaurant. And though he expressed admiration for Los Angeles's aggressive growth policies, his newspaper fought against billboards and spot zoning for retail businesses. In the 1960s he helped drive off a proposed oil refinery that would have brought hundreds of jobs. "We advise the Board of Supervisors to tell the Humble Oil Co. to take its profit on its investment and go on its way rejoicing," he wrote.

I took a walk one evening up the hill from the library to my old neighborhood. I felt furtive and a little freakish, glancing into the empty windows of the homes of long-ago friends. I suppose my younger self saw my older self walk by from the foyer of the house where I spent my adolescent years: a strange man walking up the street looking into houses would have been highly suspect back in the 1960s. I even knocked on a few doors. And while I was knocking at one, a car drove up. It was the older brother of the friend who had lived there. He shared a beer with me and told me that the friend was, in fact, still living on the peninsula.

Here for a second time I will change a name, because "Evan
Baker" did not know I was writing about my visit, nor did I
know when we got together that I might write about him.
Baker perched on a stack of discarded pallets at his shop in a
small enclave of warehouses and shops just east of Monterey.
I sat in a folding chair. It was not as awkward as such things
can be, once he got over his surprise. I was relieved to find
him looking well—the same blue eyes, upturned nose, and
thin lips. As I remembered him at thirteen, his shoulders
now seemed too broad, but otherwise he looked much as he
had, vigorous and a little sheepish.

Growing up, he lived three blocks away from me—a world
away, in the realm of neighborhood gangs—so we had not
been the closest of friends. But we had forlornly pursued two
junior high girls who were close to each other and equally
uninterested in us; we had some classes together, too. His
parents spoke with foreign accents, and he drove himself hard
in sports and his studies, despite his persistent doubts about
himself; I put a special value on him for his seriousness, and
the warmth he showed me. He had gone off to college and
eventually picked up an M.A. in economics before returning
to Monterey. After a couple of false starts, he opened his
shop. I asked him where everybody else was.

A few whom I had failed to find in the phone book were
in fact still around, in neighboring communities, like Baker.
One—perhaps my most volatile and pugilistic friend—had
won a lottery for a liquor license and now owned a bar in
Salinas; another had done some time for dealing cocaine. Most
of our old friends, though, had moved away. One was doing
laser research in Southern California; another cleaned swimming pools in Palm Springs; still another had established
himself as a cinematographer in Hollywood. They had left
this Eden and for the most part headed south, into that bub-
bling human caldron I had just left.

"Almost everybody I knew then has moved away," Baker said, so he now went south occasionally to make the rounds of old friends. "You can't stay here. There just aren't many jobs. There's a new crowd running the city, they moved here, oh, maybe twenty years ago, and now it's theirs, and they want to stop growth. They want to stop growth without spending any money. So Monterey's turning into a bedroom community for Gilroy." But he was good-humored about it all, philosophical.

We ventured into the dangerous territory of the past. He was tactful about my grandfather, who must be remembered by some, perhaps many, as a power broker who overstepped his responsibilities as a newspaper publisher. Mostly, we looked back at what had seemed, twenty years ago, an enormously complex civilization all under the age of sixteen, and we reviewed the expectations we had for ourselves and our friends then. A dangerous business. I admitted that I expected most of my old friends still to be here. Baker—my most serious, driven friend—was the one I had expected to be gone.

He said, "Well, Monterey costs too much, but I'm still here. I don't expect I'll go now." He laughed the dry laugh I remembered. "I have trouble even getting away to L.A."

———

. . . the {Monterey} Peninsula is concentrated California. . . .
—*A Guide to the Monterey Peninsula*

THE Mustang coughed and sputtered as I drove back along Del Monte Avenue toward Monterey. The gray fog of the Peninsula did not seem to agree with it, and I would have to get back on the road soon. The stretch of Del Monte just north of El Estero Park was reassuringly shabby and unchanged. Even the green facade of the old roller skating rink remained on the corner where I remembered it, across the road from the dunes where my friends and I took our sandsurfers—low-rent surfboards—during the summer. In a superficial sense, Monterey had not changed much at all. It had just spruced up and raised the rent.

I had rolled into many different corners of the country with my back seat full of travel guides from the 1930s, noting the changes and the continuities. People would tell me, sometimes in pain, that their homes—their town, their region, their trailer park, or their ranch—had been transformed so thoroughly that their childhoods had been erased from the landscapes around them. "The old tight close life broken up," wrote Sherwood Anderson in the 1940s, lamenting the decline of town life in the automobile age. But I had come to have doubts about that sort of romantic regret, because motion has always been a way of life in this country, from the time second sons and daughters began to push west in the seventeenth century. There are people in every community whose memories span generations, but they are rarely the moaners; those who've stayed on are often the people most comfortable with change. By far the larger portion of our population is quite accustomed to moving about on a regular basis, and has been since long before the automobile. So I was not entirely sympathetic to these expressions of loss, and often I found myself pleasurably heated up in the feverish climate of places like Los Angeles, where the excitement of change for its own sake shakes out the nostalgia.

Now, exploring a place where I was something more than a mere visitor, where I had a stake of memory, I had to keep in check my own querulous complaints about the newcomers and homogenizing franchise shops that were taking over "my" turf. The first few days back in Monterey, my lamentations echoed some of the folks I'd talked to in Smith Center or the Smoke Hole; but additional time allowed me to explore the strata of feeling from which they erupted. I found I was not really so much disturbed by the superficial changes in the town's character, its new buildings and highways, the young leaders who would look at me blankly, and so on. I was, in fact, disappointed at how *little* it had changed, how stagnant and sterile and touristy Monterey had become. And my real anger was not toward the newcomers but toward my own people, for failing to provide me an anchor there, a continuing presence that would pass on a private vision of the place and cultivate my memories while I traveled off on my adventures. It was selfish, but this was my childhood.

I drove back to the top of Carmel Hill and through the gates into Pebble Beach. The traffic was clotty and moved slowly along the windy, wooded Seventeen-Mile Drive. The license plates were about half out of state: Arizona, Michigan, Ontario. A major tourist attraction—an odd price to pay for protection and exclusivity.

Less than a mile in, I remembered a shortcut, and I left the line of traffic and hopped ahead of it by slipping off onto a snaky side road that went over a little hill of secluded residences. When I rejoined the main road, I was near the Del Monte Lodge.

To a California boy, the lodge and the Pebble Beach country clubs had an aura of tradition and pedigree and gentility during the era when Sam Morse controlled them. Such a notion would probably draw a snicker from those who fancy the older resorts of the South or Northeast, but I suppose the pretensions of those regions would, in turn, draw a chuckle from an Englishman. The lodge, at any rate, is now owned by a Denver oilman with a reputation for turning over properties quickly, and its patrons have surrendered any pretense of noblesse; snobbery is more blatantly plutocratic now, the province of anyone who can afford it.

I drove slowly through the lodge complex, past clusters of residences, and then onto more narrow roads, which threaded through a tall forest of Monterey pines with almost no understory. You could not drive *by* my grandfather's house; you had to drive *in*. To my left was a sloping meadow where a small gang of sheep once grazed. I drove up an oak-canopied road to the large gray gates of the front courtyard.

I wandered around the west side of the house, behind a high cypress hedge that enclosed a neat side garden of sycamores and rhododendrons and bedded plants. I had an idea that I would visit the rose garden, which lay just beyond, and perhaps grab a fading rose just as my grandfather had done years before, crush it in my hand, and throw it on the ground.

But when I reached the roses, I kept on going, around the back of the house to a spot where the hedge was cut low to frame a dazzling panorama of Carmel Bay sweeping around to Point Lobos. The sun was bright on the ocean, and the fog had rolled back like a gray carpet offshore. I could see the white froth along the beach and out by the point.

I looked back toward the patio, a maze of boxwood and brick path with the house facing oceanward behind it. I tried to imagine what sort of pride or emotion he experienced when he stood at this vantage, but I felt instead the tongue-tied discomfort of years ago, when I had looked around and wondered how one lived in this house, and listened to at him and wondered what our connection could be.

In his last years, he talked wonderingly about all the luck in his life: his good fortune to survive two world wars; the success of his paper; his romantic second marriage. But luck was just a pose for the family records. He wanted me to see, I think, what almost anyone could see: the ambition and drive and calculation involved. I still could not figure, though, how the place and the man fit together. Why did he end up here, so far from the fray, in such deadening comfort?

Well, I had known him hardly at all, and so my study of

his life was by document and interview, not shared experience. Rather coldly, I could objectify him as a paradigm of the American who creates himself from the ground up, untethered by geography or class or family ties, or even his own personal history. The strength with which he acted out his chosen character was extraordinary—a deeply felt performance, and not at all insincere. But that strength was not mine, and not what I wanted from him. Perhaps there would be clues in the office he used in the west wing, where his papers were filed and his guns were stored and the books on the shelves were the ones he'd actually read. I peered in the window. But I'd watched him at work there, and I'd hefted the guns in the cabinet, and I'd sat at that desk in his absence, and what more could I gain from it now? What I wanted was the interweaving of family and place, the warp and weft of home. It would not be there in a house that was now empty of him.

What an enormous distance it was just driving over that little hill between the Monterey where I grew up and the Pebble Beach where he grew old—a gap of more than just half a century between his world and mine. The antipodal world of his childhood, Seventh Street in Kansas City, could not easily be reached from Pebble Beach either. My grandfather had assembled about him the trappings of his chosen identity, in a tableau uncomplicated by the trivial bits of history of which families are constructed. His home gave to him what Monterey gave to California—a makeshift perpetuity and a kind of manicured serenity.

His courage and self-control never left him when he was ill and dying, and perhaps as a result, those conversations we'd had were strangely unrevealing. The garden and the house, the neat brick paths and the boxwood, the sights that had meant something to him: I looked at them now for some additional clues. And what came to mind was his description of Lincolnshire: a world of near-feudal relationship, of gentility and honor, where the brewery still made beer and the brickyard still made bricks, and the brooks went on forever. It was his atavistic fantasy. It eased the tenuousness of his parents' immigrant circumstances, erased the ordinariness of middle-class life, allowed him to ignore whatever it was about his youth, and mine, that didn't live up to his aspirations. It was sublime because it no longer was; and it was beyond the reach of his progeny because there was no touchstone for the memory, no place, really, except the one in his mind, where we could not lay hands or inhabit.

So I retreated, back around the high hedge and through the rose garden. I remembered walking with him there, and the pleasure on his face when he doctored the roses and remembered his life. These were his roses. This was his home, and I think he was happy here. I passed by the rosebushes without taking one in my hand, slipped out through the side gate, got back into the Mustang, and continued down my own long road.

Epilogue

Return to Wyoming

AS YOU drive across the unending, unbroken desert between California and Wyoming, you will pass occasionally in the dark little roadside clusters of trailers or prefabricated houses. Faint brave lights glow from behind slipping venetian blinds, even at the most exhausted hour, and you may be distracted for a moment from thoughts of your own home and family, and think instead of the sheer quantity of fragile and particularized lives that are undertaken out there, unglimpsed except by a dreamy all-night driver.

As my trip neared its end, I began imagining that as I approached each of these lonely settlements, there was someone looking out one of the windows in my direction. The someone was vaguely awake, wearing a nightshirt or underwear, absently lighting a cigarette, putting a plastic-covered kitchen chair next to the window. The light was then shaded, and the person looked out and saw first the deep bowl of

stars, then the faraway suggestive shapes of the mountains, and finally the flame of headlights bound somewhere unknowable. And at that moment our souls tangled hungrily, trying to change places.

I drove back into Wyoming on Interstate 80, the belly-binding superhighway that cinches the state's southern plains. At Rock Springs I turned north, and for the first time then I saw just above the bulge of the globe the white tips of the Wind River Mountains, visible through the low current of trembling air along the horizon, with only the meditative space of the Red Desert between us. It was early dawn, and now the fantasies of strangers' lives fell back before much stronger images: my children in their beds, arms and legs akimbo, sighing as sleep lightens and lifts off them. Perhaps the youngest has snugged in with my wife, his head by the window she opened before going to bed, being a lover of night breezes; he smells the lilac and expressions rush across

his sleeping face. On the wooden slats outside, the wind fluffs the dog's tail, and he lifts his head crossly.

Right on the heels of my happy surge of anticipation followed a contrary desire to slow and savor the approach. Just north of the town of Rock Springs I dropped off what's called the Rock Springs Uplift on a rutted dirt road and drove east into the Red Desert, an encirclement of hills that interrupts the sharp peaks of the Rockies with a unique sump of sand and rock and biota with nowhere to go. The Continental Divide splits along its borders, and water—what little falls here—flows inward and disappears. The basin is about four thousand square miles altogether, and it has some fine duny sands, some ridges Mohawked with forest, and bands of wild, roaming horses. Harsh winds, sudden downpours that turn the clay soil to slippery muck; rattlesnakes are among its resistible attractions. Two-track "roads" run crazily around in it, a maze of scars that signify both the ancient quest of

westering wagons and the careless scribing of last year's uranium prospector, fading off into the sagebrush or centering
so high that only a truck can pass; it's easy to get lost.

On many trips, the Red Desert has been for me the vestibule to the valley where I live, an extraordinary interlude of
silence after the mechanical fury of Interstate 80 and the huge
power plants of Rock Springs. Generations ago this expanse
of windblown plain was the weariest of prospects to travelers
on the Oregon Trail, who had endured so much of the empty
plains by the time they arrived here that they plunged on
blindly. Now such an uninhabited landscape is a rare thing,
with an entirely new value. After so much traveling, through
crowded cities and along shop-strewn roadways, the open spaces
and the snug isolation of Wyoming towns seem foreign and
beguiling. All over the country the builders are winning
careless victories over the landscape, and there seems to be no
enforcement of climate or topography to hold us at bay; here
the environment still stings, and a community huddles in its
own warmth.

I drove into a landscape low-slung and undulating, gray
and sienna and pale green with lichened cobble and hard clay,
sagebrush and wild rye; as the car worked its way down off a
small plateau, the most distinguished feature on the empty
plain ahead was the shadow of a cloud passing, and it was
majestic.

I heard a faint whistling noise over the sound of the Mustang's engine and looked back over my shoulder toward Boars
Tusk, a volcanic spire. To the southwest I saw a small yellow
box puttering along a narrow track. John Mioncynski would
be in the cab, traveling the track to check for vandalism or
theft. U.S. Steel used to haul taconite across the desert from
its mine in South Pass to the Union Pacific hopper cars in
Rock Springs; the mine closed recently, so Mioncynski was
hired to take these rides now and then until the salvage peo-

ple could sell the track. Mioncynski, a rangy, quiet man who raises goats and plays piano, knows the flora and fauna of the Red Desert as well as anyone, and a ride on the train was a kind of lesson.

I had ridden the little railroad car with him a few months earlier, and on the way back I climbed up on the roof with Philippina Halstead, an artist and writer from the area, so we could get a better view of the passing landscape. Both she and Mioncynski lived in the vicinity of Atlantic City, another little Wyoming town not far from mine, a little higher, a little less sheltered, a lot smaller, a lot more precarious. A century ago newcomers mined gold in Atlantic City, and now fewer than fifty people lived there year-round, barely getting by. Many of them had had jobs at the taconite mine; times were hard now, and some would have to move away. Towns are often reborn in country as handsome as this, but how does it feel to be a leftover from the last community, and what depth of history can survive such turnover? In recent years even folks I assumed were better rooted than I was— those generous people who put the new roof on our cabin when we first moved to Wyoming—would suddenly up and leave. Those who stay don't talk about it much. It would only lead to questions like: What about you? Yes, indeed, you have given some thought to moving on, much to your chagrin.

But it was so beautiful up there on that little yellow box, legs spread and toes dug in, hands gripping the riveted metal edge of the roof—a gang of five horses came flying out of the desert and crossed the track ahead of us, racing for a while— and it didn't seem worth it to get all serious. Instead, we recalled a friend from back East who had lived in Wyoming for a few years, and then returned to the coast; on a recent visit she looked around a bar in Atlantic City with a frown and said, "Who are all these *new* people?"

The Mustang was overheating again, and I pulled over at the foot of the Oregon Buttes, a salient chunk of hard sandstone rock that sits square and tall, rising up out of the dry barrenness of the desert with limber pine furring its crest. Nineteenth-century migrants followed the Sweetwater River west into South Pass, just to the north; it was a favorite passage through the northern Rockies. They passed between the buttes and the snow-capped Wind River Mountains, and sometimes they wandered a little north and found the valley where I live. A few went no farther; they set up vegetable farms and sold their goods to the westering wagon trains. I let the car rest awhile and then tried to crank the engine so I could refill the radiator. There was not even a click. I tried the lights; I tried the radio. Nothing.

I got out of the car, but instead of opening the hood and looking for the problem, I wandered away from it. The afternoon was getting on. I hiked up the side of the butte, not a difficult climb, but the sky clouded over halfway up, and a few drops of rain fell, slicking the path. Two red-tailed hawks cried _keeeeeeer_ and dove away from a stand of dead trees near the top. The top was flat, and covered with fine gravel, crunching under the boot. The sides of the butte fell away quickly, leaving a few pinnacles standing off away from the main block of the butte's flat top. A marmot stuck its gray head out at me, and then scuttled down and around the cliff facing south.

Deer, bitterbrush, lupin, marmots, bitterroot, even elk, in the winter—the top of the butte was an island, marooned by the desert all around, a floating and, because it was so small, fragile place for those creatures that survive on its grasses and lichen and rodents. In a few hundred feet you could drop from evergreen to aspen groves to sage desert. The butte's narrow confines and the inhospitable border lands surrounding it made it a most particular place, and dear to a traveler's heart. If there had been people there, they would surely be eccentric in their isolation, and, I imagined, most attractive to me.

My mind again reached forward to the valley where I live, just over the next swell of land, just across the winding Sweetwater River, around the steep flank of Limestone Mountain, across Beaver Creek, into the trough of the Little Popo Agie River, and on to town. When the dog heard the particular sound of the Mustang, he would get up, totter the way he always did, and amble over to me as I climbed out, with his crooked old tail wagging, as if I'd left just yesterday; he would put his head down and butt my leg, and do the little half hop which has replaced the leap he used to make against my chest; and then he would yip just like a puppy, and welcome me home.

And was I quite ready to call Wyoming home? Well, not quite. I would make a finicky distinction, on the pretense that I had been able to cull some wisdom from my travels. Wyoming was not my home, but the place I lived. My home was, and always would be, in California. California! Bountiful, silly, misleading California. When it's really your home, you can call it names. I have so much more hope for Wyoming. . . .

Wyoming would be, happily, the home of my children. And it *was* the place where I lived. The place I traveled away from for the pleasure of coming back to it.

It was twilight when I started back down. Like a fluffed quilt in a darkening room, the desert hills stretched below off toward the horizon. Honeycomb badlands formed a stitch running east. I heard a faint beat, then a louder glissade of violins, and finally the voice of Rudy Lewis telling us that "on the roof" was the only place he knew.

A yellow smudge by a dry creek bed, light from the window of a rockhound's tiny trailer . . . north up a dry wash, a soliltary pronghorn grazing, invisible until the sound startled him erect.

And down below I could see a faint radio glow from the Mustang's dashboard. The song sounded as sweet here as it might on the Upper West Side of New York; my trail was star-blazed now, and I kept coming down it as though it were a fire escape. Not quite the troubleproof paradise of the song, but a place with room enough, and a car that knew the way. I was singing, and my feet were doing their awkward best to turn descent into dance. It was just a few more miles to go, to the place where I live.

A blacksmith shop converted to an auto repair garage.
Arthur Rothstein.